RIDE THE
REVOLUTION

THE INSIDE STORIES FROM
WOMEN IN CYCLING

Suze Clemitson

BLOOMSBURY

Bloomsbury Sport
An imprint of Bloomsbury Publishing Plc

50 Bedford Square
London
WC1B 3DP
UK

1385 Broadway
New York
NY 10018
USA

www.bloomsbury.com

BLOOMSBURY and the Diana logo are trademarks of Bloomsbury Publishing Plc

First published 2015

British Library Cataloging-in-Publication Data
A catalogue record for this book is available from the British Library.

Library of Congress Cataloging-in-Publication data has been applied for.

ISBN: HB: 978-1-4729-1291-6
ePDF: 978-1-4729-1293-0
ePub: 978-1-4729-1292-3

2 4 6 8 10 9 7 5 3 1

Typeset in 10.75pt Chaparral Pro by Deanta Global Publishing Services,
Chennai, India
Printed and bound in Great Britain by CPI Group (UK) Ltd, Croydon, CR0 4YY

To find out more about our authors and books visit www.bloomsbury.com.
Here you will find extracts, author interviews, details of
forthcoming events and the option to sign up for our newsletters.

*The author and publishers gratefully acknowledge the permissions granted to reproduce
the third party copyright materials contained in this book. Every effort has been made
to trace copyright holders and to obtain their written permission for the use of copyright
material. The author and publishers apologizes for any errors or omissions in the copyright
acknowledgements contained in this book, and would be grateful if notified of any
corrections that should be incorporated in future reprints or editions of this book.*

Copyright Acknowledgement: Page 2: *The ABCs of Cycling* by Beryl Burton.
Adapted from Ron Kitching's *Everything Cycling Handbook*,
1970 edition © The Estate of Ron Kitching.

CONTENTS

THE MEDIA

THE ADMINISTRATORS

THE CAMPAIGNERS

WOMEN WHO RIDE

CHAPTER 1

BERYL BURTON

Housewife, Superstar

Beryl Burton was the undisputed superstar of women's cycling in the 1960s and 1970s. Born in Yorkshire – which has the same kind of relationship with great cyclists as Brittany does in France – she didn't start riding a bike until she was a teenager. Starting on her husband Charlie's road bike she was soon on her way to a string of victories that make her the female equivalent of Eddy Merckx – and some. After all, Merckx was never the best rider in his sport for 25 years in a row. No book on women's cycling would be complete without Beryl Burton – the Yorkshire housewife who became a cycling superstar.

Like Beryl Burton, I'm a Yorkshire lass. I come from a long line of tough, formidable and inspirational women – I've often said that life with my mother is like living with Beryl – and have long been drawn to the story of the housewife from Leeds who became the greatest woman cyclist ever. I originally approached Maxine Peake, author of a play based on Burton's autobiography Personal Best *to write about her for this book. Maxine was lovely but had to demur owing to her incredibly busy schedule. So the task fell to me to try and encapsulate Burton's incredible life in a handful of pages. I spoke to women who had known her – including Yvonne McGregor, who describes herself as a Burton 'mini me' – and read through the archives of her extraordinary life and career. No book on women's cycling is complete without Beryl Burton, who blazed a lonely and formidable trail for modern women cyclists. The original housewife superstar, she is the toughest of tough acts to follow.*

THE ABCs of CYCLING
By Beryl Burton

A is for ACTIVITIES, of which cycling is the best – what other recreation has such a diversity of interests? Be it touring, club runs, camping, hostelling, time trialling, road or track racing – the bicycle caters for all.

B is for BEARINGS which must be kept adjusted, clean, and lubricated to keep your cycling enjoyable.

C is for CYCLIST – be one and not just an 'athlete on wheels' – it's more fun.

D is for DOPE – the biggest one is the rider who uses it.

E is for EQUIPMENT – choose the type most suited to your needs and pocket – look after it – check it weekly.

F is for FITNESS for which you must train – each one according to his or her own need.

G is for GEARS – clean and lubricate weekly. Be sure to check the cables – it's too late in the middle of an event.

H is for HYGIENE – both dental and personal are important to a healthy body.

I is for IMMERSION in water, a thing I never do during the racing season – try a shower or rub-down instead.

J is for JOY – the feeling one gets when fit and riding the bicycle.

K is for KEEN and efficient brakes – check the cables and brake pads – your life could depend of them.

L is for LIGHTS – see and be seen – don't get caught out in the evening without good lights and reflectors.

M is for MUDGUARDS – except for racing, I can see no excuse for subjecting your body and bicycle to wheel spray on wet roads.

N is for NUTRITION – intelligent eating rather than 'dieting' is my approach. Eating healthy foods – in the proper amounts relative to your activity level – forms a good nucleus of fitness.

O is for OIL – a must for every free-running machine – don't forget to lubricate the chain.

P is for POSITION on the bicycle – comfort is my first essential consideration. Handlebars are only one inch lower than the saddle height.

Q is for QUERIES – ask the experienced riders' views, then adapt to your own requirements.

R is for ROLLERS, which help you beat the fog, smog, and ice of winter evenings.

S is for SHOES, SOCKS & SHORTS, which should be close-fitting, clean, comfortable, and good quality.

T is for TYRES – choose the type and size most suited to your needs and look after them. Check weekly for cuts and ride them at the proper inflation.

U is for the UNSUNG praises of cycling – let everyone know that you are a cyclist and proud of it!

V is for VICTORY – which should be the aim of every sporting cyclist – work for it – it doesn't come easy.

W is for WILLPOWER – it keeps you going when you're hurting – cultivate it.

X is for the eXtra care you must take in your appearance and behavior when on the bicycle. Remember, you are an ambassador for our sport.

Y is for YOUNGSTERS – encourage them to take up cycling.

ZZZ is for the extra sleep you will require if this isn't going to be wasted effort.

'I don't feel that I've got anything special about me. I've just got two legs, two arms and a body, and a heart and lungs.'

In the 1950s and 1960s two women gloried in the twin initials 'BB'. One was poetry in motion, a superstar who left men grovelling in her wake. The other was Brigitte Bardot.

Where Bardot purred and oozed her way across the silver screen, Beryl Burton – arguably the greatest woman cyclist who ever turned a pedal – was a star of the British and European roads. She never turned professional, never had a formal coach, never rode with disc wheels or a skinsuit. Yet her formidable series of records continued to hold up against riders with all the advantages of modern technology. What might she have achieved with the heft of British Cycling behind her? With the lightest and sleekest of track and road bikes and the services of a sports psychologist?

Beryl would likely have had no truck with such nonsense. She had her legs and her heart and her lungs and they took her to a phenomenal series of records that will likely never be matched. In the age of sports science and carbon fibre, her 1967 12-hour time trial record of 277.25 miles has never been bettered.

A slight, slender figure, she was always a picture of determination on the bike, her body bent low along the top tube, her distinctive close cropped curls framing the resolute face. She had the ability to get the lowest of tucks just in the drops. Not for Beryl the triathlon handlebars modern time trailers routinely rely on. She was close to aerodynamic perfection.

'If Beryl Burton had been French, Joan of Arc would have to take second place.' That was the oft quoted assessment of an otherwise anonymous French journalist. Her autobiography *Personal Best* contains an exhaustive – and exhausting – list of her achievements. Imagine winning seventy national titles at every distance from 10 miles to a 100 miles. Now add in 12 titles on the road and 12 on the track.

Then there's the medal tally at World Championship level – five golds, three silvers and four bronzes for track pursuit, two golds and a silver as road race champion. That's an awful lot of rainbow striped jerseys. Not for nothing was BB the British Best All-Rounder (BBAR) an astonishing 25 years in a row. Across three decades, from 1959 to 1983, BB reigned supreme. And how many Olympic golds might Beryl have won if there had been a women's road race before 1984 or a time trial before 1996?

When the Tour de France Féminin launched in 1984, Burton approached the British Cycling Federation for a place on the team. Surely the great BB deserved a ride by right in such a prestigious event? But she was 47 and the BCF felt she lacked road racing qualifications – Beryl had focused exclusively on time trialling on her way to her 25th and final BBAR. Then a lifeline – one of the selected riders dropped out at the last minute. But Beryl was having none of it – she told the BCF exactly where they could stick their offer.

'I remember one day I rode to Hull and back, about 130 miles. I always made sure I was back in time to cook Charlie's dinner, and I stood for about three hours after that, ironing. That's the difference between males and females from the racing point of view.'

Beryl Burton's achievements are best seen through the lens of the esoteric world of the British time trial – a very different beast to its continental mass-start road racing cousin. In 1890, the National Cycling Union banned racing on public roads – a pre-emptive strike against those they feared would seek to ban all bike racing. Cyclists were viewed as at best a nuisance, at worst a threat to the very fabric of society. And so the British time trial – a race where no one actually appeared to be racing – was born. And with it a fascinating, clandestine history of 'men in black' meeting on quiet country roads at dawn. Codes and other skulduggery were used to determine the rendezvous. There were no race numbers – instead riders carried a bell. Competitors would set off at one minute intervals in the early morning light, the better to avoid suspicion. There were no tactics, none of the hurly burly of the peloton, just a pure demonstration of speed and stamina.

The cloak and dagger approach forged a secret society, a close knit community of riders who knew every course, and the average speeds and times that might be expected in any given set of conditions over 10 or 25, 50 or 100 miles. Everyone knows their PB, their personal best, at any distance. It's the mantra of the TT world.

But the men didn't have it all their own way. A box office assistant at the Gaiety theatre in London, Maggie Foster rode for the Gaiety Cycling Club and was already smashing time trialling records in the early 1900s. And though women were banned from membership of many male-dominated clubs in 1922, by 1927 the Rosslyn Ladies Club were organising time trials on the A11 just down the road from their clubhouse. One of the first great stars of women's time trialling was Marguerite Wilson who held all 16 Women's Road Record's Association records when World War II ended her career. Like her successor the 'Mighty Atom', Eileen Sheridan – whose diminutive, feminine figure belied her huge strength and speed – she was a professional with the Hercules team.

Into this community stepped Beryl Burton from Morley. She was an icon in their world, a woman who understood that 'this, really, was what it was all about. The fellowship of like-minded folk who, in their various ways, were part of the greatest sport in the world'. But any sense of camaraderie disappeared when Beryl hit the start line. She simply blew the competition (male and female) away.

'Poor Mac ... his glory, richly deserved, was going to be overshadowed by a woman.'

September 1967. The 12-hour time trial. Otley Cycling Club. According to their website, the Yorkshire club has 'always promoted female cycling'. In 1930 they held the first 12-mile time trial open to women and in 1935 the first open 25-mile TT. But no one – least of all champion time triallist Mike 'Mac' McNamara, who was defending his 12-hour title – was prepared for what BB would do that day.

She started two minutes behind McNamara, who was on course to win the 1967 men's BBAR. Mac needed a performance of 270 miles or more in a 12-hour time trial to clinch the victory. And clinch it he did, with a ride of 276.52 miles. But it was a Pyrrhic victory. Burton, implacably churning her 62×13 gear, had cruised past in the tenth hour and ridden 277.25 miles. A new women's record that stands to this day. And an absolute record that for two years was better than the men's.

Burton recorded that iconic moment in her autobiography. With typical understatement she writes: 'I thought some gesture was required on my part. I was carrying a bag of liquorice allsorts in the pocket of my jersey and on impulse I groped into the bag and pulled one out. I can still remember that it was one of those Swiss-roll shaped ones with a white coating of black liquorice. "Liquorice allsort, Mac?" I shouted and held it toward him. He gave a wan smile. Ta love. I put my head down and drove away.'

Fuelled by liquorice and sheer Yorkshire bloodymindedness, she had achieved something no other woman cyclist had managed before or since.

> *'She just had her own ideas of what she was going to do and she did it. Nothing stood in her way.'*

In 1968, the Grand Prix des Nations was variously described as the unofficial time trial world championships and the time trialist's Classic. Its palmarès were dominated by the greatest cyclists in the world: Italy's Fausto Coppi, the first rider to win the Tour de France and the Giro d'Italia in the same season; France's Louison Bobet, the first rider to win the Tour de France three years in succession; the Swiss 'pedaleur de charme' Hugo Koblet famed for his pure time trialling ability; and the Frenchman Jacques Anquetil, the first winner of all three Grand Tours. In 1967 Italy's Felice Gimondi finally ended Anquetil's winning streak (though Anquetil's nine victories remain an outright record) and in 1968 Gimondi would equal the Frenchman's feat of winning all three Grand Tours. Gimondi proved unstoppable over the 73.5km course and took the title for the second consecutive year.

But he never caught Beryl Burton. Appearing in the event by invitation, she was given a 12 minute start over the main field. She covered the undulating course at an average speed of 41.853km/h recording a time only a few minutes behind the winner. Not bad for a housewife from Yorkshire. Gimondi ended his season with a win at the Critérium des As, an invitation-only race for the best riders of the season. BB went back to the rhubarb sheds.

'Cycling has brought me out a lot over the years. By nature I'm a very quiet person.'

Beryl Burton was born on May 12 1937 in Halton, an unremarkable suburb of Leeds in West Yorkshire. Her mother was an insular woman, often not talking to her family for hours on end. Cycling and sport in general wasn't something that the family was interested in, but BB's competitive streak was already manifesting itself. She would throw a ball against a wall in the playground again and again, setting herself tougher and tougher targets. Failure found her biting the ball in frustration. But her prowess wasn't confined to playground games. Beryl was top of her class, a bright girl for whom grammar school beckoned – until the dream exploded like a blown out tyre. She failed her eleven plus and contracted St. Vitus' Dance, which affected her speech and left her temporarily paralysed, and the rheumatic fever weakened her heart, leaving her with a cardiac arrhythmia. Recovery took two long years of prolonged spells in hospital and in convalescent homes. Beryl left school at 15 and went to work.

Was it serendipity that took her to the Leeds clothing manufacturer where Charlie Burton worked? He was a dapper young man who made a curious clicking noise as he walked. Beryl thought her future husband had a limp but it was just the cleats he was wearing after riding to work. It was the start of a lifelong love affair – not just with Charlie who would become her husband, trainer, chauffeur, nanny and mechanic, but with the bike. And it was on Charlie's bike that she won her first 100-mile time trial title, a mere 11 minutes ahead of the next rider.

She loved the social life at his Morley Road Cycle Club. For a shy, awkward teenager it was a way into the life she had lost through the years of illness. Marrying at 17, it wasn't long before Beryl was on the bike in earnest. Charlie says: 'For the first few months I used to have to sometimes physically push her along because she kept dropping back. By the time it got to the second year she was riding by the other cyclists and by the third year she was leading them.' That same determination that led her to bite a tennis ball in frustration had finally found its outlet. Four years after their wedding in 1955, Beryl won her first BBAR.

> *'When I'm at work I have a lot of heavy lifting to do and I get on with it. They treat me there like a person, not like a woman.'*

Money was tight, but nothing stood in BB's way. Not the mounds of washing that would accumulate in her kitchen after training and on a race day, especially when daughter Denise started competing in earnest. Not the 12-hour shifts on clubmate Nim Carlin's farm hauling boxes of beets and doing heavy lifting in the rhubarb sheds. Not the cheap lightweight wheels she bought for 30 shillings to ride her first World Track Championships in 1959 – they cracked and Beryl won her first Rainbow Stripes on a borrowed pair to the adoring cheers of the Belgian crowd. Not her employers at the General Post

Office who forced her take unpaid leave to pursue her World titles. Not the collision with a car that left her with 56 stitches in her head, a broken shoulder blade and two fractures in her leg at the age of 41. Many a professional would have retired, but not BB. Six months later she won the National 10-mile Time Trial title.

There's an oft-told story about Beryl and Charlie's adventures behind the Iron Curtain on their way to the 1960 Worlds in Leipzig. Stranded in East Berlin, trudging the streets for hours, penniless and with not a word of German between them, they went to the nearest police station to ask for help. As soon as the officer on duty saw the name on her passport, he was on the phone arranging hotel accommodation at the East German Sports Ministry's expense. The pair left the next morning without breakfast: 'We hadn't a bean between us and they offered us breakfast. We refused, not knowing how we were going to pay for it. We didn't know we didn't have to pay for it and we were absolutely starving', she said. There were armed soldiers on the train back to Leipzig and Charlie was all for heading back home to Yorkshire. But a little thing like an empty belly wasn't going to stop Beryl. She dominated the opposition in the individual pursuit, winning in a world record time, then used all her time trialling skills to crush the field and win the road race by over three minutes. She went home a double world champion at 23. Unstoppable.

Beryl was quiet – like her mother, often not talking to Charlie or Denise for hours at a time – but in her mind she was always busy, planning her future. 'If I did a 57, I would not gloat about it but would aim for a 56. People used to think I was being clever but it was the only way. If you tell people, then you convince yourself. You brainwash yourself I suppose', she said. And the long shifts on the farm, the mountainous piles of washing, the refusal to walk anywhere during the season paid off – her unrivalled stamina, core strength and work ethic combined to produce an outstanding athlete. She was relentless – even when she ventured off the roads of

Yorkshire and onto the continent to face the might of professional riders from Europe and the Eastern bloc.

Her toughest rival was Tamara Garkushina: 'she was five feet tall and five feet wide!' Burton recalled 'most of the Russian cyclists were attractive, nice big lasses and a cut above.' And at each world championships there was always another new Russian ready to test the legs of the other women.

Cycling has a long and complicated relationship with doping from which the women's sport has not been immune. BB won her last world championship track pursuit in 1966 then managed a handful of silver and bronze medals as women from the USSR took every gold medal for the next eight years. Beryl envied the state support Eastern bloc athletes received, telling her Morley Cycling Club mates 'I was envious at first of the Germans and the Russians, and the support they received from their government, while we had to dig deep into our own pockets to compete. But then Charlie reminded me of you lot, my cycling friends and family, and the support, inspiration and encouragement I get from you, the laughs and the commiseration. So from now on, if I start to feel a little hard done to, I shall think of you rabble ... and I will say to myself, "Smile when you lose, and laugh like hell when you win!"' Resolutely amateur, Beryl had rejected advances from Raleigh to sponsor her in a series of place to place record attempts. But what Beryl couldn't know was that the Soviet State Sport Committee was systematically doping its athletes with blood transfusions and performance-enhancing drugs like steroids.

Yet still the woman the Germans nicknamed 'the Yorkshire hausfrau' continued winning titles on the track and the road. What was her secret? Desperate to find out, the Russians sent a delegation to Nim Carlin's farm to watch the British phenomenon at work. It turned out Beryl's PED of choice was hard graft and rhubarb.

'I only gave up cycling for the three months that the bump stopped me from squeezing behind the handle-bars.'

But there were failures. After setting the women's 100-mile record in 1968 – a record that would stand for almost 20 years – Beryl set her sights on the 24-hour record. In her long hours of domestic silence she had dreamed of breaking the 500-mile barrier. It was the end of a long and successful season and she went off like a firecracker, setting a pace that rivals like Nim Carlin knew they couldn't match. After 345 miles she was over 23 minutes ahead of her nearest rival – she wasn't going to break the barrier, she was going to punch its lights out.

And then her knee gave out. It had troubled her during training and, according to the ever faithful Charlie, 'her legs seized up and they were just like boards. We couldn't move them or anything. All the veins in her legs were like solid pipes – so we just had to lay her in the car.' But Beryl's efforts meant that the winner, Ray Cromack, cracked the magic 500 barrier instead.

Like the 24-hour record, the Hour would also elude Burton. She made two abortive attempts in Milan but the terrible weather and the endless, exhausting scrabble for funding put it out of her reach. Yvonne McGregor – who would ride and beat the challenge of the Hour – remembers the woman who sat quietly through her own first successful attempt: 'She was absolutely unique as a person, an athlete, a psychology. It's such a shame she's not here to give her down-to-earth Yorkshire views on it.'

But the loss that smarted the most was not to a steroid-fuelled Russian or a male clubmate. It was to her own daughter, Denise. Following in her mother's footsteps, Denise started racing at 16 and almost from the off she rivalled Beryl. In 1972 they rode on the British team at the Worlds together. Mother beat daughter to the National Road Race Championship in 1973 and when Denise picked up a bronze at the Worlds in 1975 she recalls her mother buying her an array of bronze-coloured gifts to celebrate.

Lisa Brambani raced often with Denise and says, 'BB never really got involved with Denise's cycling career. I don't think Beryl was the sort of person who would involve herself in anyone's cycling apart from her own. I understand that she was a very driven woman who, to achieve her goals, had to become quite selfish – as most successful sports people do.'

But the tables turned in the 1976 National Road Race Championships. On the last lap of the Harrogate course, three riders remained in contention: Carol Eaton of the Paragon Club and Morley CC's formidable mother-daughter duo. Carol never stood a chance against the Burtons, but who would pull on the champion's jersey? In her usual fashion, Beryl surged, then surged again but she couldn't shake Denise and it was Burton junior who outsprinted Burton senior for the win.

On the podium, Beryl refused to shake her daughter's hand. 'I don't think she knew why she did it', Denise told the BBC recently. 'If she was alive today, I don't think she'd know. She desperately wanted to win and I beat her and she took it very hard.' Denise was refused a lift home in the family car and told to ride her bike home. In *Personal Best* Beryl admits 'it was not a sporting thing to do. I did our sport a disservice in allowing personal acrimony to intervene, and I can only plead I was not myself at the time.' Family ties collided with personal ambition. Denise wasn't pulling her weight in the house. It was a combustible mix that ignited that day on the road and on the podium when a rebellious daughter put two spokes up to her ultra-competitive mother. It was, as Beryl said later, not a romantic story but a 'real life narrative about basically ordinary people with jangled nerves and emotions'.

It was a gladiatorial combat played out on two wheels, a feud that finally came to a head at the 1977 National Track Championships. Mother and daughter met in the semi-finals of the individual pursuit and once again Denise ran out the winner. A dejected Beryl walked away from the track and Denise went after her. Suddenly, the two women were sobbing in each other's arms. The war was over.

Cycling brought one final reconciliation. In 1986 B. Burton OBE and D. Burton set a women's 10-mile time trial record together – on a tandem.

'I was right off last season. It was like riding with a ton of concrete on your head.'

○ ○ ○

It's 1983 and Beryl has hung up her wheels at the end of another winning season. The 25th British Best All Rounder award joins the other trophies and medals hidden away in cupboards and drawers. The bike is in the cellar with the others. The switch between housewife and superstar has been thrown. But something is wrong. She feels listless and out of sorts, as if she's losing her competitive edge. At 46, when many male professionals are enjoying life in the team car, has BB finally run out of steam?

An early-season accident has left her with broken ribs and a compression of the spine from which she has not fully recovered. Further tests reveals anaemia and a hormonal imbalance, asthma and an allergy to grass pollen. There's one last National title in 1986 but an era is over.

And finally comes cancer. Beryl discovers she has a tumour in her breast and undergoes a mastectomy. She speaks about it publicly. 'If I had been hit with a brick, I couldn't have been more stunned', she tells *Cycling Weekly* in 1992. But BB is indomitable. Without fuss or palaver she quietly fights back. And she continues to compete. For Beryl riding was life.

○ ○ ○

'Many journalistic interviews I have given have highlighted the "housewife" angle and, while I welcomed the publicity for my sport, it was difficult sometimes talking to people who had no concept of bike racing in the international sporting scene.'

There's a wonderful interview with Beryl Burton in the March 1974 issue of *Cycling*. Entitled 'How many Burtons?', the great historian of the British time trial, Bernard Thompson, struggles to get to grips with Beryl's personality and motivation. By turns comedically sexist and deeply incisive, Thompson paints a picture of the house-proud woman who consigns Charlie's stray bike parts straight to the garage and works through a mountain of domestic chores and holds down a full time job while racing a bike to devastating effect. A woman who speaks without enthusiasm about her greatest performances saying only that each triumph is quickly forgotten in favour of the next challenge, but who lights up when discussing family holidays. Who dismisses male riders who give up work to train full time as 'lazy in mind', adding: 'I think men are softer than women generally speaking, most of them would fall apart at the seams if they had to race and train on top of a good day's manual work!'

In his lengthy assessment of her career, 'Superwoman', that appeared in the November 1992 edition of *Cycling Weekly*, cycling journalist Dennis Donovan is every bit as in awe of his subject as Thompson. But he reveals a more vulnerable Burton than the fiercely proud matriarch. 'You have to have someone behind you if you're a female,' BB tells him, 'You get to a point when you know you can do things but that you know you need someone to boost your confidence.' For Donovan, who remembers his own time trial humiliation at BB's hands where she told him 'come on, lad, you're not trying', she is simply 'the most dedicated, determined person I have ever known'.

So how many Burtons where there? Denise remembers her mother as a solitary figure during the racing season, 'ultra-quiet and thoughtful before a race'. And she would knit, furiously: 'She'd be knitting away like mad before a race, or in-between races at a track event, because it helped keep her concentration, and it stopped her from talking to people as well.' But there were evenings out and club dinners when Beryl would don an evening dress and deliver her engaging after-dinner speeches, then change into her cycling gear and ride home.

But much as she loved her sport there was a part of Beryl that was frustrated by the lack of attention she received. Contrast the roars of approval in Liège in 1959 with the homecoming she received. No one was there to meet her at Leeds station when she arrived with the rainbow jersey in her suitcase. The newly crowned World Champion – a feat no other English woman had ever achieved – had to get a lift home with a friendly lorry driver. She became a double World Champion a year later but still her achievement went unrecognised. 'I wasn't seeking personal adulation but a little recognition would not have gone amiss,' she wrote. 'I was a double world champion in an international sport and it might as well have been the ladies darts final down at the local.'

Was Beryl's lack of recognition a result of the sexism endemic in cycling? The press were quick to dub her 'the Yorkshire housewife' and she never enjoyed the profile of an Anquetil or a Merckx – though she was their equal in terms of her palmarès – but in the world of British time trialling her star shone brighter than any other rider. Despite the recent extraordinary success of British riders, male and female, cycling has always been something of a minority sport in the UK. And Beryl turned the spotlight firmly on women's cycling in her pomp. 'She managed to get women's cycling recognised – all the sports writers knew about it', Denise told the *Yorkshire Post*. Charlie never felt his wife suffered in her career because of her gender. And BB always marched to her own drum.

She was the amateur who worked harder than the professionals. But she was also, in the words of Yvonne McGregor, 'so unassuming – there was nothing to let you know she was this phenomenal athlete who'd done all these things in cycling'. Like her heroine, McGregor has no jerseys on the wall and her medals – like Beryl's – live in a drawer out of sight. It was if BB needed to compartmentalise her different lives, to keep the housewife and the cycling superstar strictly separate. A true perfectionist, nowadays we might talk of her as being 'slightly OCD'. For Beryl it was just the way life worked best. As she told Bernard Thompson, 'I enjoy absolutely everything I do, riding a bike, housework, racing, working in Nim's rhubarb sheds. If you don't enjoy something you are doing, there is no point!'

'People will either give up or burn out before they achieve what she did. I don't think it will ever be equalled. It just can't be. It'll be a heck of a long time before it ever is.'

When Yvonne McGregor started her cycling career, she was hungry to find out anything she could about the professional sport. So she got Beryl Burton's *Personal Best* out of the library and 'just devoured it really'. But what she took away from the book – more than the titles and the records – was the personality: 'it was her persona more than her results that shone like a bright light with me. I totally identified with her.' Yvonne started racing locally and would occasionally find herself at the start line with Beryl. 'Just meeting her I was in awe,' she recalls, 'I was like her mini-me.'

Beryl Burton is having a moment. Actor Maxine Peake has written a play about her. She has been granted the freedom of the city of Leeds. There is a beautiful mural of her in full flight in her home town of Morley. Finally, she is receiving the recognition she has long deserved. But for some, like photographer Joolze Dymond and ex-professional cyclist Lisa Brambani, Beryl and her legacy have never gone away.

Joolze met the mighty BB a handful of times. She was a junior, Beryl in the twilight of that illustrious career. She remembers being 'slightly chuffed, but also tinged with sadness, when I beat her in an event'. She says she was in awe of the world beater and felt unworthy to talk to her, 'but I'm sure we wouldn't have understood each other with our thick accents!'

For the Brambani family, BB was a household name and would often come up in conversation. 'Who do you think you are, Beryl

Burton?' or 'There she goes, off like Beryl Burton.' So Lisa was aware of BB 'probably from first getting rid of [her] stabilisers!'

Lisa was a late starter, only coming into cycling after ending a promising career in competitive swimming at 16. She was shocked to see Beryl on the start list of her first race. 'I think it was more of a revelation for my parents to think I was actually racing with the legend BB, I don't think I gave it very much thought', she says. Lisa remembers finishing one place behind the legend and her parents believing she had the ability to become World Champion as a result.

'BB was, in my opinion, the first great pioneer for female cycling,' says Lisa, 'but at the time, as a young cyclist, I never really appreciated exactly how good she was and what she had achieved in a truly male-dominated sport.' Had BB been riding now, says Lisa, 'she would surely be regarded as quite possibly the finest female athlete of all time'. As it was, she says, 'I think she was happy with the self-satisfaction her victories brought and even happier to just go about her business as a true Yorkshire woman!'

Lisa walked away from her own cycling career at the age of 24, but her daughter Abby-Mae Parkinson is already breaking records and making her own mark on the sport. The shadow of Beryl Burton lies long across the landscape of women's cycling.

> *'To ease off once would be the beginning of the end; it's like packing in a race, once you've done it, it is easier to do it next time.'*

She was out on her bike, as usual, delivering invitations to her 59th birthday party, when her heart finally gave out. They found her dead by the roadside, her cycling shoes still in her toe clips, so they said. It sums up Beryl perfectly – that dedication to the bike. She never walked if she could ride. But the sheer determination that drove her to her greatest successes would eventually kill her.

'I think she pushed her body so hard, her heart just couldn't cope,' says Yvonne McGregor, who broke several of Burton's time trial records in the 1990s. 'In my 50s I think I've developed a safety mechanism where my body won't let me go into the red anymore, but she didn't have that safety switch.'

But it was that ability to bury herself, the unique blend of physiology and psychology, of grit and wit and liquorice, which made Beryl Burton the greatest woman cyclist of them all.

CHAPTER 2

MIEN VAN BREE

The Thwarted Passions of a World Champion

Mariska Tjoelker is a Dutch writer and journalist. She writes about all kind of stuff, but writing about (the history of) cycling makes her heart sing. She shared this love for cycling with her dad and when he passed away in 2010 she decided to start writing about it – as he wasn't around anymore to discuss even the smallest detail of every Tour de France stage. Since then Mariska has published her stories in Dutch cycling magazines like *De Muur, Soigneur* and on the blog Hetiskoers.nl. Her book about Dutch cyclist **Mien van Bree** publishes in 2016. Mien Van Bree's battles against the cycling establishment to become World Champion and raise the profile of the women's sport in Holland is a story that still resonates in an age when a Dutch woman is one of the greatest cyclists in the sport. She lives in Driebergen, together with Rogier and their Labrador Briek (named after the great Flandrien rider Briek Schotte).

 @tjoelkersport
🏠 www.mariskatjoelker.nl

I'm not sure how or when I became aware of Mariska's work but I was immediately drawn in by it. Like me, she is fascinated by the history of the sport and in her research on Mien van Bree has discovered one of those hidden stories about the women's sport that opens a fascinating window on women's cycling in the 1930s in a way that resonates directly with today. She was kind enough to entrust me with the job of translating the following piece about 'her' Mien and I was quickly as captivated by Mien as Mariska was. The story of 'our' Mien is by turns empowering, heartbreaking and downright bizarre …

'Kwee' they called her in the village where she grew up and – but for a few years – lived out her life. 'Kwee'. Quince. An old fashioned word with several different meanings. Hermaphrodite for one. Androgynous too, and butch. And, yes, she was big and solidly built, with hands like coal shovels. A rather asexual woman, if you want to put it politely.

In her youth, the woman in question, Mien van Bree, loves to chase after speeding buses. Bent flat over her bicycle she races them through the streets of Loosduinen then branches off to ride hard through the hilly dunes. Her fellow-villager Piet Moeskops, five time world sprint champion and in the twilight of his career, one day decides to ride out with this girl from the Trompstraat. Before long he is convinced: Mien has talent. If he can only get her on a road bike, there will be plenty of young riders who would struggle to beat her, of that he's certain. When he tells her, something begins to stir inside her. Feelings that she can't describe. Only 20 years later, when her bike has a permanent place beside her bed, does she realise what had inspired her as a young girl. Ambition. Pure ambition. An emotion she learns to suppress. Just as she learns to suppress so many other feelings.

My search for Mien van Bree begins in the most banal of ways – with Google. The websites of the Royal Library in The Hague and the Central Bureau for Genealogy bring Mien a little closer, but the picture remains hazy. Until an archivist finds me something – an announcement from 1983. 'Today marks the unexpected passing of our sister, sister-in-law, aunt and niece WILHELMINA ELIZABETH VAN BREE at the age of 68. Signed A.W. van Bree'

No husband.

No children.

The announcement mentions an address. But no one by the name of Van Bree lives there anymore.

Mien's niece, Mrs Barendse, moved to a service apartment a few years ago. She's in her 80s now but she's as smart as a whip. Her aunt used to look after her, she says fondly. She has endless happy memories: of her aunt taking her to the beach or into the city, how Mien used to let her play with water at home. 'Aunt Mien was a lovely lady.' She doesn't remember much about cycling. She was just too young, she says, and later on no one ever talked about it. But she still has some photos from Aunt Mien's house. Family snapshots. A road bike is nowhere in sight.

In 1934 Mien van Bree writes a short article for the tabloid *Het Leven Geïllustreerd*. A half page, illustrated with two photo: on the left, a proper young lady concentrating on her embroidery; on the right the same young lady, now posing in a short-sleeved shirt, bib shorts and striped stockings. Her hands rest on the handlebars of a road bike. Mien describes herself as the 'Cycling Champion of Holland', an unofficial title because 'here in Holland, women's cycling remains unrecognised'. Mien has finished third in the World Championships in Belgium and the jury has declared her Dutch champion. She writes about her training on the rollers, with the advice of Piet Moeskops, the five times Dutch World sprint champion. How she sets off on her bike for races in Belgium at 6am, arriving around noon in Brussels. That her biggest rival is her Belgian friend Mrs Elvire de Bruyn ... that there is something not quite right about Elvire she doesn't say. She writes about her ambition though: she wants to become World Champion one day. And more than that – she wants to play a part in getting women's cycling recognised as a sport just like the men's. To ensure that, when she and her colleagues ride by in their tights and jerseys, they are no longer subject to mocking laughter.

She is only 19 years old.

I decide to publish an article in the local Loosduinse paper. Surely there must be some people who remember Mien? I get five responses, two from old neighbours of hers. The other three simply tell me 'she was a big woman'.

The first neighbour is nearly 90 now. She opens the door bent double over her walking frame and holds out a small and wrinkled hand. On the phone she told me she had lived for many years across the road from the van Bree family. The war was over and Mien had been living at home for a few years. 'She took care of her mother, that woman was in bed all the time. Sad really.' The old lady sighs. She is lost in the past, thinking about the old days. But when I mention the picture she jumps back into the present.

'That was quite something', she nods. 'I was 10, I think. In the summer I used to visit my aunt in Brussels. One day I was sitting there reading the paper and what did I see? A picture of Mien! In the Brussels newspaper! I didn't understand it so I took the paper home and gave it to Mien. She just loved it, really, she couldn't get over it. She had this painting of herself and she was holding it in the photograph. She was wearing that sweater with stripes on it. A Champion's jersey, yes.' The old lady had no idea that Mien had been a cyclist. 'That was something one didn't talk about back then. No wonder she moved to Belgium.' She always felt Mien was an unhappy woman. 'A woman shouldn't be alone, you know. But Mien never seemed to find a man.'

The second neighbour describes her as a 'really good woman', but completely asexual. 'And you know the kind of bullshit people talk in small villages. Horrible. That poor woman.' Later, when I'm back with Mien's niece, she tells me she doesn't know anything about her aunt being unhappy. Nor does she know anything about people gossiping about her. She does know that her aunt was a sweet person. Really sweet, she reaffirms. 'She always took care of everyone. Everyone, but herself.'

Except during that brief period when she had the courage to live her own life.

When Mien fitted curved handlebars to her bike and started chasing buses, it wasn't something young ladies were supposed to do. Young ladies were supposed to go out to work, meet nice young men, get engaged, married, become housewives. Not Mien. She wants to ride a bike, to live the life of a sportswoman, even in those pre-war years where women in sports are the subject of so much harsh debate. Yes, young ladies are allowed to play sport but not at the expense of their natural grace and beauty. Swimming is allowed, as is gymnastics: a sport that emphasises feminine grace. Athletics is just about acceptable. But physical exertion must be avoided at all costs – the risks to health and charm and the 'female organs' are simply too great. Riding a road bike is obviously out of the question. The single woman who ventures out on a bicycle is to be laughed at and pointed at.

Mien is 16 when she and a few friends set up the first Dutch women's cycling club. It is 1931. The club is preserved in a photo, captioned: 'Cycling, Women: Women establish a cycle club in The Hague. The members line up for their first competition with Mien van Bree (extreme left), 19th November 1931.' It's cold. Mien wears a knitted cap on her thick, dark blond hair and thick gloves on her hands. A dark sweater, lighter coloured plus fours. Plain stockings. And cycling shoes inserted in toe clips.

Cycling shoes!

Toe clips!

There are four other girls, two – like Mien – with their hands on the drops, the other two riding bikes with straight handlebars. Four in trousers. One in a skirt. Medium length hair, all five of them. In the distance a group of male onlookers, some even straining forward to catch a glimpse of the ladies.

They call their club VIOS Vooruitgang Is Ons Streven – Progress Is Our Aim. And progress was what they wanted, says co-founder

Leni Bulté in an interview with *WielerRevue* in 1986. Members wore a team kit with the yellow letters VIOS emblazoned on the back of their brown jerseys, teamed with brown plus fours – bib shorts were still considered a little *too* progressive. Leni talks about how they came to race in Belgium: 'At home we read about the ladies competitions in the *Gazet van Antwerpen*.' They found someone who was willing to let them race and, voila, the girls of VIOS were off to Antwerp on their bikes. They wanted races and they got them, all the way to the World Championships. 'It was a huge race. It was taken so seriously that the organisation even filled the tram rails with plaster!'

The gulf between Belgium and the Netherlands is huge – aside from a fun race during the annual Schveningen cyclocross event, bike racing for women is absolutely forbidden in Holland. But even in Belgium, women's racing doesn't happen without a fight. After one highly successful women's race, Antwerp City council attempts to ban the sport in 1927. But their goose is cooked. The sports press gets involved, as do many supporters and opponents. A huge controversy ensues and suddenly every town and every village wants to organise a women's race: attention is guaranteed. Thousands and thousands of spectators want to see what these 'sports women' are capable of. Initially taking place on the road, women's racing soon moves to the track and single-handedly revives the almost defunct velodromes. Once Antwerp's big sports promoter Jos de Stobbeleire gets involved, the sport has even more cachet. Still, not everybody agrees to these women racing in the streets. A Belgian sports journalist comes out strongly against women's cycling, decrying the 1934 World Cup – the same event that Mien writes about in *Het Leven Geïllustreerd* – as a shameful display, organised purely for financial gain. Of the 50,000 francs offered in prize money, only 7,500 francs are eventually paid out, he tells his readers. As for the nationalities of the riders, all is not what it seems – the Champion of Luxembourg turns out to be a girl from Anderlecht! He does have a point: the number of participants from countries like France, Italy, Germany, Luxembourg and Britain is relatively small, while the organisers understand that an international field attracts a bigger audience. It's the reason why Mien's teammate Leni Bulté once ended up as German Champion. But worse than that, he continues, the entire spectacle is both annoying and humiliating. Just think of the damage that is being done to the poor creature's health! Unfortunately for the poor man, women's racing – seven years after the Antwerp City council's failed attempt to ban it – now rests on a hugely solid foundation. The 1934 World Cup is watched by thousands – some say tens of thousands – of spectators along the route.

Mien finishes the World Cup in third place, at least that's what she writes in her story for *Het Leven Geïllustreerd*. *Sport in Beeld* runs a short article about her on 25 September, noting that the Loosduinese cyclist Mien van Bree ended up third in an event in Brussels 'with which the somewhat pompous title of World Championships was connected. Miss van Bree can now be considered Champion of the Netherlands'. A column about the opening of the Six Days of Amsterdam that November in the *Algemeen Handelsblad* states that the riders had had to make way for the lap of honour of 'Miss Mien van Bree, a Dutch cyclist who, according to the speaker, was third in the World Championships'. This lap of honour is unique – despite her later successes, it will only ever happen once.

Anyway. Third. Good result.

On 17 September 1934, the Flemish sports weekly *Sportwereld* gives the results for the top 15 in the World Cup. 'First our compatriot, Elvire Debruyn; second and third, Debock and Peelman.' Peelman third. Not van Bree. According to *Sportwereld* she has finished eighth.

In the Netherlands a story appears which again credits Mien with eighth place. It is written by ex-rider, sports journalist and co-founder of the Dutch Cycling Union, G. Bosch van Drakenstein and appears in the *Sport-Echo*, the membership magazine of the Cycling Union. He calls the event a colossal success, writes of the 50,000 francs in prize money, 40 participants from countries including Belgium, the Netherlands, France, England and Italy and more than a hundred thousand people along the length of the parcours. 'The winner and World Champion was Elvire Debruyn with a time of 2h 41m 56s for 90km, giving an average speed of 33km/h, a speed that inspires respect,' Bosch van Drakenstein writes. He continues by summarizing the other results: second, De Bock; third, Peelman; fourth, Samijn. Eighth, van Bree. Eighth.

Isn't she happy with her eighth place? Is it a combination of youthful hubris and ambition – assuming that the Dutch press won't check because after all they have no interest in women's cycling whatsoever? Or does she need a better result in order to convince her parents to go along with the plan she has already had for some time now?

Because Mien has realised that the sport for which she is willing to give her heart and soul has no future in the Netherlands. Of course there are some who recognise the opportunities it presents. There is a Dutch bike manufacturer Magnet that provides Mien with a top-of-the-range road bike. For Magnet she is a valuable weapon in the push for greater brand awareness, helping it make headway into new markets. Later, Magnet even gets the first sponsored Dutch cycling team off the ground.

But Mien simply refuses to accept the way things are. She has this dream and she is determined to make it come true. And to do so she has to leave Loosduinen. Alone. In making that decision something else plays a role too. But that's something no one knows. Especially not her parents.

Mien moves to Belgium. Unfortunately no-one can tell me where she lived. Her niece thinks she ran a bar, or worked in a bar. The name? She has no idea.

'We never talked about it', she says simply.

Eventually, the family finds some photos. Photos from Belgium. Mien on a bike in a velodrome. Mien with a bunch of flowers in a velodrome. In jersey and plus fours, holding her bike, posing in front of a cafe. Casual snapshots which she would sometimes tuck into an envelope and send to Loosduinen to let everybody know she was doing just fine. But none of these images really bring Mien any closer. I'm already feeling my disappointment until I come across the last few photos. In one of them she stands under a tree. A woman stands next to her. Their arms wound tentatively around each other's waist. They laugh, though Mien is more subdued than the woman next to her. In another they both wear identical shirts with a small argyle logo on the right breast: Alex. The most telling picture seems to come from a photo booth. Their heads are close together. Their solid dark coats and white collars contrast strongly with the look they exchange. It's the same look Fausto Coppi and Giulia Occhini give each other when he presents her with the winner's bouquet after the 1953 World Championships. The look in which everything happens while the world falls away.

Did Mien also put these photos in an envelope and send them home? Or did she keep them to herself her whole life? Cherished like precious jewels, only shared with the canaries that she later bred in the kitchen?

Mien's niece doesn't know.

But she does know the cheerful, smiling woman next to Mien.

Maria Gaudens is her name. Cycling star. And the lead actress in an article in the *Soerabaijasch Handelsblad,* the newspaper that in August 1933 decides that 'The European Championship for female cyclists' might just be a nice subject for the women's section of the paper. And so a female journalist sets off on the tram from Waterloo on Sunday, 27 August 1933 not realising that her journey is the beginning of a unique story. When she arrives that morning in the small village, she finds the competitors sitting at wooden tables outside a café in the street, preparing for the race. One of the riders invites the journalist to slide in beside her, there's a free seat. Which is how the journalist makes the acquaintance of Maria

Gaudens, 'a strawberry blonde of 20, permed hair like everybody else; a strong girl with a pair of strong legs, a sympathetic face, clear blue eyes, some freckles on the rosy sunburned skin. Elbows on the table, she is completely at ease as her fingers pluck idly at a roast chicken breast.' The journalist decides to follow Maria for the rest of the day and sees the thorough preparations Maria makes for the race. When she finishes eating she disappears for a moment before returning in a blue jersey and black shorts. On her back is pinned a large, square piece of cloth. Her race number today is 22. After a final massage from her brother, she fills her jersey pocket with grapes, drinks a bottle and stashes another in a side pocket. She breaks two raw eggs, pours them into her mouth, swallows and sets off. It's time to race!

Nearly 60 riders line up for the start of the European Championships, ready to cover 70 km in 14 laps around the village. Spectators are huddled together along the length of the route. The pace is high. For the first few laps Maria acknowledges her family with a nod, but by the fifth lap, they're going full gas. Faces are redder, permed curls are beginning to droop and grimaces are turning into spasms. 'Thirty kilometres an hour!', the race speaker cries. The crowd are screaming, French and Flemish voices raised in a chant that echoes through the streets 'Elvire! Elvire! It's Elvire!' Elvire Debruyn – the star of the peloton – wins the race. Done and dusted.

After the race, the journalist finds her protagonist back at the cafe, surrounded by her family. 'She's had a crash,' mother Gaudens says. Maria grimaces as she tries to brush some caked sand off her leg. She has already been to the doctor, she says. 'My teeth felt all upside down so the doctor bashed them back into place. And I had a bump on my forehead, for god's sake. But the doctor took an empty bottle of beer and rolled it away.'

Amused by the doctor's methods, the journalist buys Maria a beer and then returns to Brussels. Later that week the story of the ladies' race appears in the *Soerabaijasch Handelsblad*, giving a unique insight into the life of a woman cyclist. Eighty years later, her words will also help to illuminate the life of Mien van Bree.

My search for Mien's home in Belgium comes to nothing. For a time the answer seems to be within reach, hidden in that picture of her posing with her bike outside the cafe. The sign in the picture says it was taken in the town of Aalst, you can even zoom in on the name of the cafe: the Wooden Hand. The place still exists. Only the cars in the parking lot outside betray the advance of time. Inside, too, little has changed says the owner. The wood panelling, wooden floorboards, wooden trellises that divide the larger room into cosy corners and, running the length of the back of the room, a gleaming bar with shiny beer pumps. Did Mien walk these same floorboards, serving one order after another? A white apron, maybe even a starched cap on her head? It's a possibility: Aalst is located in the dead centre of the old parcours and, what's more, according to the notary de Vuyst who arranged the sale of the Wooden Hand by public auction in 1940, the building has 'four large bedrooms and spacious attics'. Plenty of space for a resident waitress. Unfortunately, the current owner has never heard of Mien van Bree. And no, he doesn't recognise her photo.

It is Mien's niece who definitively puts an end to the idea of Mien serving trayfuls of beer in the Wooden Hand. She shakes her head, no, as she taps the photo with a finger. 'The pub was called Holland. Or something like that. Holland was definitely in the name. Yes, I'm sure of it. I had a picture of it. It was a cafe like that with a terrace in front.' Holland? She nods. Holland, yes. And she'd heard the name Aalst quite often, too. Why she hadn't remembered it before, she doesn't know.

The Cafe Holland in Aalst leads me nowhere.

In the silence behind the heavy barred doors of the Royal Library in Brussels, Mien comes into focus again. An article dated the 4 August 1934 in the *Het Laatste Nieuws* about the Belgian Championship to be held the next day in Leuven. There's Mien's name in the list of participants, right after that of Elvire Debruyn. On 5 August the results show Elvire as the winner and in fifteenth, 'Vanbrie' – clearly the journalist was in a hurry. The report of the World Championships in Schaarbeek says Debruyn was the indisputable winner, in front of a crowd estimated at one hundred thousand strong. Mien finishes eighth. In July 1935, in the Championship of Antwerp, she finishes third. And Mien's results keep coming. She finishes seventh in a 75 km race in Lessens, then fifth in the Belgian Championships in 1935, then second in a race in Moustier. Other newspapers start taking notice of Mien. On 24 July 1934 *De Schelde* asks what Debruyn and her Belgian teammates are going to do about the champion van Bree who has registered for the track championships in Antwerp. Elvire Debruyn wins the sprint. Mien ends up fifth.

But detailed race reports are rare and as Mien's glory days approach, results become scarce. What does appear is a series of articles about Elvire Debruyn, under the title 'How I Became A Man'. In April 1937 the daily paper *De Dag* talks to Willy – formerly Elvire – about his new life and the despair, shame and confusion that has led to his sex change. He wants to restart his career, he says, only this time as a male cyclist. But while the men's peloton gains a rider with a story, the women's sport loses Elvire, its most popular crowd pleaser. On top of that the Belgian Cycling Federation is beginning to turn against the women's sport – from 1935 it tries to prohibit women's velodrome racing, under penalty of suspension. Many velodromes ignore the ban – women's racing guarantees full grandstands, a boon to those venues that are barely keeping their heads above water. But coupled with the disappearance of the sport's undisputed star, it's the final blow. By the end of 1937 the Belgian press has lost all interest in women's cycling.

Elvire's disappearance from the women's peloton leaves the door wide open for Mien. In 1937 she becomes European Champion but her greatest ambition – the title of World Champion – remains out of reach. She finishes second. On Sunday, 16 October 1938 she tries again. The World Championships will take place in La Louviere, 50 km south of Brussels. The weather is pretty good: about 13°C, overcast, dry. As usual, Mien checks her bike herself, nervously guarding her Magnet, wary of rival supporters who have sabotaged her equipment before. She is focused, knowing she must race smart, stay alert, stay out of trouble. It wouldn't be the first time that half the peloton drops out of the race because of tacks on the road.

A few hours later Mien stands on the highest step of the podium, the victory laurels clutched to her breast. Maybe they even hung a medal around her neck. The *Zaans Volksblad* runs a little item later in the week: Mien van Bree of Loosduinen has become the women's World Cycling Champion. The 'Wayward Considerations' column in *Sport in Beeld* comments briefly on Mien's World Championship triumph: 'All respect to Mien van Bree, but to be honest, I can't say I like it. Not all sports can be done by women and cycling is one of them.' For the promotion of women's cycling, even a Dutch World Champion is not enough.

When the German Army invades Belgium and the Netherlands in 1940, Mien stays in Belgium. A year later, she goes back to Loosduinen. Her mother's rheumatism is so bad that she can no longer care for her husband or her son Aad, who still lives at home with them. She sends a letter to her only daughter, asking her to come home. And so Mien says goodbye to her life in Belgium and stores her bike by the bed in the smallest bedroom of her parents' apartment in Tramstraat. From that moment she smothers the passions that drove her to move south, suppressing them all in the unflagging care of her mother and the rest of the household. Her niece remembers that her aunt would sometimes jump on her bike during the war and ride into Belgium: 'Getting cigarettes for her brothers. Well, she knew the way of course.'

In 1944, Mien's older brother Jan – Mrs Barendse's father – is arrested during a raid. He is transported to Drenthe, then disappears into Germany to be put to work in Hamburg. During one of the endless bombing raids that plague the city in 1945, Jan is killed, because he is too ill to make his way to a shelter. The family know nothing of Jan's fate and after the war Mien's father and Jan's wife go daily to the Red Cross in search of news. Finally, months later, a group of men appear at the Van Bree's front door. They were together with Jan in Hamburg.

And so, once again, Mien's parents must grieve for a child. In 1919 they had lost Mien's sister Nelly – she died at the age of 13 in a home in Oegstgeest. But she had been born with Down's Syndrome and her parents had little expectation that she would ever grow old. Jan's death is different; he had his whole life ahead of him. Mien's mother never recovers from the blow. She dies in March 1952, leaving Mien to look after her father. Mien goes back to work, first as a packer at the local wholesaler then later as a nursing aide at Rosenburgh, a psychiatric clinic less than 10 minutes by bike from the Tramstraat. Mien's father dies seven years after her mother. Mien's brothers allow her to continue living in her parent's apartment as a thank you for the years she has looked after them. She stores her bike in the back room and, above the sofa, she hangs the portrait of her younger self in her rainbow jersey. But she never talks about her cycling career. And if someone asks, she changes the subject as quickly as possible.

In the first few years after the war Maria Gaudens and Willy Debruyn both visit Mien in Loosduinen, but after a while they lose contact with each other. Mien has little contact with her fellow-villagers. Apart from her work as a nursing aide she starts to take in washing from neighbours in her street, but any human contact is mainly limited to a business transaction.

At the beginning of the 1970s, Annie, sister of an upstairs neighbour, moves in with Mien. Annie, is 12 years older but the age difference doesn't bother either of them. Mien is already a regular customer of the liquor store at the end of the street – gin proves a good drug for washing away old memories and frustrated feelings. One day, when returning home from a visit, she opens the door to an echoing silence. Annie is gone; the apartment cleaned out. It's a shattering blow. So hard that Mien ends up in the very mental institution where she has worked for so many years. Eventually she overcomes her depression and returns to the little house in Tramstraat. She starts breeding canaries, keeps fish, has a cat. But the old Mien is gone. She allows her sister-in-law Marie to persuade her to join the Jehovah's Witnesses but Mien isn't the most fanatical of people – she prefers the oblivion of the gin bottle. Only her love for cycling remains, and she follows the Tour de France intensely. Eddy Merckx and Joop Zoetemelk are her favourite riders.

In the summer of 1983, Mien asks her niece to help her to arrange her funeral – just in case. 'It was as if she knew something would happen.' A few weeks later, her brother's phone rings. It is Mien's neighbour. She has not seen Mien for a few days. Aad's wife Janine calls round to the apartment where she finds the former World Champion. Mien is already dead, choked on her own vomit. She is 68 years old. Later, when the house is being cleared out, Mrs Barendse goes to lend a hand. 'There was this landlord around, making comments about the amount of empty bottles. I got quite angry. Aunt Mien just didn't deserve that.'

In 1959 the Dutch Cycling Federation granted the first official cycling licences to women, 21 years after Mien's first world title. In 1965 they held the official Dutch women's championship for the first time.

CHAPTER 3

ANIKA TODD

The Beast

Following a surprise silver medal at the Canadian National Time Trial Championships and a top 10 finish in the National Championship Road Race, **Anika 'The Beast' Todd** was offered a professional contract by an American team sponsored by TIBCO Software which started in January 2014. She is one of a crop of young professionals learning their craft on the roads of Europe and North America. She has represented Canada in Europe at the Jeux de la Francophonie, a youth sporting event for French speaking nations, and hopes to be wearing the maple leaf jersey many more times in the years to come. Anika's goal is to represent Canada at the 2016 Rio Olympics. She is a time trialling specialist who supports the Victoria Brain Injury Society.

🐦 @anikaxxtodd

🏠 www.anikatodd.com

Anika is an exciting young talent who, like many of her peers, uses blogging and social media to share the triumphs and downsides of her career in women's cycling. Anika was asked to write about her life so far in women's cycling and she responded with this piece, which traces her early exposure to the sport and her experiences at the 2014 Cycling World Championships in Ponferrada, Spain.

Like many of my colleagues, I never imagined that I would one day be a professional cyclist. While I enjoyed sport and competing, I was far more focused on my academic rather than my athletic endeavours. I went to the University of Victoria, British Columbia, on an academic scholarship to study biology, particularly cell and molecular biology as it relates to human health. In my spare time I worked in a psychology laboratory researching traumatic brain injury and spatial navigation, volunteered at the local brain injury society, took up running half marathons and marathons, learned how to knit, and dabbled in several different styles of yoga.

Fast forward a year and my typical day is much different, centred around training and racing: wake up, have breakfast, train, shower, lunch, yoga, dinner, sleep and repeat. I will finish the season with over 60 race days and having rarely been home for more than a week. Never did I imagine that my life would become consumed by sport or that I would count myself among the lucky few who get paid for sports. I am living the dream.

The highlight of the 2014 season and of my athletic career thus far was the 2014 UCI Road World Championships in Ponferrada, Spain. I was beyond excited to have the opportunity to test my legs against the world's best and honoured to have been selected for TIBCO's team time trial squad. The course was perfect for me – just shy of 40km, smooth roads, lots of flat or slightly downhill sections, only a couple of technical corners, and just a short climb in the finishing kilometres. It was the kind of course where my love of a huge gear and low cadence would work to the team's advantage. The plan was to use my power on the flats and downhills over the first 30km to buy the team some speed and time, and then to use the sprinters and climbers on the squad for the climb, descent and finishing kilometres. I was planning on riding my big ring (54T) for the whole course, but had changed my small chainring from a 39T to a 42T just in case I couldn't make it over the hills in a 54.

We arrived in Ponferrada a couple days before the race and had some time to settle in, preview the course, and experience the local culture. While I have been to southern Spain numerous times, this was my first time in northern Spain. It was beautiful! Driving into Leon from the Santander airport, we saw huge fields of golden sunflowers, red cliffs, rolling hills and herds of the glistening black bulls and elegant Andalusian horses that Spain is famous for. When we went to pre-ride the course, the magnitude of the event really started to sink in: the roads were barricaded, we had a police escort, and media was everywhere. Only 24 hours until the real race and time was flying by. I woke up the next morning feeling nervous but excited. I had slept well, eaten well, my legs were feeling fresh, and I was feeling confident and ready to race. Today was going to be a good day.

Before I knew it, I was on my Kurt Kinetic trainer rocking through my warm-up. I had made a new playlist that started with a motivational song titled 'Why We Fall', all about chasing success and overcoming adversity, before getting into my usual mix of Tiesto and gangsta rap. Little did I know how relevant the lyrics of that song would be.

Almost an hour later I was ready to race, got off my trainer and went to get my helmet, caffeine power gel, and aero booties. It was 13 minutes to the start and time to head over for bike check. I grabbed my bike, saw the severed shift cable and panicked. Somehow the cable for the rear shifting had been cut and I barely had enough time to get to bike check, let alone re-cable my bike. Shit.

Panicking was obviously not helping the situation and so I forced myself to take a deep breath and fought to keep my emotions under control. The worst thing I could do would be to panic and distract my teammates mere minutes before the start. I called our director, Ed Beamon, over and showed him the problem. The panic must have been written all over my face as the first thing he did was to give me a big hug while I fought to hold back the tears of anger and disappointment that were threatening to spill over. With Ed taking control of the situation I was able to breathe, refocus and get it together. He gave me the spare bike and sent me over to the start. At that point I was convinced I would be doing the race on the spare bike. There were less than 10 minutes before the gun.

With three minutes to start we stepped onto the start ramp, lined up and focused. With 30 seconds to go I was clipped in, focused on my breathing and the opening metres of the race. 15 seconds to go and I closed my eyes waiting for the beeping of the timer to start the final countdown. The yell from our mechanic, Jo, yanked me out of my trance – 11 seconds to go and Jo was throwing my TT bike over the barricade about 10m from the bottom of the start ramp. She yelled at me to get my bike! Screw the timer, get the bike!

So I jumped off the spare bike, sprinted down the ramp as quickly as one can sprint in bike cleats, grabbed my Fuji TT bike and sprinted back up the ramp ... cyclocross season was starting so it was probably good training for that. I made it behind the start line just as the rest of the team started and threw my leg over my bike getting one foot clipped in without too much fumbling around. The adrenaline had me shaking and my mind was foggy; all I could think was that I need to get rolling and catch onto the back of the train. With one foot clipped in, I rolled down the ramp and started chasing my team, immediately realising that my bike was in the small ring, the 42, and shortly after that realising that it would not shift into the big ring: big problem. The start of the course was fast, on a bit of a downhill and for a minute or two I did not think I would be able to catch the team with such a small gear. It's a good thing I had started doing cadence pyramids in training because it took about 200rpm to generate enough speed to finally catch onto the back of the team. The overwhelming wave of adrenaline was definitely helping things as well.

Finally in the draft of my teammates, I took a second to breathe and evaluate the situation. There was absolutely no shifting on the front indicating that a cable had been cut, come loose or been disconnected. There wasn't really anything I could do to fix that. Running through the course profile in my head, I decided the best thing I could do would be to try to take long pulls on sections with wind or slight uphills where I would be able to generate some speed and power despite the small chainring. In the downhill sections and through the technical sections I had no option but to fight to stay on the back of the train. If I let a gap open, I was fairly certain my chances of chasing back were slim to none. By the time I had settled down, come up with a plan and informed the rest of the team of my mechanical problems, we were already 10km into the course and I barely remembered any of it.

My body, saturated with adrenaline, was feeling no pain and I was able to pull on the front repeatedly and at a ridiculously high cadence until about 25km into the course when I finally hit the wall. Hard. Suddenly the acid was stronger than the adrenaline and my legs screamed in protest. Forced to spin, I was unable to give them any real reprieve without risking being dropped from the team. All I could do was harden the fuck up and do my best to recover a bit in the team's draft. The pain made the next 10km seem to drag on for hours and, by the time I saw the finishing climb ahead of us, I had resigned myself to being dropped from the train before we reached the top. There was just no way I could push through more pain. Just as I was starting to allow myself to look forward to the physical relief of sitting up and dropping off, one of my teammates yelled out that she was done as she dropped from the train. We were now down to five riders, four needed to make it to the finish. Halfway up the climb another one of my teammates was dropped and we were down to four. I panicked.

It's a good thing my computer was still on the spare bike as I'm pretty sure my heart rate at that point in the race had gone from the 'this hurts' zone to 'stop or your heart is going to explode and you'll drop dead off your bike' zone. My three remaining team mates did everything they could to get me up that hill and, with their help, pedal stroke for pedal stroke, through wheezing, desperate gasps for air, I somehow made it to the crest. On the descent we reached over 70km/h and my legs just about spun right off, but the finish was now so close I could taste it. Another wave of adrenaline brought a second wind and the final kilometre flew by. In what seemed like mere seconds we were at the final corner, sprinting for the finish line 500m away and then, just as quickly as the race had started, it was all over.

Of course we were all disappointed with how the race went, but that is the way that sport goes. Nothing is ever perfect. At the end of the day, it's how you react to the cards you're dealt that matters. In the grand scheme of things, what happened to us was not so bad: no one was hurt; it brought us together as a team; it forced us to really fight. We will come back stronger. Personally, I am still making the most of this amazing opportunity – absorbing the experience of competing at that level, learning all that I can, and taking the disappointment and frustration and using it as a burning source of motivation and focus in the training building up to the 2015 World Championships.

While I love what I do, I have noticed that it is easy to be entirely consumed by the sport. I now make a conscious effort to maintain balance in my life. Yes, cycling is my top priority, but I deliberately make time for other sports – yoga, running, rock climbing and paddle boarding, to name a few. Looking forward, I am also going to continue my education to keep my mind challenged and open doors outside the world of sport. Perhaps one of the most important things for me is to maintain old friendships from my pre-bike days. Making time to regularly be around those friends keeps me balanced by providing a time-out from bike and race talk. Sometimes you just need to crack open a beer, sit back and talk about a hockey game.

CHAPTER 4

BRIDIE O'DONNELL

From Lab Coat to Lycra

Bridie O'Donnell *graduated from medical school and began her career as a doctor before being accidentally lured into the world of cycling. She won the Australian Championships in 2008 and quit her job to try to qualify for the Beijing Olympics. For the next 5 years she raced in Europe, experiencing cobbled classics, the Giro Donne and three World Championships. She thrived in the AUS National Team, and survived two professional Italian teams and a US-based women's team, Vanderkitten. Writing, blogging and social media became a connection to home when she lived in Italy with no English-speaking teammates and was published regularly in Australian newspapers and cycling magazines. She's now a Melbourne-based doctor, medical educator and passionate cycling advocate. She manages and races for Australian domestic national road series team, Total Rush Hyster, and is forced to follow the professional European women's cycling scene from the Southern Hemisphere.*

🐦 @Bridie_OD

🏠 www.bridie.com.au

🏅 **Major palmarès:**

Oceania Road Champion (2010)

Silver medal – Australian Time Trial Championships and RR
    Championships (2010)

Oceania Time Trial Champion (2008, 2009)
Australian Time Trial Champion (2008)

I contacted Bridie to contribute to this book as I'd always loved her frank and funny blog. She responded with a series of short pieces that outline the ups and downs of her cycling career – from divorce and her career as a doctor to the rigours of life on the road as a professional athlete to her eventual retirement – with her usual wit and individual style. Sometimes scabrous, always interesting, and never one to shy away from the tough questions, Bridie continues to be one of the most outspoken voices in the sport, blogging about the issues that face women's cycling as it rides into a period of unprecedented growth and interest.

Today was the first stage of a hard, short tour in the 2011 Giro del Trentino. It's used as a lead-up to the women's Giro d'Italia by lots of the UCI Women's Pro Teams, and there are steep mountains, technical descents and it usually rains. In other words, Tour d'Fun!

But there I was, after the stage, sprawled in the bag of the team van as we drove to the next hotel, feeling pretty good, happy even, despite 'arriving late' in a small group. My legs felt ordinary, and I neither climbed nor descended like the fearless Italian Vincenzo Nibali. (I'm not getting his rumoured new team salary either, maybe that helps with the skinniness and the fearlessness. I'll let you know when I become a ProTour bloke and get my contract with Astana).

As I watched famous scenery rush by, incredible craggy Dolomites and fields of corn, I thought about this day's frustration compared to some more *difficult* things I've endured, and a few events in particular.

When you study psychiatry, you learn about the top 43 most stressful life events (to avoid, if you're lucky). I've ticked too many in the last 12 months.

I got divorced. That was pretty shit, to put it mildly. I can't recommend it, although for me, it was better than staying married.

Divorce was accompanied by its horsemen: being a bit place-less, having your life in boxes, searching for a home to call one's own, finding out who your friends are, and relying on the generosity or hospitality of those that remain. Bless them!

Following that, my very good friend, coach, mentor and a great driving force behind my transformation from zero to hopeful-hero in cycling endured a terrible and devastating tragedy when her 12-year-old son died. I was around the family in the days immediately following, and I still feel terribly sad, angry and scarred by what I saw. I can imagine my friend wonders how the world continues to go on, after such a loss. But she is indeed living her life, forging ahead. I hope, every day continues to be a little better than the last.

Next, and high on the list of things to avoid, is cancer. My wonderful and inspiring mother went and got herself breast cancer again, and the only thing worse than cancer is having to make incredibly hard and important decisions about surgery, treatment, pretending you're informed and calm instead of frightened and overwhelmed. Mama had to find all sorts of new ways to endure hospitals and the doctors housed in them. (On behalf of the medical profession, I would like to issue an apology to all cancer patients for any repeated lack of sympathy, empathy or just our often totally ineffectual methods of communication. We are too often better at cutting, dosing, watching, waiting and trying than we are at listening and imagining ourselves where you are. Sorry.) But I'm digressing.

There I was in the orange *furgone* (team van) emblazoned in sponsor logos, watching Italy rush by, with my tired legs and tight back, and all I could think was 'How lucky am I? I have the whole back seat to stretch out!' (Granted, there's no seatbelt, so it could have been a James Dean tragic scenario in the event of an autostrade collision. Senza trenchcoat and cigarette). I have a job where I get paid to ride a bike in Italy! If you Google 'professional + cyclist + Italy', you'll find a job that lots of people I know would like.

In fact, fools that they are, more people want my job now than when I was a doctor making an actual salary, wearing different clothes every day (and not a cute bear logo in sight), and not sparing a thought for the caloric value of my next meal.

My job now certainly isn't quite how many people perceive it to be, but it does mean I have this great, strong, fit body that does nearly all the things I want it to (except be a world champion already!) I stress it, test its capability, see the improvements, and most of the time it doesn't feel old and tired. Actually, that's a total lie. It feels old and tired every morning. But Italian espresso seems to be helping.

My job motivates me. I have desire each day to improve. I still want for more, to be better (which of course, leads to being permanently frustrated or disappointed, but aye, there's the rub). I have people who love me. Good, kind, supportive, funny and generous people who (mostly) understand why I'm doing this and who believe in me. My great family, wonderful friends, the support staff at home in Melbourne, my inspiring masseuse (a 60-year-old mountaineer and masters hockey player), and the amazing companies that give me first class equipment, ways to measure progress and accoutrement to make this life easier. I'm totally kicking Nelson's arse in that department. *He* doesn't have a custom-painted Parlee Z5 or TT bike with beautiful birds on it.

Oh, and then there's the disappointment. I got dropped today, I didn't even figure in the equation or make any impact on the race. But this is road cycling in Europe, man. It's all about managing disappointment.

So, after a shower and a massage, I wandered down to team dinner, tired but already managing the frustrations of the stage. Next to me at the table was the perfectly rotund Berto, our acting *directeur sportif* (DS), who could pass for a silver moustached circus ringleader. He regarded me a while, then asked how I was.

'*Non c'é male*' (not bad), I replied.

He gave me a wonderful look, one that only a kind man who has seen hundreds of days of bike races in his lifetime could reveal. You see, Berto knows about managing disappointment too – about putting the useless emotions away and preparing to be great the next day. He patted my shoulder and said '*Oggi é passato. Domani é nuovo giorno.*' Then he poured his eighth glass of house red and raised it to my glass of water. '*Cin cin!*'

Surviving the Giro

They say that 10-day tours get easier the more you do them. I hope so, because my first one in 2010 was damn hard!

The Giro d'Italia Femminile (or Giro Donne, rebranded in 2013 as the Giro Rosa) is always held in July, when it's nice and hot in northern Italy. It's famous for having hard mountain stages, ruthless time cuts and plenty of DNFs (Did Not Finish).

I was riding with instructions from our DS, GianCarlo Montedori: 'Breedie, the Giro, it's hard, no? You must finish, *si*? And you must help Monia e Tatiana, *si*? *Va bene*.' Terrific. Let's not get too specific on how I go about that!

Team Valdarno had been waiting for this race since the beginning of the season, and 2009 Road Race World Champion, Tatiana Guderzo, was our General Classification (GC) contender. She was fit and in form, and her new custom painted Pinarello Dogma (complete with subtle rainbow stripes) was ready for the tough mountain stages in the last three days.

She had two other climbers to assist her: a Russian who spoke a bit of Italian (Tatiana Antoshina, Russian TT and Road Champion); and Evgeniya Vysotska, a Ukrainian who barely spoke Russian. Evgeniya was a tiny climbing machine, brought to the team three days before the Giro. She was a revelation, even when she described her legs as being 'kaput!'

We also had Italian road champion, Monia Baccaille, vying for wins in the early sprint stages. Unfortunately, she was involved in a huge crash inside the last kilometre of stage 2 that brought down a lot of riders, including Australian Rochelle Gilmore (Lotto-Honda Team), the Brit Sharon Laws (Cervélo TestTeam) and three national team riders, Tiffany Cromwell, Kirsty Broun and Emma Mackie.

Monia wasn't badly hurt, and went on to finish the Giro well, but couldn't manage a stage win. Sharon Laws fractured her clavicle and was operated on in Switzerland, and Gilmore started the next two stages but was heavily bandaged and pretty sore. She couldn't trick her body to continue and pulled out on stage 5.

My role and my plan of attack required daily vigilance: eating enough, staying safe in the peloton, drinking enough fluids in the 39°C heat and then listening for a teammate's call over the radio to get to the front to (a) chase back a break or (b) keep pace high into a climb (meaning I hit the start of the climb in the top 5 and then 100m later, I'm in 100th place!) or (c) assist Monia in the sprint.

If I was being kind to myself, I'd say, yes, I did do all those things. But the quality and experience of Team HTC-Columbia Women, the USA National Team and Cervélo TestTeam was enough to overwhelm any meagre efforts by lone Italian team domestiques!

Ina Teutenberg (Team HTC-Columbia Women) took the first two frantic sprint stages, and then surprised even herself by winning the 17km time trial in stage 3. Oh, and then won the stage 4 sprint finish too. Outstanding displays of skill and strength, both by her and the team.

By stages 5 and 6, the alleged 'non-hilly' days, all were a little tired and hot. The average temperature had been 37°C and we knew which mountain passes were coming in stages 7 to 9. We had changed hotels every single night, and the novelty of a carpark shower then three hours in the back of a hot van was starting to wear off! What is it with cyclists and a fear of air conditioning? Legionnaires' disease? Italian bird flu?

Marianne Vos, current world no. 1 and riding for the Dutch National Team, took the next two stages solo, in technical finishes that suited her aggressive cyclocross style. Judith Arndt (Team HTC-Columbia Women) had consolidated her second place and Guderzo was in third.

For stages 7, 8 and 9, we covered high mountain passes, technical descents and the challenges of getting a bidon from your 70-year-old visually impaired soigneur. I learned how to climb in the sprinter's bunch, at *just* the right pace to make time cut safely, but not so hard that the bunch splinters on the 42 switchbacks of the Stelvio Pass (2758m). Besides, no one wants to get yelled at by Teutenberg for not doing it right.

I also learned that your legs can feel fine at 25km/h in a warm-up ride to the stage start, instilling plenty of positive vibes of 'yeah, this is fine, I'm really not that tired ... ', but when the race starts with three 6km laps at Livigno (1875m), and the peloton takes off at 40km/h before a nasty climb, non-tired legs will just not cooperate. And that's the day, done and dusted.

Uber-climber and yoga instructor Mara Abbot (USA National Team) won stages 8 and 9 and sealed the maglia rosa. Her teammate, Shelley Evans, won the final stage bunch sprint into Monza and our leader, Tatiana Guderzo, finished up 3rd on GC, with the best Italian rider jersey. We also had the full eight on the finish line and won best team (with Vysotska sixth and Antoshina eighth in the GC).

10,654m climbed, 1,125km ridden, a kajillion litres of water drunk and I stayed upright. Gotta be easier the second time around, right?

CHAPTER 5

CONNIE CARPENTER-PHINNEY
From Silver Blades to Golden Bikes

Connie Carpenter-Phinney is an American cyclist who won the first-ever Olympic women's road race in 1984. She also competed at the 1972 Winter Olympics as a speed skater at 14 years old, becoming the youngest ever American female Winter Olympian. Connie is married to Davis Phinney, and together they have two kids – Taylor and Kelsey Phinney. She makes her home in Boulder, Colorado, where she is an entrepreneur and also on the board of the Davis Phinney Foundation. Connie is a graduate of the University of California, Berkeley, and has a master's degree in science from the University of Colorado.

🐦 @bikecamp
🏠 www.davisphinneyfoundation.org

🏅 **Major palmarès:**
Gold medal – Olympic Road Race (1984)
13 times US National Track Pursuit and Road Race Champion (1976–1982)
World Champion Track Pursuit (1983)
Silver medal – World Road Race (1977)
Bronze medal World Road Race (1981)

Connie Carpenter-Phinney is one of the pioneers of the women's sport, not only as a rider but in her efforts to promote and develop women's cycling in the US. I was introduced to her by her son Taylor, himself one of the brightest young talents in the men's professional peloton. I asked Connie for her perspective on women and cycling, and she responded with the following piece that outlines not only her illustrious career but the issues that she and her peers faced – and that women cyclists continue to face – in gaining recognition for their sport.

Some say it's not what you know, but who you know. I might suggest that both are true, but in my sporting life it's the people I've met who have sculpted and shaped not only my athletic career, but me.

Speed skating was my first true sporting endeavour. I dabbled in the very few other sports that were deemed appropriate for girls in the 1960s – I tried gymnastics (too tall) and diving (too slow) and figure skating (too rigid).

During the long cold Wisconsin winters before the advent of colour television and long before the personal computer age, there was little to do in the winter apart from ice skate. I was lucky to grow up across the street from an elementary school playground. It was fun in the summer but more fun in the winter when it was flooded with water to make ice from December through February. Lights were strung proficiently around the perimeter and they flickered on every night precisely at 7pm for two hours. This was the best baby-sitting my parents could have imagined: my three brothers and I all fed, then fled across the street eager to play.

The local village constructed boards for the boys to hone their hockey skills over half of the playground. The other side was easily the size of a soccer field (it seemed ginormous at the time) and was dedicated to free skating (no hockey pucks allowed!). There, the neighbourhood gathered to play games – an endless cycle of them. We played a version of tag called pom-pom, and the more elaborate and tactical game of capture the flag. Those games were thrilling especially for me as I was easily one of the fastest skaters on the rink of any age.

If you have never skated under lights on a dark night, you may not know the acute sensation of speed that accompanies the lessening of peripheral vision that darkness brings. The skills I learned allowed me to be elusive when chased – and effective when I was the chaser. That gave me a sense of power beyond my age.

I was shy and awkward, except where sports were concerned. In the vernacular of the day, I was a tomboy. I wished I had been born a boy; my brothers had more opportunities than I did. But I played hard – and my three brothers played hard. Even my dad played hard. They occupied the space within the boards playing hockey. Girls did not play hockey. It was never presented as a choice and, even when I dared cross that line and pass the puck a bit with my brothers or my dad, it was only for a few minutes until the action picked up and I was sent back to the other side. For my part, I eschewed the normal figure skate and had my dad grind the toe picks down so they handled more like hockey skates.

The city of Madison, Wisconsin, hosted annual skating championships. They were straight-line sprints that required qualification by neighbourhood rinks and finals held at Vilas Park. The winners got their pictures in the newspaper. It was a tradition and, for me, a blast. I won every year from kindergarten through sixth grade. And every year the local speed skating club would call to ask me to join the team. I'd ask my parents, who would politely decline.

'Oh honey you don't want to do that,' they'd say. And I'd say, 'Wait – why don't I want to do that?' 'Because it takes too much time blah blah blah …'

They were caught up in youth hockey and didn't have the energy or time to take me the three miles across town to practices. No one on my side of town speed skated so I couldn't carpool. It wasn't until sixth grade that my parents relented after I went to a local skating race hosted by the club. I won – wearing my corduroys and baggy sweater, I'd beaten the kids in their flashy red skating tights. That result encouraged my dad to take me to another race the following weekend. There, I'd beaten myself. I was leading in a 1½-lap race when the bell sounded. I rounded the turn after the bell, clearly in the lead and then stood up and coasted. I thought the race was over. The rest of the field skated past me. I was so naïve that I did not realise the meaning of the bell lap.

I spent the rest of the afternoon crying in our family station wagon out of sheer pre-adolescent embarrassment, but my dad used that time to meet the parents, discuss opportunities and sign me up for the club.

In an instant, my life changed and for the first time, I belonged. It was my first sports team. Sport gave me an instant sense of community and a purpose that had structure: a season filled with meets scattered between Champaign, Illinois, and St. Paul, Minnesota. I was hooked on the lifestyle; packing into someone's family car to go to a race because my parents were generally and understandably consumed by hockey. Speed skating was a family sport and I believe that is why women have always had equal opportunity in the sport. It was never questioned, and no one ever complained about having me crash in their hotel room and share their snacks.

There was a huge upside to the fact that I was the solo speed skater on my side of Madison. It allowed me to escape the social pressure of junior high school. The sporting pressure was no problem for me; in fact, I thrived in competition. I could be one person in school (a rather mysterious, good student) and another person across town (athlete and a good one at that).

When I began to train year-round, I had to find a way to escape the harsh scrutiny of those times. In those days, running wasn't something you did casually, unless you were running away from something – like a robbery. I rode my trusty Peugeot three to four miles across town to the University Arboretum or to a large park known as Picnic Point – there I could run in anonymity on trails in the woods that were seldom used. Of course, in and around the university, there were some others running and occasionally I'd meet up with other skaters to train. But skaters tended to train alone. There was sort of a secret society aspect to the training. No one really shared and I could only imagine that everyone was training more than me.

I made my first Olympic team in 1972, precisely 3 years after I joined the local speed skating club (thanks for that Dad!). I was fortunate to have had exposure to a top coach in 1971. Finn Halvorsen was brought over from Norway to coach our national team. Most of the 'old guard' in skating already had coaches, so I was a bit of a project for Finn. He taught me how to train and sparked a life-long curiosity in exercise physiology that would see me earn a graduate degree in the topic.

Though I was just 14 years of age, it didn't feel as if I were out of place. The top ranked girl on the squad was a 16-year-old phenomenom named Anne Henning. My other roommate at the time was 19-year-old Sheila Young (now Ochowicz). Both Anne and Sheila became Olympic gold medallists in speed skating (Anne in 1972, Sheila in 1976). I would wade through two other sports, and train another 12 years, until I joined their fraternity and finally reach the top step on the Olympic podium.

I was drawn toward – and introduced to – the cycling track because of Sheila. Apart from our sporting choices, we could not have been more different – I was long and lanky, she was short and muscular. She was a sprinter – super-fast twitch. I was not. Off the bike, she took to simple pleasures, which belied her alter ego. On the bike, she was a fiery dynamo. In fact, Sheila Young-Ochowicz was the first seriously tenacious competitor I had met. She first won the 1973 World Sprints in San Sebastian, Spain – seemingly unencumbered by the handful of staples in her head that were necessary to close a wound in the run-up to the exciting finale. Her victory marked the end of the 15-year Soviet reign at the top of women's sprinting, and, even more notably, Sheila was the first athlete to be world champion in two different sports in the same year. It was a feat she would duplicate in 1976 (World Sprint Champion for Speed Skating and Cycling).

In 1975, I spent many hours riding the track with her. Track training was fun in groups and allowed me to do intensive intervals that were required of me as a speed skater. Take the bike away, and the speed skating position is quite similar – the active muscle groups are more or less the same. Long road rides were not as beneficial for the shorter efforts of speed skating so the track was a good cross-training tool and it opened up an active and engaged community – much less secretive than the speed skating tribe.

My older brother Chuck also dabbled in road cycling during the summers and often I'd accompany him to the races, though at the time, I didn't consider racing as a likely option for me. He was a stand-out hockey player, rowed on the crew at Yale, and bike raced in his spare time. I definitely took his lead in sport and in life.

In 1976 I failed to make the Olympic speed skating team. I had been dealing with chronic tendonitis in my ankle during an era when access to physical therapy was limited and orthotic inserts were virtually unknown. The peroneal tendonitis – located on the outside of my left ankle and running behind the bony bit known as the malleolus – was responsible for sustaining my body weight through the turns (speed skaters only skate counter-clockwise, to the left). Coming out of a turn in one of my final workouts prior to the Olympic trials, it snapped. Technically, it was more of a micro-tear, but it felt like a snap – and in an instant, I was hobbled.

When they failed to call my name as one of the Olympians, I was quite suddenly an 18-year-old without a plan. When I looked around me, it felt like my whole world had shattered. After the waterfall of tears and several days of despair came a trip to the hinterlands of the Midwest with Chuck and his friends who were on Christmas break from college. What I discovered almost instantly was that a whole wide world existed beyond the ice rink and it was waiting for me with arms wide open. My ankle, which didn't move side to side very well, could quite easily move up and down. I could cross country ski (classic style) and I could ride a bike. Voilà.

I returned to the University of Wisconsin, and I turned my energy to studying and my athletic prowess to the bike. I was happy to be free of the confines of frozen winters and ribbons of ice, and loved the open roads, warmer weather, and perhaps more than anything, the camaraderie of bicycle racing in the 1970s.

I never looked back.

By the end of my first season of bike racing in 1976, I won the US national championships by defeating the previous champion and former World Championship medalist Mary Jane 'Miji' Reoch in both the individual pursuit and the road race by very narrow margins. Later in the summer, I viewed the 1976 Olympic Games track cycling events from the infield with Sheila (courtesy of her VIP status) and competed in the World Championships for cycling on the road and the track. I was no longer a speed skater, but a fully immersed world-class bike racer and I was having the time of my life.

Miji Reoch was much more than just a competitor I beat in that first year, she was also the most generous and open-hearted friend and the one who tugged and prodded me to plow through her wake on my way to the top of the sport. She, like many before her, came to cycling very late and with very little athletic background. She didn't start riding and then racing until her mid-twenties, while also supporting her husband as he went through law school. A tenacious woman on the bike, most of what I learned in the early years of racing was channelled through her. I stayed in her home and chased her through the streets in and around Philadelphia where she lived. She drove me up to the Trexlertown track for Friday night races.

Miji was a style queen and, I thought, the epitome of fine taste, on the bike and at home. Everything was cooked or prepared to perfection and the table was always set as if expecting royalty. She spoke French fluently, having been an au pair in France during college and she cooked with a lot of flair (not to mention a healthy dose of butter).

Most importantly for my cycling career, she taught me how to dig deep and race aggressively, primarily in men's races. In the late 1970s, most women's races were run simultaneously with the masters men, the junior men or a lower category men's field to save time. If there was a women-only event, it quite typically was a short race – sometimes as short as 5 miles, maybe 10 but hardly ever more than 15. Fortunately, I could race in the women's race and then a few hours later, race in the elite men's field – a pattern I continued through most of my career.

I raced a lot when I started out; it is one aspect of the sport that allowed me to get good fast. Coming out of a winter sport with a short season that depended on frigid conditions (all long-track speed skating was outdoors until the Calgary Games of 1988), it was a pleasure to race as often as five times in a week in the summer. Two nights a week, I rode the track in Kenosha and Northbrook. The track series were always fun and diverse, including many attempts by me to ride the team event known as 'the Madison' with an intrepid male or female partner. One night a week we had an intense mash-up club race on the roads of an abandoned military base outside of Madison. Those races honed my cornering and breakaway skills – and put me right where I needed training-wise – on the rivet. And on the weekend, there were races in and around the Midwest. Cycling always had a festival-like atmosphere. It was fun.

Later, when Miji gave birth to her daughter, Solange, and moved to Dallas with her husband (from whom she would later divorce), I invited her to be the coach of my team through the 1984 Olympics. Monica Van Haute was our manager – she did the heavy lifting of getting us from place to place and helping with the challenges that we all shared living on the road as much as we did – but Miji came in for big events, and helped us strategise and focus. She became an integral part of my team.

If at this point you think that things came easily to me, I would argue that there is no easy way – I suffered mightily physically, and emotionally. However, one thing is true: I was definitely a quick and very eager study. And I loved pushing myself to be better. And honestly, I loved winning. More than that, I was supported and encouraged by my family despite their concerns. I was a magnet for – or had the good sense to be surrounded by – great people. As for the not so great people, I tried my level best to ignore them.

After completing a few years of study at the University of Wisconsin, I took a break to bike race and moved to the warmer climate and active cycling college town of Berkeley, California. My boyfriend at the time raced at the highest level; neither of us made much money, but we were definitely living the counter-culture vagabond cycling life. We graduated from living in the spare and sparse room above Peter Rich's Velo Sport bike shop in Berkeley, to a one room studio with a mattress on the floor. The urban roads around Berkeley were a stark comparison to the country roads of Wisconsin. We rode to the east – on the Dam road, out past the Pig Farm, toward the ever-looming presence of Mont Diablo. To get out of town, we'd 'tunnel up' or 'spruce out' depending on the route, giving me access to climbs that did not exist in Wisconsin. And we always finished back in town at Peet's Coffee. What a life!

A note to all you hipsters out there, you would have loved it.

I obtained in-state residency (a tuition savings that made my college experience almost free) and applied to the University of California in Berkeley and resumed my studies during the winter quarter of 1979. I was already growing tired of the lack of opportunities presented to me by women's cycling and was motivated to get my degree, perhaps more so because it was expected of me than because I had a grand career plan. There is a sidebar to this story – and that is that I rowed on the crew for precisely a year and a half while at Berkeley. In that time, true to form, I was a quick study. I made the

Varsity Eight after rowing for six months and we finished second at Collegiate nationals.

In the late seventies, one race stood apart from the rest and that was the Red Zinger (later known as the Coors Classic) and it changed the course of my career. It was like a bright shining beacon on the top of Mount Olympus – only it was in Boulder, Colorado; the rarefied place I now call home. It was sponsored by the makers of Red Zinger tea, Celestial Seasonings, and was led by its enigmatic founder, Mo Siegel. Mo was a huge early benefactor for the fledging sport.

The Red Zinger did have a women's division in 1975 but I was not yet racing so my first year was 1977. We had three stages, and I surprised myself by winning at altitude and by winning big. The festival atmosphere that I had grown accustomed to in the Midwest was raised up a notch in the funky college town of Boulder, Colorado. It was fun, cool, hip and thrilling. I was beaten in 1978 and 1979 – due to race promoter Michael Aisner's commitment to bringing the top Europeans in to race against us, thereby raising the ante of women's cycling to a whole new level.

Dutch racer Keetie van Oosten-Hage was the reigning queen of women's cycling (much as Marianne Vos is now) – an imposing athlete almost 10 years my senior and a multiple world champion. She was feisty, tough and relentless on the bike, and very quiet off the bike. Whenever she won (which was often), she would throw up her hands in a manner that suggested she had never won before. She'd celebrate with her hands to the sky and her face was lit up like a Christmas tree.

I have to admit, it drove me crazy. I really wanted to beat her. If you have ever pushed yourself on the bike to a very high level and had someone take off and attack you from that level – well, that was Keetie. She could break my chops just about any day of the week. I had to work extremely hard to beat her. Once, I flew to Holland and spent several weeks in her back yard – chasing, attacking and taking advantage of the local peloton politics to break away and win a few on my own. She had thrown the gauntlet down in my hometown, it was the least I could do to return the favour.

I recruited a few other younger friends from Madison who were successful speed skaters – Beth Heiden and Sarah Docter. They were instantly successful due to their impressive fitness level despite a relative inexperience with the sport. In 1980, Beth Heiden turned her Winter Olympic disappointment (she medalled in one event, but had been widely expected to do more) into a win on one of the toughest World Road Championships courses ever. She was not enamoured with cycling, however, and quickly turned to cross-country ski racing where she earned a national collegiate title while skiing for the University of Vermont. I wasn't alone in my success in diverse sporting interests.

We were a generation somewhat unconfined by convention, floating between two different schools of thought. The generation before us quit sport early – if they pursued sport at all – to start a family. Once the landmark Title IX passed into law, universities across the country were required to include more gender equality in all collegiate sports. It did not happen all at once, but quite suddenly the call to sports for women was widespread. That didn't ensure longevity or financial success in sport but it changed the face of team sports in particular.

For the duration of my sports career, and while I was supporting myself through sponsors, like AMF, Cateye, Puch, Levi's and Raleigh, I was an amateur. We were allowed to win prizes up to a certain amount per day and my average annual income was equivalent with the 'amateur' men. There was no professional division in cycling for women and the Olympics were 'amateur only' (and in cycling, only for the men until 1984).

After finishing crew season at Cal-Berkeley in 1979, I had only six weeks to prepare for the races in Colorado and I was clearly not at the top of my game. What could I expect? I'd been running, lifting weights and rowing 20 plus hours per week, not cycling. In 1980 I rowed pretty much full-tilt but opted not to race my bike at all. It wasn't until I visited the Coors Classic to watch that I realised how much I missed it.

During that off-season I started dating Davis Phinney. One of the first things he mentioned quite casually to me was that he didn't see that I'd lived up to my potential. Ouch. That stung me to the core, but he was right and he encouraged me to come back and race after I graduated later in 1981. I was more motivated to race than I was excited about getting a real job. My timing could not have been better as it was announced formally that women's cycling would be included in the 1984 Olympic Games in Los Angeles. One race: a 79km road race on the opening day of competition. I was 'in' for the duration and looking to live up to my potential.

Yet the biological – or perhaps more importantly – the cultural clock was ticking. There was pressure to marry, have kids, be normal (please!) In no small way, the goal of winning the Olympics legitimised my journey and allowed a grace period in my life.

When I finished up at Berkeley, Davis and I loaded up the VW Rabbit and hit the road. After a year away from competition, it would take a lot of racing to find my form and so we travelled the length of California hitting all the local races, camping out in cheap motels or spare beds in homes of friends, before I eventually settled into Davis's hometown of Boulder, Colorado.

New sponsors were coming in to the sport and primarily into women's cycling due to the Olympic inclusion. We crafted a team of like-minded women who wanted to race hard and work together. We were good and we had fun, but the lifestyle was tiring and the pockets were not super deep. One teammate stood out, and that was Sue Novara-Reber, who had already won the World Sprint title two times but wanted her shot at the Olympic Games. No track events were scheduled for the women in the 1984 Olympic Games.

Sue brought her sprint game to the team in races and in training. From experience, I knew that at least 95% of all races end in some sort of a sprint, so I worked on my sprinting systematically in training. The luxury of having an in-house master cannot be overstated. Working with a sprinter of her caliber, week in and week out, made me quicker, and boosted my confidence. She was competitive in town sign sprints and organised sprint training, and she was physically intimidating despite being one of the sweetest girls you could ever meet (off the bike that is). She could give Davis and the guys a run for their money when we sprinted over hill and dale in pursuit of the elusive town sign sprints. Sue knew how to take advantage of the terrain, her competitors and the bike. Moreover, she was fun to train with – motivated, talented and highly skilled. Above all else, she understood me and supported me as a friend.

One particular comment became etched in my mind. We were doing what we thought we needed to do to improve – and that is to race in Europe with the national team. Our federation had flown us to Belgium so that we could drive all the team vehicles to the south of France. And we were fried from the drive. Our first stop was in the hills of Provence where we all stayed in a school. Our team was given one half of a room, with five beds lined up 'Little Orphan Annie style'. The other side of the room featured the Swiss national team. The shared bathroom was down the hall.

A few days later, we were miserably cold and wet, and had checked into yet another school for our accommodation and food. There was no heat on in the building, no blankets on the beds, and the food lacked any nutritional content. We piled all of our clothes onto our respective beds to generate enough warmth to slumber. After a restless frigid night, we awoke to more of the same.

As we looked out the window to the courtyard below, Sue said, 'They treat us as women imitating men, not as female athletes. We don't belong here – we are not one of them.' To be honest, her sentiments were not meant to be elitist. It was, however, simply true.

We had moved far beyond merely surviving as female cyclists, and were unwilling – or unable – to endure the huge lifestyle step-down required to race in Europe. At the time, there was no World Cup or international ranking system, but I knew I'd only return to Europe to race in the World Championships, not to squander valuable time or my talents in no-name races on partially closed roads for no real reason. I knew I could prepare better in the US.

Thus began a quest to chart the ideal preparation for the 1984 Olympic Games. From the time that I saw the course in January 1984 to race day at the end of July, I raced almost 80% of my races with the category 1 men. This afforded me more quality time to train, less time loss in transit, and a more aggressive style of racing. I resisted the temptation to race the full distance in races that were too long because I wanted to be fast and going the distance was not an issue for me. I focused on faster shorter races that required bike handling and tactics, and forced me to stay at or near my limit for a good portion of the race. At the time, many US men's races were 1–3 hours in length and were criterium or circuit style which was perfect for my preparation. I raced up and down the coast of California, and across the country in races ranging from the super-fast Athens Twilight Criterium to an aggressive stage race in North Carolina – and of course several races in Colorado – all with the men.

Davis and I married in October of 1983. His run-up to the Games included a long stint in Europe. In the non-information age, we primarily existed with a huge void of time and space between us, which was the hardest part of the '84 season. We would scarcely speak to each other for weeks on end. I was my own coach and had been for a long time, but I relied on Davis's advice in all aspects of racing and life. I missed him.

Fortunately my sponsors also bought into my plan. I wasn't winning races but I was getting attention and the Olympic hype was already in full gear, and we'd crossed into the mainstream media. Our team had a full-time publicist and we were deflecting as many interviews as we were taking. The highlight of this blitz was a photo shoot in Death Valley with the iconic photographer Annie Leibovitz for the January 1984 issue of *Vanity Fair*.

It was a great disappointment for me that Sue's quest to make the team did not succeed. She couldn't overcome the true sprinter's classic struggle with gravity – and her inability to sustain her power over a long climb meant that she did not perform well enough at our Olympic Trials. Alas, she was due the honour of being an Olympian just as Sheila Young should have earned it before her, but the Olympic road race course was hilly and it didn't suit her skillset. Sue retired one race ahead of me, and went on to became national team coach and Olympic team coach before settling fulltime back home in Michigan.

Who were my competitors in 1984? Besides the legendary French woman Jeannie Longo, the Italian Maria Canins and a few strong young West Germans, I knew that my US teammate Rebecca Twigg would give me a big challenge. She had risen from a track specialist to a worthy contender on the road. We weren't friends – our age difference (five years) meant she was more reliant on the national team coach at the time (Eddy B). She was book smart but it didn't translate to her interpersonal skills. Or maybe she was just shy. In any case, my job was to beat her, and it was never easy.

The Olympics in 1984 were huge. It was a gigantic undertaking by a gigantic city and they pulled it off flawlessly. Our relatively small field of women convened on the start line on 29 July before a massive audience to race 79km, most of which would be shown on national TV. Together we made history that day. The race itself played out as I had imagined it would, with a small group of strong women riding away from the pack over the very challenging terrain on a very warm day. The resulting group sprinted to the line 79km later; I won by only a few inches utilising a technique that I had refined under Davis's tutelage, with Sue's insistent voice in my head to bring it home. I can honestly say, I did my best and it was just enough.

And that was the end of my career in bike racing.

Epilogue

Taylor was born in 1990 and his sister Kelsey followed in 1994. Davis turned pro in 1985 and retired from competition in 1993. Davis and I ran a successful mom and pop business called Carpenter/ Phinney Bike Camps since 1986, and Davis was doing commentary for television among over things. Our days on the bike led us to be entrepreneurial off the bike, which allowed us to continue our lifestyle.

In 2009, I was asked to be on a committee chaired by the Governor of Colorado to help find a way (meaning sponsor) to bring the Bike Race back (the Coors Classic which had concluded its run in 1988). I showed up at the first meeting in August with Taylor introducing himself to the Governor of Colorado as my 'arm candy.'

I said, 'I am not here to bring a men's race to Colorado. The men have enough races on the calendar. What I really want to see is the historical footprint of the original race upheld and to see the women racing on the same day, over similar terrain, in front of the same audience.' Moreover I wanted the US women to have the opportunity that I had, to race at the highest level at home. I readily admit that I would not have become Olympic Champion without the training and proving ground of the Red Zinger/Coors Classic race.

Everyone on the committee agreed with me from the outset and over the course of the next 18 months until the sponsor came in and the promoters came on board. Then, the women's race as a concept simply vanished from the conversation. The men's race hit the ground running in 2011 and was an instant success, except for me; I felt I had failed the women's cycling community and myself.

Former pro cyclist Jessica Phillips succeeded in creating a three-day stage women's race in Aspen in the first two years, but it suffered from lack of support from the 'big show' and fizzled.

However, out of the blue at the conclusion of the 2014 race in Colorado, it was announced that there will in fact be a women's component in 2015. When asked how many days it should run, I said: 'All of them. Let's go big.'

So it's back to the future we go. Yessss!

Hallelujah!

Dedicated to those who shaped me, pushed me, tolerated me and love me – still. How lucky I have been and continue to be.

Notes:

Mary Jane 'Miji' Reoch was killed in Dallas by a hit-and-run driver in 1993 while riding her bike during a coaching session with a client. She was 49 years old. More than anything, she is missed but not forgotten.

Sheila Young-Ochowicz is a middle-school PE teacher in Northern California, the mother of 3 (including a 3-time Olympian speed skater) and the wife of Jim Ochowicz, Taylor's boss.

Sue Novara-Reber is a successful real estate agent in Flint, Michigan. She has two grown daughters.

Cornelia 'Keetie' van Oosten-Hage retired in 1979 from a very successful career. She has been seen around the races in Holland helping to promote women in cycling.

Rebecca Twigg is a single mom living in Seattle.

CHAPTER 6

KATHRYN BERTINE

A Pirate's Life for Me

Kathryn Bertine is the 2014 Caribbean Champion and a professional cyclist for Wiggle Honda. Off the bike, she is a journalist, author, filmmaker and activist for women's rights in sports. In 2013, she co-founded Le Tour Entier with Emma Pooley, Marianne Vos and Chrissie Wellington to petition the Tour de France to add a women's event and in 2014 *La Course* found its way into the history books. Her film *Half the Road* explores the issues female pro cyclists face, and her latest book *The Road Less Taken* is an essay collection on the same topic.

🐦 @kathrynbertine @halftheroad
🏠 www.kathrynbertine.com www.halftheroad.com

As one of the movers and shakers behind Le Tour Entier, Kathryn Bertine was obviously someone that I wanted to contact to contribute to this book. But she was – unsurprisingly – busy, not only training to compete in the race, La Course, *that she had been so instrumental in setting up, but in writing her own book and putting together her film* Half the Road. *Instead she gave me a chapter from her book* The Road Less Taken, *which is a collection of her writing over her years as a professional cyclist. Here she writes about the typical lot of many women cyclists on the road – the kinds of conditions that she is so keen to address and mitigate in her work with Le Tour Entier.*

I've spent the past four nights sleeping with Johnny Depp. I'm exhausted. It isn't Depp who's worn me out, though. It's the 150 other female cyclists I've been racing for the past week. This doesn't explain Depp, but I'm getting there.

My teammates and I are at the San Dimas Stage Race and Redlands Bicycle Classic, two of the most high-profile bike races in America, set just outside Los Angeles. Stage races are multiday cycling events that sound like a good idea while signing up, but not so much during the events. They hurt. Bad. But it's a good bad. While cycling offers rewards such as physical fitness and the thrill of victory, there are also crashes, road rash and mind-numbing physical exertion that borders on delirium. Apparently, we elite riders find this fun. Or perhaps we have deep-seated emotional issues stemming back to childhood. No one really knows what drives a person into the world of cycling, but the ones that stick around truly love it unconditionally. Especially the female racers.

While most men's pro teams have larger budgets and corporate sponsors, the women are still working their way up the ladder of global recognition. For the majority of elite female racers, that means taking a no-frills approach to the sport: Flying to events is a luxury. Most of us drive to races, playing games like 'How many cyclists can you stuff in a Volkswagen?' We often pay for our meals and gas out of our pockets, and we're lucky (and grateful) when team managers/owners cover entry fees and the occasional dinner. Our bikes are usually loaners, as the irony of the sport is that most elite cyclists can't afford their own stellar carbon-fibre machines at retail price. And then there's the lodging. Hotels during stage races are usually not in the women's race budget, so we rely on home stays to keep us sheltered. And Johnny Depp to keep us warm.

Home stays are local families near race venues who kindly agree to take in pro athletes, for free. We use their kitchens to cook our pre-race meals and sleep on their beds, couches and floors. For this trip, my Trisports Cycling teammate, Marilyn McDonald, and I are given a home stay with a family in Redlands, California. We share the room of the family's four-year-old son, who is in turn relocated to the living room couch. Thanks to SpongeBob's absorbing presence on the living room TV, this transition goes remarkably smoothly. His two-year-old sister, however, will soon borrow my laptop for a game of 'Let's sled down the stairs'. Marilyn claims the futon in the four-year-old's room. I take the bed, which is a replica of a pirate ship, sails and all, complete with a *Pirates of the Caribbean* bedspread.

After the first day of racing in the four-day event at the Redlands Bicycle Classic, I find myself a bit further back in the time trial results than I hoped. This is bike racing: sometimes you soar, sometimes you suck, sometimes you settle somewhere in between. And when you're physically exhausted, mentally dejected and in a strange bed far from home, sometimes you question everything. I whisper to my teammate:

'Marilyn?'

'Hmmm.'

'I'm 34 years old, and I'm asleep in a pirate-ship bed of a four-year-old, neither of which belongs to me. Is this weird?'

'Kind of.'

'Aren't I supposed to have a four-year-old?'

'Probably.'

'How did I get here?'

Marilyn laughs. She knows I'm not referring to my decade-old Volvo wagon with 153,000 miles that we drove to California from Tucson, Arizona.

'We love bike racing?' she suggests.

'Right,' I say. 'Thanks.' I turn over, considering this truth. I do love this racing life, as bizarre, exhausting and underfunded as it is. I especially love how it found me – suddenly and wholly.

As a sports journalist and elite athlete, I was offered an assignment in 2006 by ESPN. The company wanted me to investigate what it takes to get to the Olympic Games. The catch? I was both the reporter and the guinea pig. For two years, I attempted to qualify for the Beijing Summer Olympics in road cycling. While I had a short career as a mediocre pro triathlete (and an MFA in creative writing) heading into this assignment, it wasn't quite enough to get me to Beijing. Oddly, though, after two years of road cycling, I came quite close. Too close. When my assignment with ESPN concluded in 2008, my love of cycling did not. In fact, it grew. And so too did my muscles, ability and results. I decided to shoot for the 2012 Games as a member of the St. Kitts and Nevis Cycling Federation, which is why, at the end of the day, I'm in a boat-shaped kiddie bed in a stranger's house setting sail with the Pirates of the Caribbean and a flask of electrolytes.

Or it might not. Like most women in their early 30s, I've done some thinking about my life path. I've compared the 'What I've got' list with the 'What I thought I'd have by now' list. Here's a brief rundown:

What I thought I'd have at 34:
Husband
Kids
Stable career
Dog
Cute wardrobe
Routine
Predictability
Happiness

What I actually have:
Singledom (though that has changed, too)
Bicycles
Freelance work
Cactus
Farmer's tan

Spontaneity

Stories

Happiness

Funny how the road to happiness can take such different routes. Occasionally I suffer from grass-is-greener-itis, thinking I want or need the things my conventional peers have. Sometimes the cycling life makes me angry, annoyed and inconvenienced. But for the most part, it brings me great joy. Sure, I often live out of a suitcase. *But I also get to live in the moment.* I have to be on best behaviour in home-stay settings. *But I meet wonderful, interesting people.* I worry if I'll make ends meet. *But I am getting by.* I don't know where this cycling life will lead. *But no one knows where any life will lead.* I decide that's enough thinking for one night.

Sometimes – especially during a stage race – it's best to remember that not all life questions need to be terribly deep.

'Marilyn?' I whisper.

'Hmmm.'

'Do you think Johnny Depp is hot?'

'Yeah. But not so much as a pirate.'

'Aye,' I agree. But I'm glad he's here with me, anyway.

CHAPTER 7

MARIANNE VOS

The Reluctant Queen of Cycling

Marianne Vos is the undisputed queen of women's cycling, and the finest rider of her generation. The comparisons with Eddy Merckx are more than apt and reflected in her nickname 'The Cannibal'; though with palmarès that include dominance in track, road, mountain biking and cyclocross, she is a more complete rider than even the great Belgian. 'Vosje' or the 'Little Fox' as she is also known, is a passionate advocate for her sport and was instrumental in setting up Le Tour Entier, the pressure group that successfully campaigned for a women's race at the Tour de France.

 @marianne_vos
 www.mariannevosofficial.com

🏅 **Major palmarès:**

Vos's palmarès are almost too numerous to mention, but highlights include –

Winner – La Course (2014)

Winner – Women's Tour Britain (2014)

Gold medal – Olympic Road Race (2012)

Winner – UCI Women's Road World Cup (2007, 2009, 2010, 2012, 2013)

Winner – Giro d'Italia Femminile (2011, 2012, 2014)

Winner – Fléche Wallonne (2007, 2008, 2009, 2011, 2013)

Winner – Tour of Flanders (2013)

World Champion Cyclocross (2006, 2009, 2010, 2011, 2012, 2013, 2014)

World Champion Track (2008, 2011)

Gold medal – Olympic Track (2008)

Dutch journalist Mariska Tjoelker had the opportunity to talk to Marianne in her native country Holland about her career – including 'that' day on the Mall in the 2012 London Olympics – the future of women's cycling, what it feels like to have Alberto Contador as a fan, and how she'd like to end her career: on the cobbles of Paris–Roubaix.

Although she is happier away from the spotlight, in recent years the rider has sought the limelight more often. Not for herself, no. She does it for what she loves doing best: cycling. That women finally rode over the cobbles of the Champs-Élysées in 2014 is as a direct result of her efforts. She is Marianne Vos – the reluctant queen of cycling.

In 2012 she wrote her name into the history of the Olympics when she won the women's road race title. It was a heroic race that had viewers on the edge of their seats. Even the most hardened fan of men's cycling – and I count myself among them – found themselves yelling at the TV screen. It was like watching a stage in the Tour de France. But these were women. Flapping ponytails. Tawny skin. Wider in the hips than the men. I'd never been that interested in the women's sport, until that race. When Marianne crossed the line cheering and crying, I cried too. In front of the TV. It had been truly exciting. There were tactics. There were games. Watching each other. Holding back. Watching again. There were bluffs. There was suffering. Everything that makes bike racing so beautiful was in this race. A woman's race. When I tell Marianne that this race had me yelling, for the first time, at women on bikes, she laughs. Yes, she's heard that often. And yes, it was a brilliant race. Because everything came together, she thinks. 'In the 1970s and 1980s women's cycling was making a big noise, and then it stalled, started to go backwards even. In the period prior to the London Games, women's cycling was back on the rise and it got a huge boost from that race.'

The growth in the 1970s and 1980s was substantially different to that of the last few years. If women's cycling is enjoying a new found popularity, it's not due to the traditional cycling countries but rather to the 'new' cycling nations like the United States, the United Kingdom and Australia. And there's the crux: where the traditional cycling nations often tended to sneer at the efforts of these women riding their bikes, the Anglo-Saxon countries don't even understand that there should be any difference between men's and women's cycling. Or, as Marianne puts it 'they find that inequality is really bizarre'.

But that wasn't the only thing that was so beautiful about London. There was also the race itself. 'As you said yourself, that race was very exciting, a beautiful and attractive competition for the public. That was the reaction we got from the public. And that was exactly what the sport needed, I think. We have a lot of attention now because we managed to generate it at exactly the right time. You need moments like that to advance the sport. Now you see women's cycling really expanding: the level is higher; the races are more interesting; we have more teams, hence tactics amongst the teams play a greater role. And that makes the sport so much more fun to watch. More exciting, yes.'

Marianne would love to see every big race generating a similar boost, but she is no stranger to reality. The World Championships gets a lot of attention but is not always pretty to watch – in that respect there is no difference between the men's and women's sport. The peloton usually waits for the finale before lighting the fuse under the powder keg 'whereas you always hope that these events will be super exciting from beginning to end.' La Course – the women's criterium race held for the first time in 2014 before the final stage of the Tour de France – was a special case, she says. 'Everyone wanted to show something beautiful. It was perhaps not the most exciting of races, but that shouldn't surprise anyone because on the Champs-Élysées the riders can see each other all the time: getting away is not an option. But the vibe we had in the peloton was so amazing and we wanted to put that feeling out there. That really succeeded, I think.'

That the women's sport is not yet where it needs to be, Marianne knows only too well. A race can be really thrilling but, if no one sees it, it doesn't capture people's interest. People will only talk about you if they know you, it's as simple as that. That's what motivated Marianne to step out of her preferred place in the shadows, she says. 'I'm a cyclist, I love cycling more than anything, but I realised that the sport needed more sponsors to step in so that more women could become professional cyclists. Otherwise the talent base is too small. And we had to bring our sport closer to the audience. No, not for me, but for the growth of the sport. And I was willing to use my reputation so the sport would get a bigger stage.' Vos is convinced that a greater stage for the sport isn't simply about throwing money at it. 'It's about the value we have as a sport, as athletes, that's where it starts. And we have to create that value for ourselves. Calling for greater prize money doesn't make any sense if the sport doesn't have value.' It is, she agrees, a typical case of chicken and egg: more media coverage, means more fans, means more sponsors, means more money. But where do you start?

'We have to show the outside world how beautiful our sport is. Our experience: the struggle, the sacrifice. And people need to identify with a rider and a team. Yes, just like the men: this team has put everything behind their sprinter; this rider is going for the general classification; this rider has a score to settle; that one had a bad day yesterday – all those elements that determine the course of the race and make it so passionate and engaging to follow; but to really show these stories takes money and time, plenty of time. Plus it shows that we're all fishing in the same lake: the people who already love cycling.'

'We Own Yellow', a campaign set up in 2014 to create a platform to encourage more participation in cycling, with a special focus on women and girls (the 'we' are Loes Gunnewijk, Marijn de Vries, Marianne Vos and Roxane Knetemann), is 'trying to tap into a new audience'. Marianne enjoys being involved, not only because in doing so her sport – if all turns out well – will gain greater exposure. 'Cycling gave me so much and I really like sharing that with other people. It's nice to let other people see what this sport can do to you.' Ultimately, the participants in We Own Yellow get to know more about the riders and become more involved in the sport. And then? 'We hope they become fans, fans who will follow us and want to know how we do in our races. If we can achieve that, we've created an added value. And that will suddenly make us much more interesting to a sponsor.'

In the summer of 2011, Marianne was a guest on a Dutch television show which covered the Tour de France. In the morning she was sent off with a cameraman for the team buses. And although the presenter Mart Smeets spoke highly of Marianne, I found it – sitting on my comfy sofa at home – a little embarassing. These men won't know her at all, it will all go wrong, they'll laugh at her, why have they exposed her to this – thoughts like that were running through my mind. The ignorance! 'Cause, oh yes, Alberto Contador knew her very well. 'The Machine' he called her, before casually listing some of her results. Yes, he followed her. And yes, he had a lot of admiration for this woman who was capable of doing such great things! I squirmed deeper into my sofa, my embarrassment at my own ignorance growing with every word Alberto said about Marianne.

There was definitely some sniggering in the men's sport about women's cycling, Marianne says now. Women getting involved in cycling – what was that all about? The recognition of someone like Contador was important. 'It all starts with recognition and appreciation. Today men and women train together more often, because many men's teams have their own women's teams. That professionalism has been very important for us; we suddenly have a proper structure. Structure, imagine! We really didn't know what was suddenly happening to us!' And along with that structure also came greater appreciation. During training sessions male riders realised that 'those women' trained just as hard and made just as many sacrifices as they did. In 2015 the recognition and respect of their male counterparts is the most natural thing in the world. And what about the physical differences between men and women? 'That's just a given, nothing more, nothing less', she laughs.

Marianne has high hopes for the future of the sport. It's hardly surprising: the number of women in cycling is increasing, there are more teams and more organisations wanting to hook up with them. But with that success comes a risk: that it is all too much too soon. 'We shouldn't skip any steps,' Marianne warns, 'The Vuelta a España, the Tour of Poland, the Tour of California – they all want to organise women's races. But we, the teams, the riders, need to be ready for that. The talent base is still narrow, and if we do too much too quickly, it's easy to attract negative publicity.' She does have some examples of events that have given the sport a negative image. 'We still see riders of different levels of ability at the start of the same race. The result is that some teams end up riding just behind the motorbikes. Yes, that happens, in the Giro Rosa [the women's Giro d'Italia], for example. And in the criteriums after the Tour de France. It's fantastic that we're given the opportunity to ride them, but don't forget we ride those crits really flat out. The result is that even some of the professional riders end up getting lapped several times. And the public sees all that, you know. You can imagine that after that some of those people won't take women's cycling that seriously anymore.' One solution she suggests is the introduction of various different categories – but that hasn't happened yet. When it comes to further development in women's cycling she has a lot of confidence in the UCI (Union Cycliste International, cycling's governing body), she says. 'To the outsider it might look as if some of the decisions they take in Aigle (where the UCI headquarters are based) are inhibiting the sport, but I think they're doing good work to develop the conditions under which the sport can develop in a healthy way.' Marianne's voice is heard by the UCI: she works with them in an advisory capacity, acting as an intermediary transmitting the thoughts of the peloton to the governing body. And yes, she is aware that some riders are frustrated and find the pace of change too slow. She doesn't feel that herself, she says. 'I mainly see the progress we are making.' She has the same attitude when it comes to money in the sport. There is a huge gap between the women's earnings and those of their male counterparts. 'Of course there are girls who find that disappointing, I can well imagine that. But it doesn't bother me so much, if I'm honest. I never got into cycling because of the money, and I still feel like that. At the same time, however, I'm really grateful that I earn my living by riding a bike.'

Although she's won everything there is to win in cycling, even Marianne Vos still has dreams. The biggest? 'Paris–Roubaix for women. Yes, that would be fantastic! Paris–Roubaix is a race that everyone has always said is too hard for women. That attitude has change; that's another step forward that we've taken. Of course it's an incredibly hard race and of course we'll suffer and of course once we're on the road we'll be saying to each other: Never! Ever! Again! But once we're under the showers in the velodrome, we'll forget all that, I'm sure of it.' She believes she'll still be a pro cyclist when the first women's Paris–Roubaix takes place. The first real Tour de France for women, no, she probably won't ride that one as an active cyclist. But Paris–Roubaix? 'I really think so, yes.' I tell her I'll get off my sofa and out standing by the cobbles to cheer her on – because, hey, there's only one who should hold the cobblestone above her head on the top step of the podium, right? But she takes me by surprise, by saying victory wouldn't be the most important thing. 'No, I'm serious, really.' Then, after a pause: 'That is, that's how I feel at this moment. Let's wait and see what happens when the final kilometres arrive.' Queen of cycling – oh yes!

CHAPTER 8

MARIJN DE VRIES
Of Teen Dreams, Quick Pees and Tough Mothers

Marijn de Vries is a Dutch professional cyclist and journalist, who turned professional at the age of 30. She took up cycling as an experiment while working on a programme for Holland Sport called Can You Still Be a Top Athlete in Your Thirties? *In 2010 she won her first professional race, the Hilversum Criterium. She achieved her ambition of riding in the World Championship team time trial in 2013 and has her sights set on individual participation in the World Championships time trial or road race. Though Marijn now considers herself primarily as a professional cyclist with her Giant-Shimano team, she continues to write for publications like* Wielerrevue, Rouleur *and her own blog.*

🐦 @marijnfietst
 http://marijndevries.nl

Marijn de Vries is the kind of woman other women are supposed to hate – smart, funny and talented, she developed a high profile career in journalism before becoming a successful cyclist. But Marijn is exactly the kind of woman other women celebrate for her achievements, her warmth and her talent. As a fan of her excellent blog I knew this book wouldn't be complete without a contribution from Marijn. Here she shares some of her writing, including her celebrated instructions for the 'quick pee'.

Marijn on Training

This is the way to train on Mallorca:

You need to be at 'Number 6', on the boulevard, at 10am sharp. If you arrive a minute later, the group will be gone. You can only come along if you know someone else in the group. Or if you are approved by The Boss.

The Boss is daddy Kreuziger, clad from top to toe in Astana kit. Each gesture, every look, his entire body language shows he's in charge of this group. He is brutally strong but also exceptionally caring, especially towards the girls that follow his pack.

'Are you okay?' he asks now and then. He looks you in the eyes to see if the words you utter match with the look on your face. 'If you want to train less than five hours, I'll tell you the way home', he offers. 'Oh, you want to come along for the entire day? That's fine with me.' And he does another check on how we position ourselves on the bike and grins encouragingly.

The group is very mixed: true pros, semi-pros, almost pros, former pros and two women. Every once in a while someone takes a right turn, towards the mountains, to improve their climbing skills or do a shorter training session. But most of them will follow along for the entire ride.

But beware if you don't master the group-riding skills: if you are afraid to follow a wheel, or when you are not completely stable. If The Boss hasn't spotted it himself – he's very alert – someone else in the group will brief him. The Boss doesn't appreciate bad riders.

The Boss is the one leading the group the most. For a straight half hour he gives his all against the wind and determines the pace. He's brutal and so are his facial features. With an average speed of around 40km/h, we cruise along the Mallorcan flatlands, towards the eastern tip of the island. 'Always be cautious' is his motto. Don't cross like a madman, don't overtake turns, don't speed through tiny villages. But once the pack is at top speed, everyone must follow that pace. In the wheel of this fast train, life's good for two girls.

Nature breaks are only permitted by The Boss. Men at the right and women at the left side of the road. Not done yet? Bad luck. It's your problem and you have to get back to the group on your own. The result is that the two girls are doomed to do a mini team time trial with their pants still halfway up their legs. We don't complain though, because we wanted to tag along, which means we have to follow the rules of the pack.

O O O

Yes, us women do pee while out training. That is *the* answer to the most asked question by men. Second question on the list is always: how do you do it? The race waits for no one and especially not for women taking time to get undressed and pee on the side of the road. Unless there's a train passing, which doesn't happen all that often.

How do we do it? I only learnt how to 'quick pee' last summer. This piece of knowledge also comes in useful if you are not a professional cyclist, because when you are just riding your bike around you don't want to get partially undressed either.

(To all male readers, stop here if you prefer to think that women are creatures without kidneys or bowels and only enter the toilet to clean. This information in is not at all interesting for you anyway, unless you feel like sharing it with the women around you, which would be great. Anyway, you have been warned.)

Ladies, to explain this technique in words is somewhat difficult:

1. Pull one of the trouser legs up as far as possible.
2. Hold it from the inside with two hands: one at the front and put your other hand behind your back and grab the bib shorts from that position. Now pull the trouser leg as far as you can towards the opposite leg. The position of the hands

is crucial in this respect. If you don't follow the instructions correctly, you'll end up with wet hands. If you do it correctly, there's an opening big enough to pee through.

3. Squat and pee.

The great thing about this technique is that it's not only fast but decent too as there's hardly any exposed flesh. If there is a passer-by, he or she won't see any nude body parts, let alone intimate nude body parts. And if you are a racing woman, it's fast enough to hop back on the bike and find your way back to the peloton before the last team car has passed.

○ ○ ○

When we're back we wave and say bye. Tomorrow, at 10am sharp, at Number 6. Whoever shows up, The Boss will be there to guard his pack.

On Racing

The Ronde van Drenthe (an elite women's one day race, in Holland, that forms part of the UCI Women's World Cup). I've never ridden this course over familiar ground. Saturday will be the first time. Once the race starts, we'll be rushing through Oosterhesselen at about 12:20pm. If I look left over the flat land, I'll already be able to see the church tower of Sleen in the distance.

We used to make it a game when we were kids, my brothers and I, in the back of our Volkswagen Jetta – who would see the tower first? At the end of the summer holidays we peered especially eagerly, because seeing the tower again was extra special after such a long time. It meant we were back home. Within minutes we could grab our bikes, which always felt special after not riding for three long weeks.

The farm of the Heeling family at the left side of the road, the river Jongbloedvaart at the right side – where they for sure are already building the kindling for the Easter fire. The asphalt road changes into *klinkers* (cobbles), we bounce into the village of Sleen.

Along to the Slener Bazaar. Oh, the Slener Bazaar! You could buy anything at that local shop, according to my mum. After a long and futile afternoon in the city center of Emmen, looking for an egg cutter or the right kind of hoover bags, she always sighed, 'Okay, let's take a look in the Slener Bazaar, then.' And of course she always returned with what she was looking for. Always.

I used to buy marbles and birthday gifts for my classmates there. This was a pretty tricky business, because everyone else in my school did the same. So before you knew it, we had all bought the same box of Lego for the birthday kid.

In front of café Het Wapen van Sleen: sharp turn to the right. There used to be a phone booth in the middle of the green there, from where we called sex lines, howling with laughter.

Along to the old police station. The station where my little brother reported a crime once. He was five years old and had lost his slippers. He probably left them somewhere in the street between school and home like he always did, and this time my mum had told him: 'You can't come home before you've found your slippers.' So he walked to the police station on his tiny legs, rang the bell, and told the officer who opened the door that his slippers were stolen. Or lost. I don't remember exactly how this ended, but I would give the world for the document the officer had to type that day.

Along to Bakkerij Schepers, the local bakery, where as a teenager I worked every Saturday. At 6:30 in the morning, the delicious smell of fresh croissants lured me into the warm bakery. Waldkorn bread for 3 guilders 15, a square casino brown loaf for 2 guilders 60.

Now along to Tankstation Oudeboon, the petrol station, which we always visited first at Sint Maarten fest (Harvest Festival) because they didn't give the kids mini candy, but the real stuff – full-size Snickers and Twixes – which were still called Raiders back then.

Keep left along the grocery and the snackbar, which turned into a bar and later into a restaurant, where I used to drink a lot of beer after the volleyball matches I played every Saturday.

Next up, the bus stop. Line 21 Assen – Emmen. I always went to secondary school by bike, unless the weather was really bad. On those days, the wet-dog-smelling bus was packed with school kids, who wrote with their forefingers on the foggy windows.

Turn right on to the big road. The ice skating rink is on the right, the Eerste Bosje on the left: end of Sleen. It's almost 12:30.

Eighteen years of my youth have gone by in barely 10 minutes.

On Being a Cycling Fan

I am visiting my parents as my mum asks me: 'That Tyler Hamilton book, about his doping confessions, you haven't read that yet, have you?'

She walks to the book shelf and scours the titles, looking for *The Secret Race*. After a while she pulls the book off the shelf and hands it over to me. 'There you are. Very good book, you know.'

By now, I've sort of got used to my mum being a cycling fan, but if she says things like these, I'm still flabbergasted. Even five years ago she would say things like: 'All those men riding a bike through France, what's that good for?!' And: 'Races are so boring! Hours and hours on a bike. Stupid waste of time.'

Nowadays, the TV is tuned in to the Tour de France, even if my mum is home alone. When I was a kid, my dad used to follow the important races; in my memory, the radio played Radio Tour de France the whole summer, the house filled with the scent of freshly baked pancakes, and me washing my sandy feet before joining the family at the dinner table.

When I started cycling at 30 years old, my mum really didn't like it. Why would I want to do that at my age? she asked. Racing, suffering, crashing, breaking bones … And especially: that stupid act of just riding a bike all the time. She didn't understand. She wished

I would stop immediately, so she didn't need to worry about me crashing all the time.

Once she accepted I was fully captivated by bike racing, my mum decided to stop resisting and started to show some interest. Suddenly I found her at the side of the road at the Ronde van Drenthe, with a camera. She was so nervous about seeing me race that all her photos turned out to be totally blurred, because she was shaking all over. The next time she tried it she put her camera on a big stone to make sure the photos would be good.

Just after I started racing, my brother was diagnosed with cancer. Testicular cancer, the same type of cancer Lance Armstrong suffered from. The doctors found it out in an early stage, there was no reason to think my brother wouldn't be cured, but he had to be treated with chemotherapy and they operated on him twice. My mum read Armstrong's *It's Not About the Bike*, and the book gave her hope. She started to wear the yellow wrist band.

Not long after, my mother bought herself a race bike: one with straight handlebars, to be a bit more comfortable and to make sure braking was easy. She was 62 already and she had never been on a race bike in her life. She started to train. And she signed up to the Alpe d'Huzes – a challenge to ride up Alpe d'Huez up to six times in one day – to raise money for fighting cancer. She climbed Alpe d'Huez. Easy. My mum! She could even have done the climb several times, I am sure of that because she was in a great shape, but she didn't dare to ride down. So it was just one time.

My brother is healthy again. My mum doesn't have a goal to ride her bike for anymore. She doesn't need a goal. Riding a bike is the goal now. She rides to relax, to enjoy nature. Just like it happened to me, she's totally captivated by riding a bike. Tomorrow, she's going on holiday, together with my dad – who also bought a race bike. They are going to ride in the hills in Germany.

Meanwhile, she will surf the internet, looking at all the cycling pages she can find, to make sure she'll see the results of my races as soon as they're published. She knows exactly where and when I race, even if I don't tell her. She cheers for me and my teammates on Facebook. And she texts me a good luck wish every single time.

You're never too old to become a cycling fan. You're also never too old to start riding a bike. And you're absolutely never too old to be proud of your tough mother.

CHAPTER 9

MATRIX TEAM, THE 'YORKSHIRE ROSES'

Five Riders, Five Bright Futures

The 'On the Drops' project was born in 2009 with the twin aims of achieving racing success and developing the sport of women's cycling in the UK. With riders like Dani King and Jo Rowsell in the team, race victories came thick and fast in their first full season in 2010, and the joint work of the team with its sponsors ensured women's racing in the UK was shown on television with the birth of the Matrix Fitness GP, part of the highly successful Tour Series. Stability for its riders, sustainable growth and reward for its sponsors have been the key goals of this highly successful domestic UK team Following on from a successful partnership with the UK's Vulpine clothing brand, from 2015, with sponsorship from Trek Cycles and a new name plus a squad composed of Britain's Golden girls, the cream of UK talent and experienced overseas riders, Matrix Fitness will become Britain's second fully professional women's team.

🐦 @penny_rowson @jesiwak @harrieto93 @saaaraolsson
@mellowther @onthedrops
🏠 http://www.onthedrops.cc

I'd followed the fortunes of the Matrix team in its various guises through the years and had been impressed by the quiet way they had gone about building such an impressive team without the big budget of some of their rivals. I knew I wanted to include a team profile in the book and so contacted their team manager, Stef Wyman, who gave me what access he could, through email and their blogs, to his talented young team as they rode the 2014 season. The result is a snapshot of life on the road for a group of young women who are going places – their motivation, their highs and lows, and the advice they would give to other young riders who would like to follow in their footsteps.

When Matrix-Vulpine (now Matrix Fitness) were selected as the only British-based domestic team in the inaugural UK Women's Tour in 2014, it was the culmination of a project to raise the standard of women's racing in the UK. 'We decided to shoot for the stars,' says *directeur sportif* Stef Wyman, 'from those humble beginning has grown a stronger team, with increased backing, and bigger ambitions. We will not be going to the Women's Tour with an attitude of survival; we will be looking to achieve.'

Penny Rowson is one of the 'Yorkshire Roses' – described by her team as a 'light but gutsy rider'. She's a multidisciplinary talent at home on the road and the track with a real gift when the road starts to climb. She was delighted by the fact that someone had written 'GO PENNY' on the roads of the Women's Tour, which was 'very illegal yet awesome at the same time!' And it's that positive attitude that she wants to pass on to other young women who'd like to follow in her footsteps. 'Go for it, why not?! If cycling's something you love, it doesn't matter how good you are now; it's about how good you believe you want to be and what you're willing to do to achieve it', she says with enthusiasm, adding 'it can be a real fun job but you have to stay positive as cycling's tough on the mind and life's all about balance.' How can riders achieve that balance? 'Work hard but enjoy the journey too.' She feels that riders new to the sport should challenge themselves: 'a good start into the cycling career is not choosing the easy options, you really have to work for it then you know if it's for you or not.'

It's advice Penny applied to her appearance at the Women's Tour, saying about the experience: 'I thought this race would either make me or break me. And yet it didn't do either; the race made me realise how good I am as a bike rider but more so how good I want to be.' She finished all five stages, even managing to get into some of the action at the front of a race that included the best riders in the world: Marianne Vos, Lizzie Armitstead, Laura Trott, Emma Pooley and Georgia Bronzini, to name a handful of the world-class riders that took to the roads of southeast England in May 2014. What did she learn about herself as a rider? 'I must have good bike skills because twice I've followed Jo Tindley's wheel and she's taken lines that have made me jump traffic islands and ride down stairs!' she laughs. But it made her hungry for more, excited to be part of such a professional race in such a professional set up.

Penny, like many of her teammates, started riding as a kid. 'My older brother started to learn how to ride a bike and it became a race as to who could take the stabilisers off first,' she remembers. 'I just loved it and have never stopped.' Her biggest inspiration as a rider also comes from Yorkshire, like Penny herself. 'Lizzie Armitstead inspires me, I've seen how far she's come, she's from Yorkshire so she's easy to relate to', she says. 'It's been nice to believe in her and watch her achieve so much.'

The high point of Penny Rowson's career to date has been winning the first-ever women's Newport Nocturne in 2012, which she described as an 'amazing result'. She was also second in the National Under 23 Road Race that year. But, still only 22, she knows her best years are to come. So where does the she see herself in five years' time? She is full of ambition saying she wants to win stages in the Giro Rosa, the elite, mountainous Italian stage race and have taken some individual world cup wins. She'd like to represent her country at Olympic level. She hopes to achieve all this with her current team as a professional rider. But more than that, she says, she wants to have 'travelled the world, meeting new people, gaining experiences, and enjoying pedalling up lots of climbs with breathtaking views. Basically loving my life/job!'

o o o

Jessie Walker has a wide open smile and eyes as blue as her dad's, Chris. Cycling is in her genes – Chris was a multiple national criterium champion and Milk Race winner, riding with the likes of Rob Hayles and Bradley Wiggins; mum Lynne rode for Great Britain as a junior; and brother Joey rides for the RST/NFTO Junior team. It was Joey's success as a rider that encouraged his sister to get on a bike herself after seeing how much he enjoyed it.

It's been a good season for the young rider from Sheffield who has family connections to the sport that go all the way back to her great grandfather, who was a noted time triallist. The rider herself ranks her 18th place on stage 1 of the Friends Life Women's Tour as her season's highlight: 'It was crazy and exciting at the same time sprinting against the world's best,' she says, citing the race as her big inspiration because 'racing in it this year gave me such a high and made me realise how much I love the sport so that really motivates me to achieve great things.'

The 19-year-old had mixed feelings going into the race: on the one hand she would be competing in one of the biggest women's races in the world, and on home soil; on the other she had never raced at that level before and would be lining up with one of her cycling heroes, Marianne Vos, an experience she described as both surreal and amazing. To ride on her wheel and gain a top 20 finish gave her a huge buzz and the entire experience 'made me extremely driven to become pro as this is what I love.'

But cycling hasn't always been plain sailing. Riding in a French Road Cycling Cup race in 2013, she suffered a horrific crash, in what she calls her worst moment in the sport. On a course that ideally suited her capacities as a *rouleur* she was caught out on the first lap when the road narrowed suddenly: 'The girl in front didn't see it so she hit the curb quite hard. I had nowhere to go so went over the top of her. I banged my knee really hard. I jumped back up and carried on but the peloton was gone.' But they make them tough in Yorkshire and she was soon back on her bike and catching the rest of the pack. 'I kicked to get round the corner and my rear mech completely smashed to pieces so I couldn't ride', Jessie remembers. 'I was then at breaking point as everything was going wrong so it definitely was a race to forget. Turns out I had snapped my forks as well so I was lucky they didn't break first otherwise I would have been straight over the handlebars.'

Having finished her A-levels the year before, 2014 was the first season where she had been able to concentrate full time on racing and training, as her results reflect – and as far as Walker is concerned the only way is up. Where does she see herself in five years' time? 'I hope to be racing the hardest races in the world and mixing it with the world's top riders,' she says with the confidence of one who knows she can mix it with the best riders in the world. So what advice would she give to other young women who'd like to follow in her footsteps? 'You get out what you put in. Basically, never give up, just keep at it and the results will come.' Jess Walker certainly practises what she preaches.

○ ○ ○

Another high-performing rider for the team this season has been Harriet Owen, who advises aspiring young riders to 'work at the basics first, make sure you get them right and everything else will come to you.' Harriet has certainly taken her own advice – one of the fastest riders in the UK, her team describe her as a rider who is technically very good and always looking for the right break, and she's already scored a medal at the Junior World Track Championships and won a round of the Tour Series, winning in Peterborough in 2012.

Like her teammate Jessie Walker, Harriet got into cycling when she would go and watch her father racing: 'Just local races, nothing too serious but I used to go watch and there was always youth racing on beforehand. I thought I'd give it a go and it went from there really,' says the 21-year-old from Oxford. Her big inspiration as a junior was Nicole Cooke, one of Britain's greatest ever riders, 'but now I wouldn't say someone is my inspiration, I just respect riders and what they do.' Graduating to the senior team from the Matrix Fitness Racing Academy, Harriet's career to date has seen some ups and downs – she cites her greatest achievement as finishing second in the scratch race at the Junior World Track Championships, an experience she describes as 'daunting', but after a relatively poor second season as a junior she was let go by British Cycling. 'As a first year junior I was there for experience so it made it even more special to podium', she says, adding that parting company with British Cycling was 'an odd sort of jump, from being so looked after by British Cycling to then being completely on your own, not really knowing what to do when, but because I've been doing it for so long, I know how to train. It's definitely been a shock – but now I'm quite enjoying having a bit of freedom to do what I want.'

Joining Matrix Fitness has been a definite 'up' in Owen's career and she is a long way from the rider who fell off her bike on the start line of her first ever race, something she describes as her 'nightmare moment', though she says crashing on the first day of the Women's Tour 'still hurts now as I had big hopes for the race'. But when the racing is good and you get the result you hoped for? 'You just have a constant grin on your face, you're not really sure why,' Owen laughs, 'It's a good morale boost, it keeps your spirits high – but alongside that, when you have a bad race, it's quite hard on the head – but over time, you had to live with that.'

Owen has declared that she will stay in cycling, even when she can't race anymore, but at the moment her sights are set on a bright future. Where does she see herself in five years' time? 'I'd love to be settled in a women's pro road team, battling for world cup and world championship victories', she declares. 'We will see what the future brings!'

○ ○ ○

Like Harriet and Jessie, Sara Olsson was inspired to get on her bike by her family. 'I started cycling at five years of age, my first club championship prize is from 1995', says the 24-year-old from Sweden who has joined the team from the Norwegian Hitec Products outfit, for whom she rode the team time trial at the World Championships in 2014, finishing ninth. She brings a huge amount of experience to the team and says she is 'super excited' to ride for the team, praising their plans for the future and saying 'it all feels like it will be a perfect fit for me'.

'Cycling has always been a part of my family's life; both my parents competed as youths and my older brother started two years before me, and there it began,' she says, adding that her experience gained at Hitec – where she rode with the likes of experienced procyclists Elisa Longho Borghini and Audrey Cordon, who now ride for the Wiggle-Honda team – has helped her learn and develop as a rider and she can't wait to line up alongside the likes of Harriet, Jessie and Olympic gold medalist Laura Trott for her new team.

Sara looks to her compatriots for inspiration, saying she admires sports stars who are 'not only good at what they do but also show happiness and humility, like the Swedish skiers. Charlotte Kalla and Anna Haag are two fantastic sports women.' So what advice would she give to other young women who might want to get into cycling? 'My best advice is to never give up and not always take the easy way', Sara declares. 'Many times it can give you more by working harder, for example, on a lower team level than going straight in to a UCI team before you are really ready, both mentally and physically.' Her own secret of success is 'always go with your gut, have fun and do your own thing!'

In 2008, as a 2nd-year junior, Olsson shone brightly, gathering great results in time trials. 'I was top 10 at Europeans, Swedish champ in TT and won bronze in the road race despite a broken navicular earlier in the season.' Success continued into the seniors when she won the Swedish Cup in her first year and again in 2013. She followed up with a criterium title in 2014 after riding solo for 45 minutes. But she says her biggest achievement involves her biggest nightmare on a bike: 'In 2007, in my first race as a junior, I had a terrible crash after my brake touched a sign on the side of the road and at 45km/h I crashed head first on the asphalt. I needed 20 stitches inside my mouth, 7 on my split lip and I lost a few teeth – that was some of the injuries it caused me.' Olsson also suffered a heavy concussion, was left with injuries all over her body and wounds to the left side of her face, had a splinter of bone in her hand and suffered a bad sprain. The after effects of the crash were long and slow to heal: 'my mouth took more than six and a half years to get totally done again and today I have four porcelain teeth instead of normal front teeth'.

But the injuries weren't just physical. The crash left her with mental scars, too. 'After the crash I was freaked out from only racing in a group of 15 girls, especially in the rain where I had less control over what could happen', she says. 'From that to where I am today has been my biggest achievement and I still today have things from that to work on and I probably will for the rest of my career', she reveals.

Sara is confident that the team can help her achieve her ambition – in five years, she says, she sees herself as one of the top women riders in the world and 'hopefully I'll have spent some time in the blue and yellow with a Swedish national title and am fighting for medals in big races and championships.' And beyond cycling? 'I'll probably be studying or working, but will always in some way have a relationship with cycling.'

Unlike her teammates, Mel Lowther didn't spend her childhood in the saddle. Instead she grew up in the pool, putting in long hours of training as a swimmer before getting an overuse injury in her shoulder and being forced to cut back on her training. It was her mum who put her on the path to a new career: 'My mum went on the internet and found a local triathlon club for me to go to. After a while I started doing the local youth races and just decided I wanted to move totally to cycling.'

Injuries have plagued Lowther through her career – she was forced to undergo shoulder surgery in 2012 after a promising season and then broke her collarbone while riding in Holland. She calls that day her worst, especially as she had to return to Leeds by car the same day. But it hasn't stopped Mel from gaining a place on the Olympic Development Programme giving her the opportunity to represent Great Britain at international competitions as great preparation for the sterner tests of international competition at senior level. It's an honour she shares with teammate Bethany Hayward.

Only 18, Mel is another of the Yorkshire contingent at the team, having been born and raised in Tingley. Her local paper describes her as a 'cycling startlet' and she has a great love for racing on her native roads, recording strong results in the Otley and Sheffield GPs in 2013. 'Being a proud Yorkshire lass I love racing at Otley,' she writes in her blog, 'the crowd and the atmosphere is always buzzing.' It's been a huge year for cycling in her home county, with the Grand Depart setting the public imagination alight and filling the roads with would be roadies. What advice does the girl from Tingley have for anyone who'd like to follow in her footsteps? She has a typical no-nonsense Yorkshire attitude. 'Have goals to achieve, but don't be too fixed on them, be flexible,' she says, 'I have learnt that in cycling not always the "best" rider in the best form wins, so you have to persevere and keep trying. Don't expect to win every race, when you do win though, celebrate it and make sure you always look back from where you started.'

Still only a second-year junior, her team describe her as 'an aggressive rider known for her breakaways, who is already showing she has the capability to step up into elite racing', but her focus this year has been on the track. She showed her aggression and attacking style when she rode to an excellent win at the 2013 Junior National Track Championships in the scratch race. Up against the newly crowned junior world sprint champion in a race that is often decided in a mad dash for the line, Lowther knew her best chance of victory was to attack and, with nine laps remaining, she seized her chance. 'For the first lap into the attack I rode hard, coming into the second lap away I sneaked a glance at how far the bunch was behind me, turns out that they weren't, in fact, that far ahead of me,' she remembers. 'I came up to the back makers with about four laps to go and then just rode trying to keep on the back of them and I finally got my podium spot! Top spot too, first win of the season at the national championships, I was very happy, and shocked after the season I'd had.'

That success was followed by a top 20 finish at the Prudential Ride London Grand Prix where she improved from 23rd in 2013 to 13th though, as she says, 'there is always a part of me who wishes I was in the top 10.' Then came another race on home turf – the Pontefract GP – and a Matrix Fitness clean sweep of the podium. Lowther was competing for the first time against teammate, and fellow Yorkshirewoman, Jessie Walker with whom she often travels to events in the south. It was a very wet race, she recalls, making the *parcours* particularly treacherous. But that didn't stop Lowther from attacking. Having already spoken to Walker beforehand, the pair had decided that 'if we had enough time on the rest of the field, we wanted to race it out between us. So when I knew we had enough time I decided my plan was to wait for a sprint', Mel wrote on her blog later. But her teammate didn't quite see it that way: 'Jessie, however, had different plans and started attacking me with around five laps to go. She definitely didn't make it easy for me. I managed to get on her, just, at each attack and coming into the last lap I was ahead, looking back all the time. It felt like we were racing a track sprint. In the end I just managed to get past Jessie before the line. I'd rather have her as a teammate than an opponent!' It was a tough day but a rewarding one, as Mel recalls on her blog: 'just when we thought the day couldn't get any better the race was sponsored by Haribo and so we all got a pack of Haribo each!'

○ ○ ○

Haribos and heartache, crashes and cheers – such is the lot of a professional woman cyclist. But what I learnt from talking to the women of the Matrix Fitness team is the deep love they all share for one of the hardest, most demanding and difficult sports you can compete in. To come back from the mental and physical scars of a terrible crash as Sara has done, to keep pushing to always be your best, like Mel, to learn how to juggle academic and sporting demands and pressures as Jessie does, or to bounce back from the lows and disappointments that Harriet has faced takes guts and determination, and true strength of character, especially when the opportunities and financial rewards are a fraction of those offered by the men's sport. As the Matrix team rides into the big league, I'm excited for the future of women's cycling and for these young talents who will light up the roads for years to come.

CHAPTER 10

ROXANE KNETEMANN
Fun

Roxane Knetemann is a professional cyclist with the Dutch
Rabobank-Liv Women Cycling Team. She is a multiple national
champion, both on the road and track, and won a silver medal
in the World Championships in 2013. Roxane is the daughter of
Gerrie Knetemann, one of the greatest male professional cyclists
the Netherlands has produced.

🐦 @RoxaneKnetemann

🏅 **Major palmarès:**
Dutch National Track Champion Points Race (2009, 2012)
Dutch National Track Champion Madison (with Marianne
   Vos, 2012)

*Roxane Knetemann is an old friend of the greatest living cyclist, Marianne
Vos. But she is a talented rider in her own right and has a story to tell that
has more than its fair share of the usual ups and downs that all women
cyclists seem to encounter in their careers. Growing up as the daughter
of one of Holland's greatest-ever male racing cyclists meant the teenage
Roxane had more than her fair share of pressure when she took to two
wheels – and an additional burden to deal with when her father died
unexpectedly. We arranged to talk by Skype and she was unfailingly polite
and positive, even when we experienced a string of connection problems.
It seemed to me that it was this cool unflappability that helped Roxane to*

deal with the emotional rollercoaster of her life – that and her insistence that her cycling be 'fun': 'When you have fun you can be serious, but when you have no fun and you're serious it's not a good combination.'

When I suggest that Roxane Knetemann must have grown up surrounded by cycling memorabilia, or her father's World Champion jersey hanging on the wall, she laughs. 'No, there was nothing like that,' she says in her warm, lilting voice, 'but I always wondered why everyone knew my father.'

This is Roxane's first interview by Skype and it's not going well. The connection keeps dropping out and I can hear sounds of domesticity, of plates clattering and drinks being poured, in the background. At one point her boyfriend, Wim Stroetinga, a fellow Dutch professional cyclist, asks 'have you finished yet?' Through it all she remains unflappably polite, answering my repeated calls with a cheery 'Hoi!'

We start at the beginning – how it felt to grow up as Gerrie Knetemann's daughter. Knetemann was one of the greatest Dutch cyclists, winning a World Champion's rainbow jersey, two editions of the Amstel Gold race nearly 10 years apart and a clutch of Tour de France yellow jerseys in the 1978 race. He shares the Dutch record of 10 stage wins at the Tour with Classics specialist Jan Raas and 1980 Tour winner, Joop Zoetemelk. His are big cleats to fill. Roxane says that it's weird as she didn't realise that having a famous father was any different 'because it was always like that'. She says she was eight before she had an idea of how well known he was and that, until she started cycling, it was never an issue 'because he was just my dad, and the parents of the kids at school knew him and we live in a village'.

But being Gerrie Knetemann's daughter, the cyclist, was much harder. 'Everyone had expectations of me,' she remembers, 'and it wasn't always nice – for example, when I won a race that was never enough, it was always "oh but she's the daughter of ..." So when I lost a race, or came second or third, they made it bigger than it was, even though it's not a shame to lose.' Things became a big deal, she says, when they shouldn't have been. That must have been tough? She pauses and I can see her literally shrugging it off as she replies: 'It was always like that, but I don't know how it would have been if my father was not my father.'

Knetemann didn't start cycling until she was 14, 'which is really late in Holland', preferring to spend her leisure hours riding and playing tennis. She says she never really liked cycling until one day she decided to give it a try 'and my father said "No, it's not happening, you're better to keep doing athletics."' Perhaps her father wanted to shield her from the inevitable pressure of following in his illustrious bike tracks. But Roxane wouldn't take no for an answer: 'when I asked again later my mum said "Maybe you have to try it" and my father said "No, you're not going riding."'

Gradually his persistent daughter wore him down and 'in the end he said "OK, we'll go training, but first we have to do a home trainer session." So he put me on the home trainer and it was really, really heavy but I kept going and he came back after an hour and I was *still* going. I was halfway through, I was still on the bike and he said "you're still on the bike?" I said, "Yeah, I want to keep going," and he said, "OK you can get off, tomorrow we'll go training on the track." And that's how it started.'

Father and daughter hit the track the next day: 'I think he saw that I really enjoyed it – and it's weird to say but I was actually pretty good immediately and he saw that I was really motivated for training and I asked if maybe I could do some races? So I rode my first race and I didn't stop after that.'

And then tragedy struck. That November Gerrie Knetemann went for a mountain bike ride with friends as usual. He never came home. The great star of Dutch cycling was dead of a heart attack at the age of 53. For a young woman who had always been closest to her father, it was a devastating blow. The next day she went to the track and rode lap after lap, pushing herself harder and harder, riding faster and faster as the tears streamed down her face. 'My father died and after that my career wasn't so good for a few years,' she says simply. 'I wasn't motivated and I didn't know where to start and what to do on the bike and I was really lost. I thought "I have to stop."' Her father had always taught her that cycling should be fun 'but I really didn't like it. It was no fun anymore on the bike.'

Meeting Wim changed all that. The Dutchman was training for the 2008 Beijing Olympics at the track in Alkmaar and the pair started chatting, then walking on the beach, then going for dinner, and then, somehow, they were together. What Roxane really liked about him was that he clearly enjoyed his riding: 'it was weird to see how much fun he had, because for four years it had been no fun for me. So I thought "yeah, it's nice when you have fun on the bike. I think I can like it again!"' You can hear her love for the bike as she speaks, and imagine the way that watching her boyfriend enjoy his training so much began to bring her back to that life. She followed Wim to Beijing and watched some of the track events. She was in the velodrome when her old rival Marianne Vos won the gold medal in the points race: 'I was so jealous and a bit emotional because I'd decided to stop and then it was weird to have that emotional feeling.' She decided to give the sport one more year of her life 'not for results, just for fun'.

She started training in December 2008. 'I was really bad,' she remembers, 'but actually I got better pretty fast and it was really fun.' At first she would get dropped a lot, she says, and then she didn't get dropped so often. The races went better and the most important thing was that she was having fun. The word again, that simple little syllable that ties a daughter to a father in attitude and belief. That is the common thread that runs through a life in cycling. We all – men and women, professional and amateur – ride because of those three letters at the end of the day. Roxane found herself on a small team and they had a good time together; by the end of the season her condition was pretty good and the podium places were coming her way again. 'I hadn't decided whether to stop or not,' she recalls, 'but I did the National track championships in October and then I won the Points race so I thought "OK, maybe it's not the time to stop."'

She kept going and in 2012 she signed for the Rabobank-Liv team: 'Every year between 2009 to 2012 I got better and better, in stage races, going uphill. I'm the same age as Marianne and in the juniors we were always together and she always looked out for me. She and a teammate, Hannah Barnes, had started a team and they invited me to join.' What is the world's greatest female rider (some would argue best rider period) like to ride with? 'I really like her – she's very nice to work with and she's really nice on and off the bike and the whole team is really good together. I joke sometimes that they're my second family, but actually they are because we travel together so much and they're a really nice group of people. Other people have expectations and that's hard, but it's nice because they look after you and it's great to be part of that team.'

2012 was an Olympic year, and after Vos and Lizzie Armitstead's glorious tussle on the Mall, where the Dutch rider emerged victorious and the world fell in love with women's cycling, Vos was ready for a new challenge. 'She wanted to do something different and I joked, "Maybe you can do the Madison with me on the track [at the Dutch National Track Championships]", and she said, "yeah, yeah"', Roxane remembers, 'but when I asked her again she said "yeah, let's do that." So we trained together and said we'd see what happened.' Knetemann says: 'it was one of the hardest races of my life, because everyone was riding against us, everyone thought that we were thinking "oh we'll win this!" but actually we were very nervous, Marianne as well – *we* didn't think we'd win! We pedalled really hard for that victory! Afterwards we were really tired and when we talk about it – not often! – it was one of the hardest races we ever rode.'

We talk more about Vos, who has had such an extraordinary career across so many different disciplines – track, road, cyclocross and mountain biking. 'She's very easy,' Roxane enthuses, 'she's a good person to work with, she never gets angry, she never asks for crazy things, she never pushes herself forward, she's always at the back – she's a really nice person.' Knetemann says few people know the real Marianne, they only see the great bike rider. 'But I think she's a greater person than a bike rider, she's really special, a really nice person.' The deep affection is obvious in Roxane's tone when she talks of the way her team leader will always help out, even if she's busy, then adds laughing 'she's not always 'nice' of course – she's only human! She's really hard on herself and sometimes she does crazy things because she's a top sportsperson and they do crazy things!' Roxane doesn't elaborate but you're left with the impression that however crazy Marianne might get, she retains her teammates respect.

I ask her about life on the road, the season-long grind of one-day races and stage races that make up the women's calendar. Roxane talks about the morning meetings on the team bus to discuss the plans for the day's racing. 'We meet in the team bus and have a drink and catch up with each other. Then we discuss how we're feeling and the tactics with the *directeur sportif* and make the plan for the day depending on what kind of race it is, but how we're feeling is the most important thing.' Once the peloton hits the road 'we talk to each other during the race because the plan never works out exactly how we discussed it, because things always change in the race. Then we have to discuss whether to stick to the plan. But it's always relaxed, never stressful,' she says, before finishing 'and then we ride hard on the bike.'

Rabo-Liv were one of the star attractions at the inaugural Women's Tour, ensuring a much anticipated rematch with Lizzie Armitstead who was there with her Boels Dolmans team. And they delivered yet another victory for Marianne Vos – the dream outcome for the first Women's Tour. 'We talked a lot at dinner about all the people out on the course, it was really incredible!', she says. 'All the schoolchildren were yelling Lizzie's name of course.' She describes the experience as 'really great' remembering the thousands and thousands of people who lined the route in the rain: 'Every day we said "it's crazy!" – all the people were so enthusiastic on the finish line and we're not used to that in women's cycling.'

But 2014 was the year that women's cycling started to believe that huge crowds and massive public support is exactly what the sport should get used to. The Women's Tour and La Course were landmark events. Roxane was disappointed in her World Championship results that year, preferring to look back to 2013 in which had been the best result of her career so far – a silver medal in the team time trial at the World Championships. 'That's been the best feeling so far,' she says, 'I didn't expect to ride in Florence and then I was selected and we got the medal and it was great. And actually last year, in 2014, I was third in the World Cup race in Sweden and that was really cool.' She reflects for a moment – I can hear the sound of liquid pouring into a glass, imagine Roxane and Wim settling down for dinner together – before saying 'actually in 2014 I surprised myself all the time with the things I did, I had a really glad season. A few weeks ago I looked back at my results and I thought "yeah, it was actually a great season!"'

Does she have any regrets about her career – about what might have been? 'I really wish I'd known what I know now when I was younger – how I do my training; I never did that when I was younger, I was just pedalling on my bike. I think now about how it would be like if I was serious earlier. But it is how it is.' You sense she is keen to focus on the now, and I ask her what she most enjoys about being a professional cyclist. 'I really like riding my bike and they pay me for that which is really great – I like that! Of course you have days when it's not that nice but you have that when you work in an office.' Again, the love of cycling shines through in her voice: 'I really like to ride with my head in the wind, thinking about everything, getting my brain in order. And when I'm training I see different things, even when I'm training in my home area – I really like that. I think more women should know that. You see so much and it's different every time and I'd really like other women to know that. That's why I cycle. Of course sometimes I ride fast, but I like to ride really slowly, just looking around.'

So what advice does she have to other women inspired to follow in her footsteps? 'Keep working! It's a sport where you have to work really hard and believe in yourself. You can't think you're not good enough.' She pauses, before continuing. 'A lot of people told me I wasn't good enough, that I had to stop – but if you think you're good enough, keep going! It's your thing and the most important thing is to have fun and not to be too serious. When you have fun you can be serious, but when you have no fun and you're serious, it's not a good combination.'

I think back to that first training session with her father – how Gerrie Knetemann had pushed his daughter and how she had proved herself, proved she could have fun on the bike. Who has been her biggest inspiration? 'Good question! Of course my dad in the beginning, and then later on I really like to watch how my boyfriend is doing his cycling.' She thinks about it for a moment and then says that she really likes to inspire herself: 'I like to see I can still be better than last year, for example, and that inspires me.' And her team, of course, her 'second family': 'because we do such nice things together and they all inspire me – especially when I'm lazy and can't follow them and I don't want that!'

At 27, it seems as if Roxane Knetemann is in a good place. Three years ago she moved in with Wim and they share a house in Nijkerk, the house I can imagine from those sounds of domesticity in the background. Gone are the days of crazy hair colours, of weight gain and rebellion, of not having fun on the bike. In August 2014, both she and Wim won their respective races at the Omloop Bosberg. They are the family that wins together, too.

So how does she relax? 'We have two 10-day training camps with the team where we do things together like power kiting, we have dinner together, it's a nice relaxing time to get to know each other.' She has been part of the core Rabo-Liv team for two years now and says, 'We know each other really well, so we know our goal and we do everything for each other. When someone wins, we all get a good feeling!' With Marianne in the team, and Pauline Ferrand-Prévot becoming world champion, she must get that feeling a lot.

Where does she see women's cycling going after 2014 and what Tracey Gaudry, the Vice President of the UCI, has described as a 'grand year' for the sport? I say that a lot of the goodwill surely comes from Marianne's success, 'and Lizzie of course!' she is quick to add. 'I hope the guys realise we also do a good job, but it's just the beginning and there's so much to improve but every day there's more racing on TV and it's shown in a really positive way.' She talks about the negative coverage that has dogged the women's sport – how the cameras have gone out of their way to show poor crowds, or that the bunch are riding slowly, or that 'there are only five good riders in the peloton who can do anything'. But she is adamant that men's and women's cycling needs to work together: 'we need the guys to help improve our skills and I hope they'll see that we need that. We have to show women's cycling in a good way and last year was better than the year before – for example, the Women's Tour had the same prize money for women as for the men and it would be great if more organisers did that.'

So what are Roxane's ideas for the future? It's the first question she shies away from, saying she has no opinion on it: 'It's really hard because they think we're being really feministic if we ask for more prize money or point out how good women's cycling is, and I'm against that because it's not the best way. But if they make rules that organisations have to have women's races, like the Amstel Gold Race, Tour of Flanders or Liège–Bastogne–Liège. They need a women's race. And the UCI needs to make that happen because when they do it will be a big step forward. And we ride already on the Champs-Élysées and that's a really big step – maybe they need to organise a race for the last week, for the women, in the same area as the men's race, things like that. It's really easy but they still don't do that. Nobody knows why.' We both laugh ruefully, agreeing that it's a mystery why nobody seems to know how to make such a simple thing happen.

Dinner plates clatter onto the table and I have time for one last question about achievements and ambitions. She says her best memory is of that 2009 Dutch National Points race title 'when my second cycling life started.' And the future? 'I want to work on my time trialling skills, I want to be on more podiums in World Cup races. I have a lot of ambitions!' She pauses again. 'Actually I want to be in the best group of riders in Holland so people aren't asking "is she there?" They'll *know* I'm there.' To show all those people that put pressure on you in the past that you're the best, I suggest. 'I want to show all those people I can do it in my own way, but I'm doing that already!'

I thank her for her time and leave her to get on with her life with Wim, with her Rabo-Liv team, with Marianne and the girls. I think about the 17-year-old who nagged her father to let her try cycling. About the lost years when cycling stopped being fun after her father died. About her second life in cycling and a woman who trains as much to pause, think and reflect on herself and her surroundings. I hope she gets her women's Tour de France and the chance to win on the Champs-Élysées as her father did. I hope she keeps having fun.

CHAPTER 11

SUZIE GODART
Going Her Own Way

Suzie Godart started cycling late, at 32, and was immediately successful on the national level, winning numerous national titles in mountain biking, cyclocross and road racing. Supported by her husband Marc, directeur sportif of the continental team Differdange-Losch and also the pro teams Suzie has been a member of, her daughter Trixy, now also a cyclist, and her son Franz, who prefers dirt biking and freeride, Suzie continues to compete at 50, saying the sport is the drug that keeps her young.

Cat Armour, who has been following cycling in all its disciplines across Europe for the last two seasons, is a naturalised New Zealander who sold up her life in Auckland to travel the world and follow professional cycling. A passionate fan of the sport, she writes about the difficulties Suzie has faced in her extraordinary career in one of the hardest disciplines there is – cyclocross.

🐦 @meowclank
🏠 http://www.suziegodart.com

Cat spent a day with me by the sea and we talked about our mutual love of the sport of cycling. Cat shared some delicious gossip and rumour from her year spent following professional cycling – men's and women's – around

Europe and beyond. I urged her then to start writing about her experiences but she said she didn't know where to start. In Suzi Godart – multiple national champion, teacher and mother, competing at the highest level in her fifties – she has found her subject.

This is only my second season as a cyclocross (CX) fan. When I first saw a live stream of a race online I thought 'Wow!' Then I went to my first meeting and I was hooked. If you are unfamiliar with CX, by all means go to the UCI web page, but let me save you the effort and reproduce their 'About' page here:

> *Cyclo-cross races last approximately one hour. Races are held on technical and hilly circuits of 2.5–3.5 km. Cyclo-cross provides a real education in cycling as it requires accomplished bike handling skills and unfailing physical fitness. Competitors have to carry their bikes over some sections. The first Cyclo-cross World Championships were held in 1950.*

Thank you for that gem, UCI. Let me just add that riders not within a certain time of the leader, usually 80%, get pulled out of CX races. There's no such thing as getting lapped or being held up by a backmarker.

This year I went to Cauberg Cross, a UCI World Cup meeting, for the first time. It was a gloriously sunny October day in Valkenburg, Holland and, as there had been little rain in this part of the world for some time and the ground was hard with minimal mud, I knew the racing was going to be fast.

Through the trees I could see the riders in the women's race and hear the state of play over the speakers. As the racers get closer the cheering for the front group gets louder. I could hear them coming. And there they were – the elite of the elite of women's cyclocross riders: Helen Wyman, Sanne Cant, Sophie de Boer and Ellen van Loy. Further down the field at this point in the race was eventual winner, USA champion Katie Compton, then Swiss champion Olivia Hottinger, and then, bringing up the rear of the main bunch, there was an older woman who I could not name. Dressed in blue and bearing the number 44, she was pushing her bike up a little steep section of the course.

So who was she? At the end of the race I made my way to the finish line area where the riders and support crew were milling around – riders getting their faces cleaned and taking on drinks after a hard race – and there she was again, with the biggest smile. Someone had had a really good day. Eventually I found out that the woman in question was Suzie Godart and – despite being more than eight minutes down on the winner – she had not been pulled out. She had finished the race, and there were several riders who Did Not Finish that day.

Being an advocate for women's cycling I felt guilty that I did not know who this woman was. So, as soon as I got home I hit the computer.

Born 20 July 1962 – that makes her … 52?

I had to find out more.

As it turns out, Suzie Godart is an extremely approachable person and amazingly, it seemed to me, gave unstintingly of her time to a new fan. So this is a snapshot of the story of this incredible woman and how, despite the cycling 'powers that be' not wanting her there, she just kept on going.

In the beginning there was a bike for Christmas at age 5. Then, there was the first 'men's bike' bought with pocket money at 15. Then, weekend touring with her husband. Two children later, there comes the mountain bike fun, UCI licence and a whole lot of national titles in mountain biking, road cycling and cyclocross. That is a short summation of the life of Suzie Godart, but obviously there's more to it than that.

Like her childhood hero, Pippi Longstocking, Suzie Godart is her own person with the strength of mind to follow her own way and not care about what others might think. This fearlessness comes out in her love for sport, be it cyclocross, mountain biking or skiing – as a youngster she loved all the technically skilful sports and quite happily played alongside the boys. It would seem that nothing was out of bounds for Suzie and, although her parents encouraged her towards more academic achievement, she was always active.

It may seem strange, but Suzie had never considered a career in sports. Her first thoughts were with her family and then her job as a school teacher. Sport was just about having fun. In fact, before trying her hand at cycling, she had already had a family and it wasn't until after the birth of her son in 1991 that she took up mountain biking 'just for fun'. This was principally because her husband had been doing a few duathlons, so she trained a bit with him, but immediately fell in love with the technical skill. Both her and her husband, Marc, applied for a licence together, but it was Suzie who was getting the better results so Marc gave up his licence to follow her. He is the major support behind her continued success as well as her coach and mechanic. They will be celebrating their 28th wedding anniversary next year!

Suzie caught the competitive bug after that. Her palmarès make reading any rider would be proud of – she is a multiple national in cross country mountain biking and was Luxembourg cyclocross champion every year between 2001 and 2009.

That's a lot of championship jerseys!

On a more serious note, it would seem that the Luxembourg Cycling Federation have been remarkably resistant in recognising the talent that Suzie has shown over the years. And it all comes back to her age.

'As I started very late with cycling, I was considered a little bit as "exotic" by both the public and the riders, but over the years I made my place in the bunch and for the moment I really enjoy every moment of every race with so many people cheering for me.'

Suzie got her first licence at the age of 32; an age when many are actually thinking about retiring, but Suzie did things the other way round. Her first successes came in mountain biking and road racing and she signed her first UCI licence with Team Fat Birds alongside

Helen Wyman, Catherine Williamson and Emma Pooley. Although her part in the team was fairly short-lived, it brought her much more attention.

But because of her age she has never been given the opportunity to represent her country, even though at times there was actually no other female rider in the country to challenge her. So what possible reason could a National Federation have for not sending their National Champion to represent them?

Take a closer look at her palmarès and you'll notice that there is no cyclocross championship before 1997. The UCI did not recognise women's cyclocross before that time, although events had been contested for many years and several countries already had National Championships prior to 1997. But nobody has ever accused the UCI of being proactive.

In 1997, Suzie's first cyclocross race was won on a bike borrowed from a friend, but she bought a bike of her own for the National Championships that year, which she won without any competition – the other riders simply never made it to the start line. Apparently, it had snowed and she believes the others were too scared of riding on the frozen ground. She admits that this time she was scared too, as it was one of her first races, but she did it anyway. This is a familiar and recurring motif in Suzie's life.

Suzie's cycling career has been a bit of an uphill struggle, but despite being recognised only as an 'older' rider and not being considered by the Luxembourg Federation for any national selections, Suzie and Marc just got on with racing under their own steam. Suzie rapidly discovered she had enough UCI ranking points to make it into the top 100 ranked riders. Finally, this was something the Luxembourg Federation could not ignore and so she was able to participate in World Cup races, but never the World Championships. It appears she was 'snubbed' because of her age. It's easy to think that this sort of thing is all in the past, but it happened as recently as 2007 when she won the National Road Race title, but still it was the younger women who were selected in her stead. It seems that, regardless of how good you are, if you're over 40, your place is deemed to be in the masters category. However, there was a silver lining for Suzie – it drew her to the attention of Team Fenix in Italy, who proceeded to give her the chance to ride the Giro d'Italia Femminile as a domestique for team leaders Svetlana Bubnenkova and Monica Bacaille. Although she admits this was an amazing experience, she missed the technical aspect of her sport and returned to cyclocross.

Sometimes we need to remind ourselves that discrimination isn't just about gender. The thinking that 'she has her future already behind her', as Suzie puts it, was not just wrong in an ageist way, but literally and factually incorrect, because Suzie just kept on winning. Cycling is full of 'if onlys', but what might have been if the Luxembourg Federation had allowed her to compete for the previous 10 years? Is it always just about getting medals for national federations? Clearly they're under increasing pressure to justify their existence because they spend tax payer money, but shouldn't sport also be about recognition? Isn't it also about having a representative good enough to compete?

Since she started racing in 1994 Suzie says she has seen many changes. There were no races for women in Luxembourg at that time and although that small country loves cycling, there is still not much in the way of cyclocross racing. The UCI have, however, decided to hold the world champs in Luxembourg in 2017, so hopefully this will rekindle and stimulate interest in the sport. Back in 1994 though, women's racing in general was very unprofessional and a bit haphazard. Now with the UCI taking notice the races are organised and all aspects of women's cycling have become much more professional, but there is still a great divide between the big UCI teams and the smaller teams that are struggling to survive.

The nature of cyclocross courses has also changed with more technically difficult sections, such as long sand pits, to please the crowds – and they do! And the organisers do their bit by placing beer tents by those sections of a course where possible. Suzie believes that mountain bike cross country courses today are 'technically as difficult as downhill courses in the nineties'. Of course there are many more women participating in cyclocross now and the sport has diversified, attracting entrants from many different countries. The recognition from sponsors, like Twenty20 Cycling – who provide equal prize money at Koppenberg Cross – and Bpost Bank – who've been responsible for moving the women's race up the race day order, instead of being held at some time before dawn – has made a difference. The full impact may not be known for a while yet, but when the crowds come to the races earlier in the day and are able to call out the women's names, I tell Suzie I think this is huge. Suzie worries, however, that the expectation on organisers and sponsors may make it less affordable to put on a race. We have a way to go to get women's cycling TV coverage, unfortunately, although fans can only hope that this increase in popularity will see channels like Sporza or Vier actually showing the racing live instead of putting out packages of recorded highlights. Races like La Course help to make women's road cycling more popular but, as Suzie says:

'CX fans are different from road race fans, the courses are shorter and the entertainment value is bigger: look at races like Koppenberg, that's not a race, that's a big "fiesta". And this is the point why I adore cyclocross. It's the interaction between spectators and riders.'

And this is why we, the fans, love Cyclocross, too.

There have been huge improvements in equipment over the course of her career too. Suzie bought her first cyclocross bike in 1997, the year the UCI first acknowledged women's cyclocross competition – it was a long way from that first cyclocross race, ridden on a bike borrowed from a friend. Her first cyclocross bike sported an aluminium frame which, at the time, she thought was state of the art. Now, with developments in carbon frames, shifters, brakes, pedals and virtually every aspect of bike technology, she can't imagine riding anything else. Suzie currently rides a Guerciotti cyclocross bike 'but it costs *la peau des fesses* [the skin off your arse] as the French say and sponsors are very hard to find especially in women's cycling.' Hopefully, this will change.

Suzie doesn't worry too much about sports nutrition and is quite happy tucking into pizza, pasta and cookies. There's hope for many another carb-happy 52-year-old yet! She tells a similar story about her training schedule. It's a story many working mothers can relate to – Suzie works in around the family and being flexible to adapt to sickness and afterschool activities is paramount. She says she actually finds that competition itself is the best intense training.

It is a simple statement of fact that in order to be any kind of successful athlete a person has to be dedicated. To be a female cyclist, that dedication has to be accompanied by a support network, a massive love for your sport and, usually, a second career to pay for it. As well as the support from her husband and children, Suzie Godart is a physical education teacher at a local school with students ranging from 6 to 12 years. She loves her job and says her principal aim is to give children the chance to discover the joy in physical activities. She hopes that she can help each child to believe in themselves and to reach their potential – even if, like her, they don't realise that potential until later in life.

There have been some extraordinary highs and some deeply painful lows for Suzie over her career. One of the highlights of her career was in 1998 when she won her first national road race title, especially as she won cyclocross and mountain bike titles that year too. Her children had T-shirts made up saying: 'Mummy Suzie you'll win, we know you'll win!'

Last year she got to stand on the cyclocross podium in Luxembourg with her daughter, Trixy, who is following in her footsteps, but has taken her own path to success. Other highlights include that national road race title in 2007 at the age of 45 and her subsequent selection by Team Fenix to ride the women's Giro. But that was overshadowed by the death of teammate Liane Bahler in a car crash on her way to the airport. On stage 3 she received a phonecall to tell her of her mother's death. Another painful memory was the death of Magali Pache – who was also involved in a car crash – at the Trophee d'Or in 2000. The death of young riders such as Amy Dombrowski and Annefleur Kalvenaar is something most in women's cycling find very difficult to cope with: 'Especially in cyclocross we are so few riders that you feel like a huge family and it's terrible if someone's missing.'

So what does the future have in store? 'There were moments I wanted to stop. At the age of 40, I got a dog and thought about just walking him around, but it never lasted long until I felt like something was missing and started again. Finally I'm not racing for a federation, but for my pleasure and I just go on as long as I'm taking pleasure in what I'm doing and as I'm not making myself look ridiculous.'

As a teacher it won't be difficult for Suzie to fill her time when she finally stops applying for a racing licence. She has always seen racing as a bonus; an opportunity to travel, meet people and enjoy riding. She was worried that her two children might have missed out on some aspects of family life because of her participation in cycling, but thankfully they feel quite the opposite. Not only did they feel they haven't missed out, they feel they got to experience a lot of things that they would not have done otherwise. With daughter, Trixy, now participating in racing she won't be far from the sport she loves; though Trixy does not intend to make a career of cycling – she has other interests and is not ready to give up that life just for the bike. Sadly, should cyclocross ever be made an Olympic sport, there won't be a Godart representing Luxembourg just yet.

But it's a sad state of affairs that the Luxembourg national champion rarely got the opportunity to actually race in her home country, on her home roads and it's hardly surprising that those nations who field the most competitors are those with most races and the highest level of consideration for their riders. Take Belgium – for many the spiritual home of cyclocross – though for many years they didn't recognise the women's sport, they have more than made up for that oversight now. And the more races I go to the more I see local people recognising the women riders and taking them to their hearts. There are still some, like my friend at Koppenberg, who give their disparaging opinions freely, but mostly, as a dedicated fan of and advocate for the sport, what I see is acceptance of women's racing and, more than that, respect for the riders' athleticism, hard work, commitment and achievement. There is still a long way to go before the general crowds come to see women's racing with the same excitement as the men's, but then the men have had over 60 years, head start – it's hard to ride not just against your competitors but against 60 years of history.

CHAPTER 12

YVONNE MCGREGOR

The Ride of Her Life

Yvonne McGregor became the first British woman to win an Olympic cycling medal when she took Bronze in the individual pursuit at the Sydney Olympics in 2000. She is also a Commonwealth Games Gold Medallist and World Champion, who was awarded the MBE for services to cycling in 2002. Yvonne now runs her own sports massage business.

🏅 **Major palmarès:**

British National Track Champion Pursuit (1994, 1995, 1996, 1997, 1998, 1999)

British National Champion Time Trial (2001)

Gold medal – Commonwealth Games Points Race (1994)

Bronze medal – Olympic Individual Pursuit (2000)

World Champion Individual Pursuit (2000)

World Hour Record (1995)

I'd forgotten about Yvonne McGregor until I saw mention of the fact that she was considering an attempt on Land's End to John O'Groats. But when I remembered her, the memories were rich and powerful ones and I recalled what an inspiration she had been – the nearly-40-year-old who had finally fulfilled her destiny in her final season, winning the first ever cycling medal for a British woman and then capping it all with the rainbow jersey of the world champion a few short weeks later. I remembered roaring her on and willing her to do it for all us older women. So when the opportunity arose to interview her I dialled her number with not a little fan-girlish trepidation. I needn't have worried – she was exactly as I'd hoped she'd be: down to earth, funny, passionate, committed and happy to tell her story, which is not just that of a talented athlete finally making her mark, but of the whole revolution in women's cycling in the UK.

'Did the gun go off on my side?' That was the question Yvonne McGregor asked herself that September evening in the Dunc Gray Velodrome in New South Wales, Australia. In the ride off for the pursuit bronze medal, 39-year-old McGregor had been unable to get ahead of the 24-year-old New Zealander Sarah Ulmer and the metres were running out for her to avoid a repeat of the heartbreak of Atlanta. It was her very last chance and McGregor wasn't going to let it slip away.

She knew the gold medal was out of her reach – Holland's Leontien Van Morsel had smashed Frenchwoman Marion Clignet's 'unbreakable' record in the semi-final and it was clear that those two riders would go head to head for the ultimate prize. But the bronze? That was there for the taking and McGregor knew she had the form of her life.

'When they called me to the starting gate, I had this smile on my face, I knew. I said to myself, "Yvonne, just go out and enjoy it – you've done it thousands of times before, just go out and enjoy it."' She'd spent hours doing visual training on her start, her great weakness. She was never a sprinter, never had their raw power out of the starting gate. But she knew her numbers – the hours of training with sports science guru Peter Keen had told her that once she got up to speed she could hold good power through that 3,000m of intense and gruelling effort.

Her qualifying ride was, she says, 'the biggest ride of my life – you had to qualify top four and I rode a personal best.' She was slower in the second round but, crucially, she was quicker than Ulmer throughout qualifying. But each round is a new race, a new challenge, and in Atlanta she'd buckled under the pressure, walking away empty handed. At 35, she was convinced it had been her last chance. But here she was, cycling around the track, waiting to start her ride ...

'I knew I was behind after the first kilometre; I had a slower start and was pushing a bigger gear – but even with a lap to go I was about second behind and that's normally insurmountable in pursuit terms.' Slowly but surely McGregor begins to haul back the deficit, clawing back her opponent centimetre by endless centimetre, her slight body and lightweight frame eating up the wooden track. 'Even though it was close, it was quite surreal,' she remembers. 'In my body it was like 'this is my medal'. After everything I'd gone through in my whole career, the ups and downs, I hadn't come this far not to get a medal. I felt at peace and unrushed, I was pushing, pushing, pushing and I knew I was coming back at her and I remember Pete's arms punching, but within myself, my being, I was totally calm. It was mine.' McGregor still gets emotional when she talks about it, she says, 'because everyone was screaming and shouting "come on!" and Hugh Porter [ex-World Champion at pursuit and BBC commentator] was saying 'don't do this to me, Yvonne!' And to me it was all so ... I don't know ... and the feeling of my dad looking down. And I was pretty sure the gun went off on my side, although it was almost simultaneous.'

McGregor was right. The gun had gone off on her side. She was finally, at 39, an Olympic medallist, by 8/100ths of a second. 'I had to cycle halfway round the track to see the scoreboard,' she says, 'and then the tears came, tears of relief. And I thought of my dad. He was always incredibly proud of all of us, he was just a lovely guy and he came immediately into my mind; in his own way, he has followed my journey.' Initially it was a relief, she says, to have finally delivered the performance she knew she was capable of at World and Olympic level. 'I could have retired there and then, it was such a weight off my shoulders, and to do it on that stage was just incredible.' She thinks back to when she was training for the 1994 Commonwealth Games, when she had to travel to Leicester velodrome, the days they never got to ride on the track, just stood and watched the rain come down. 'And then fast forward to 2000,' she says, 'from there to there, it's amazing what your body can achieve, for a little kid from Bradford.'

For a cyclist of her achievements, McGregor was a late starter. 'I was always competitive,' she says, 'but I just never envisaged getting to the level I got to – never in a million years did I think that I'd get to the Olympics. They're other people's dreams.' She was, she says, an OK runner, always the competitive one, always pushing herself but she never had the innate speed to be successful at international level. But she knew she had the engine; she represented England in the World Fell Running Championships, Great Britain in the European Long Course in Triathlon Champs – and she'd beaten all the boys at school. 'These days, with talent ID, I'd have been spotted and gathered up and directed towards finding the sport that was right for me.' But it was the 1960s and 1970s, and light years away from lottery funding and Olympic success.

It was an Achilles tendon injury that changed McGregor's destiny. 'I was only cycling to commute to work and training sessions and I started doing the odd turbo session with a bloke I met by chance in a bike shop.' She had taken the decision to take six months off through the winter and focus on the bike. She had never done bike training and had fully intended to go back to running. Instead she walked into a Bradford bike shop to get her antiquated, second-hand bike checked out and changed her life forever. 'There was a guy, probably in his late sixties, early seventies, and he just came up and talked to me as if I was his long lost daughter.' He was George Robinson, a senior coach with the Association of British Cycle Coaches who ran turbo training sessions at Jer Lane Cricket Club in Bradford and would go on to coach the Nigerian cycling team.

McGregor is typically self-deprecating about her first training session: 'I don't think he saw I had talent. I hadn't raced, and you're just there on a bike going nowhere, you just put your head down and go. But I had that tenacity, that part of myself that just buried myself in every session, thrived on it.' Off the turbo, she would just go out on her bike after work, doing longer rides. 'I didn't use a heart rate monitor or anything like that,' she says, 'it was a million miles away from Athens or Beijing, but you didn't know any different, you just did what you did even in professional cycling.' But McGregor was bought up with the work ethic, had always loved sport and the opportunity to test herself and push herself – even when she wasn't at a great level as a runner, she still enjoyed the competition, the social side. It is, she says, a part of her being.

Eventually George suggested she try doing a race. Her first attempt was a time trial, a discipline that has long been at the heart of the British cycling scene. She has always been, she says, a time triallist, comparing the experience of running to the solo effort required on a bike. She remembers that first race as being 'horrendously wet and windy and I just had my 80 quid road bike, standard drop handlebars'. She says that first 25-mile time trial hurt like hell: 'I never wanted to do it again, I just wanted to chuck my bike over the nearest hedge.' She was so clueless she didn't even know whether she'd done a good time until other riders started coming up to her and telling her what a good time she'd done for her first race, bearing in mind the conditions. 'It didn't make me feel any better because it just seemed to go on for ages,' she laughs, 'but I'd done it and I just thought I'd continue riding and going to George's sessions, still thinking I'd go back to running and triathlon the following year.'

But in November 1991, McGregor suffered a huge personal tragedy. Her father, who had been so proud of his tomboy daughter, collapsed and died suddenly. It was a complete shock, McGregor says. 'I had a few weeks where I was completely out of it but I slowly got back into going to the training sessions.' Her family was always active and being fit was central to their life: 'when we went away it was the cricket bats and the tennis racquets that went in the suitcase first. I remember me, my brother and my sister all won the Bradford Schools Cross Country Championship on the same day in our respective age groups and they were so proud; so genetically they must have given us something.' She says she was always the quiet one, the tenacious one, who got a kick out of pushing herself. She says she perhaps wasn't quite as bad as Chris Boardman, who she would come to know when they attacked the Hour record within months of each other – he was a real 'perfectionist' – but for women 'there were less opportunities so you went out and did your own thing and hoped you got recognised. It was very amateur.'

McGregor started competing in earnest in 1992, riding to and from races as well as competing in them. Like her parents, she had never learned to drive. Despite Yorkshire's strength as a county, she started getting results – first top fives and then top threes. Without triathlon bars and on her 80 quid bike, McGregor was getting herself noticed.

1992 was also the year of the Barcelona Olympics, where Chris Boardman won Olympic gold in the individual pursuit. Seventy-two years after Great Britain had last won an Olympic medal in cycling, the Wirral man they called 'the Professor' set the nation alight. McGregor remembers watching Boardman triumph and feeling encouraged and inspired: 'it rallied me a bit more, but I still never dared believe I'd get anywhere in the sport. I was enjoying it because it was a new challenge.' She never had a bike as a kid. 'I didn't get a bike until I was 17 to go youth hostelling with me mates.'

1993 dawned and McGregor finally knocked her running career on the head. She had a good winter training base and started to set herself targets. She was going to get a medal in the national 10 and 25-mile time trial championships. She came away with a bronze. She entered the National Road Race Championships in Wales and finished 6th in her first attempt. It poured down, she recalls, but the tough, hilly course suited her abilities as a rider. 'I remember the national coach coming up and the first thing she said to me is "how old are you?" And when I said I was 32, it was as if I was too old. But I didn't know anything, I just answered the question. I've just always let my legs do the talking.' She never understood what all the fuss was about her age, saying that in endurance sports like cycling women are often stronger in their thirties.

After she got her first national jersey when she was selected for the World Championships, she says it was a turning point, the moment when she realised she could do something in the sport. 'I felt physiologically it was the sport for me. I didn't have the speed to do what Paula Radcliffe did in running, and though cycling is down to speed, you need bags of strength and endurance which was my forte. I'd never do anything in a bunch sprint, not in a million years, but physiologically the 25-mile and the hour were my ideal distances.' She admits that the pursuit was actually a bit too short for her as a distance: 'but I definitely got the best out of myself'. National selection forced her to make a commitment to the sport, to sit down with herself and decide to give it a couple of years to see how far she could go. She wasn't interested in regrets, in 'what-might-have-beens'. She would give it her all.

McGregor had moved back home shortly after her dad had died to help her mum cope with the shock. It gave her a roof over her head and she decided to go part time at work to devote more time to her cycling but existence was precarious. 'I remember being in the Co-op in Bradford and looking at how many coppers I had in my hand and how many carrots it would buy. It was literally hand to mouth.' But she refuses to feel she made a sacrifice – it was, she says, simply a decision she made.

1994 was a Commonwealth Games year. And McGregor was determined to get selected for the team going to Canada. Not only did she tick another ambition off her list, but she came away with a gold medal. 'It was totally unexpected. It was an event I'd never done before', she recalls. She was entered in the points race, an event in which riders sprint for points after a predefined number of laps and which often comes down to a bunch sprint. But a tough and canny rider can hope to get a lap on the field and automatically lead the race. The national coach at the time was Doug Dailey – who would go on to become logistics manager for British Cycling and discover Chris Froome – and he convinced McGregor to ride. 'He begged me, forced me! He said he'd sort me out a points race bike, but in the end I did it on my pursuit bike. It was a low profile, small wheeled bike and they just fitted normal handlebars.' McGregor laughs at the memory: 'Now bear in mind I've never done a points race in my life, I hadn't done that many pursuits to be honest, but what was in my favour was that it was an outdoor 333m track, so it was more like riding on the road for me.'

She describes what it felt like to line up at the start of a race that didn't really suit her style or capabilities: 'You start holding on to this barrier and my tongue was stuck to the roof of my mouth it was so dry. And I was holding on to this barrier thinking I was never going to be able to let go. We never had any expectations of a medal out of it.' But Dailey and McGregor had a plan – she would wait until a few sprints had happened and her rivals were tiring. 'Once there's been a sprint everyone sort of spins up the track, especially in women's cycling, and they kind of roll around the track before they wind up for another sprint. So we decided I'd nip down on the inside and just go for it!' McGregor bided her time and at half way, the moment came. 'I swooped down on the inside, put my head down, just out of fear more than anything and they were quite slow to react so I got half a lap quite easily.'

Her complete inexperience worked in her favour and the bunch let her go, obviously thinking that the novice wouldn't be able to stay away. 'I remember Phil Liggett telling me the next year, because he was commentating on it, that he said to the guys in the commentary box "if they don't chase her now, she's going to stay away because she's a very strong time triallist."' She gained the lap and was now leading the race – all she had to do to take the gold was stay out of trouble. 'And I crossed the line and I was Commonwealth gold medallist!' she says, still delighted by her unexpected achievement 20 years later. She says the whole experience was 'ridiculous, surreal and bizarre', that she had no idea what to do on the podium and raised her arms 'in a kind of a shy way because it just hadn't sunk in', but she does remember 'feeling "this is it, I've made it!"' Soon afterwards she was approached by Chris Boardman's coach, Peter Keen. The decision was made in the winter of 1994: she would go for the women's Hour record.

On 17 June 1995 McGregor's slight figure spun through a 15-minute warm-up on the 250m track at Manchester velodrome, before she settled into the position she would hold for the next hour pushing a 54×14. The Hour record is one of the purest tests in all cycling – just a rider, a bicycle and an inexorably ticking clock as the athlete strives to ride the furthest distance possible in the space of 60 minutes. The 34-year-old held the black line as if it were magnetic, only an occasional movement of the head betraying the intense effort involved in challenging the Hour. After 30 minutes she was down on her target of 47.750km, but, crucially, nearly two laps ahead of the record set by Catherine Marsal in Bordeaux that April. But that target started to drop further. Through the second half of her ride, she stopped gaining on the record. But like the Duracell bunny, she pushed on and through, breaking Marsal's record with a lap to spare. The new Hour record stood at 47.411km, beating the Frenchwoman's record by 299m. On such fine margins is the Hour record balanced.

McGregor says that the building of the Manchester Velodrome had a huge impact on cycling in Britain, and that while Sir David Brailsford gets all the accolades for delivering the phenomenal gold rush in British Cycling, it was Peter Keen who had the vision of Britain as the dominant cycling nation by the end of the decade, and the foresight and the scientific brain to push that vision through. Her attempt at the Hour, under his stewardship, was a small team effort. Unlike Jeannie Longo, the French superstar, who was making her own attempt on the Hour record and who could go to Mexico and wait for the precise, right conditions, McGregor had to book the track when it was available, travelling to the Wirral each week to stay with Boardman or his manager, Peter Woodworth for an intensive Kingcycle (a glorified turbo linked up to a computer with a power reading) session. She was, as ever, doing her own thing. 'When I look back on my career, probably a good 90% of the time I was training on my own and that's how I worked best ... with no distractions.' Like Graeme Obree, who had battled Boardman throughout those eight glorious months in 1994 when the men's Hour record changed hands four times, she was an individual who always enjoyed her training and could motivate herself to do it, even in the depths of a Bradford winter. She revelled in the sports science, the working to heart rate and power monitors that Keen introduced her to. 'There was a reason behind every session I did.'

McGregor's Hour would serve as a blueprint for Chris Boardman's own attempt at the Manchester Velodrome in 1996. Keen, the quiet genius of the track, would spend years coaching the reserved Wirral man, the willing monster to Keen's mad scientist, and the stars aligned that evening in September 1996. McGregor was there to watch Boardman set his best performance Hour record of 56.375km.

So what is it like to ride the Hour? To know that when you settle into your riding position you are locked in for the next 60 minutes? 'It's relentless. When you do a time trial you can freewheel, change gear or use a tailwind, things change on the road. But for the Hour it's constant, it's relentless ... nothing changes but your state of fatigue.' She breaks the ride down into sections. The first half hour is fairly comfortable, she says, you've trained for it and physically you're within yourself. But over the next 15 minutes, the fatigue begins to set in and it becomes a psychological rather than a physical challenge. 'You know you're stuck in this gear, in this position and you've got to put up with it and keep going like a metronome.' But it is the last 10 minutes that decides whether you will succeed or fail – as Boardman says, there is no hiding place. 'The last 10 minutes is just … it's really gruelling. You're not really thinking, you're just waiting for the hour to be up. It's just pain.' The sigh of recollected anguish and relief is audible.

McGregor succeeded, but was disappointed to miss her projected target of 48km/h. 'I still got the record, but being the person I am, I know I could do more.' She says her form had probably peaked the week before, that she'd been suffering with a 'sniffle', but that she got the record and elevated herself to world class, which had been her goal. 'It's a high-pressure situation and from where I'd come from, to be on that stage, putting myself under that pressure, was massive. And I was proud to put myself under that pressure and get a bloody world record!' But getting the best out of herself when it matters is what Yvonne McGregor is all about.

After the tremendous highs of the Commonwealth Gold and the Hour came the massive down of Atlanta. She had reasonable form, not 'stonking', but the experience was a nightmare. Four girls slept in a room meant for two students and the toilets overflowed. British star rowers Steve Redgrave and Matthew Pinsent took one look at the accommodation and left for a hotel. Worse, it was a three-hour round trip to the track and it was tiring – McGregor says she could feel her form 'just seeping away'. She was suffering with a back injury, bad enough to see her undergoing an MRI scan and 'psychologically was on a downward spiral'. She remembers standing in the starting gate in Atlanta, her foot shaking in the pedal, knowing she was not at the right level to put in her best ride. She was fourth, a second and a half off the bronze: 'I was just in tears – I was 35 and I thought it was my last chance of being at an Olympic Games, my last chance of being up there after the Hour record. I thought I'd let myself down, really.' She returned from America on a real low and then 'had the winter in Bradford to get through'. She says there were two points in her career when she thought about quitting: 1996 and the aftermath of Atlanta.

Though she improved the Hour record in 1997 and took a bronze in the World's pursuit, McGregor felt she'd reached a plateau. And time wasn't on her side. 'In the back of my mind I was thinking "I'm going to be 39 when Sydney comes around" – well, 39 and a half actually – it just didn't seem real.' But in 1998, things slowly began to turn around. 'I knew when I was going well; when my mind was good, my body was good, and I had these moments when it was almost an out-of-body experience, where everything just flows. I remember competing in the pursuit at the National Championships, operating only three or four beats from my maximum pulse, and I looked down at my legs and they were moving and pumping yet I didn't feel anything, it was complete synchronicity. Memories like that are all that you take with you. You don't have photographs of that.' Most importantly, in 1998, the decision was made to fund elite sportsmen and women through the National Lottery. McGregor experienced what she calls 'a massive psychological switch': 'every time I went out on my bike, I felt this was my job; there are no other stresses to worry about apart from focusing on your performance. The physical effort I put in didn't change but mentally it felt a huge shift.' The biggest grant she ever had, she says, was £21,000, but she got all her bikes and equipment supplied for free as well

There were other advantages too, in the form of warm weather training camps. For the kid from Bradford, used to the rigours of training in those harsh Bradford winters, 10 weeks in Melbourne was compensation for all the days people didn't see, the nights coming in from Bradford winters in tears: 'I couldn't feel my hands and I couldn't take me helmet off for half an hour because my hands were so cold I couldn't undo the buckle. When you're going into a gale-force wind and barely moving, you're thinking "why am I doing this?"' Days she would use the hand drier in a pub toilet en route just to bring some feeling back into her red raw fingers. But she kept plugging away, remembering the old mantra of 'form is temporary, class is permanent'. There are no easy rides in Bradford. Melbourne was her reward.

Eager for a new challenge, she started road racing, joining a European professional trade team and taking a more than decent sixth place in the Flèche Wallonne Classic in Belgium that finishes with a climb up the Mur de Huy, a sharp and brutal 1km ramp that hits a maximum gradient of 26%. She was a good climber, she says; her power to weight ratio was ideal for a mountain goat and she did well in the season she spent with a small Spanish team, finishing on the podium at the Tour of Majorca and winning another smaller stage race. She could, she says, give Jeannie Longo a run for her money on her day. 'Graeme Obree said to me, "If you'd been born in France, Yvonne, you'd have been lauded so much more because cycling is so much more passionate abroad." And he's right, in those days we were pretty much second-class citizens in a second-rate sport. How it's changed is phenomenal.' Before she learned to drive, she says, she remembers going to a race in Lancashire. 'I got the train, I had my tent in my rucksack, I chained my bike to a tree – and this was in the early 1990s. But I did it because it was a means to an end.' It's McGregor in a nutshell – strong willed, independent, doing what needed to be done, determined to keep pushing herself. The pioneer woman, alone, camping out in the wild.

She was there at the beginning of the seismic shift in British cycling. Would she like to have been in Beijing when the project finally came to fruition and Britain announced itself as the new superpower in the sport? She says she'd have liked to work with sport psychologist Steve Peters or to have ridden the team pursuit – she was always a good team player, always enjoyed riding as a *domestique* supporting the women road racers – but most of all she'd have liked to have ridden the bikes, seen the times she might have set, because it was all about her performance.

But in 1999 she suffered another setback. She had a recurrence of her back injury so severe that in December that year she couldn't even sit on a bike and touch the handlebars. Sydney was nine months down the line but it might as well have been nine years. Eventually the pain was so intense she was given an epidural and told to stay off the bike for a month. 'Looking back after Sydney I saw this was another part of my cycling destiny. I was a prolific trainer and at close to 40 years of age my body needed a big rest and recuperation and it needed something like this to stop me in my tracks, force me off the bike, to allow that to happen'. Slowly and surely she got back on the bike and there was no pressure to perform: 'I'd go to the camps and the girls would go to the races and I'd train very specifically, often twice a day following Peter's schedule.' She says it wouldn't have been enough to be selected, that she would have turned down a place in the team if she thought she was only going to do the qualifying ride 'that wasn't how I wanted to end my career.' But she kept following Keen's advice and, sure enough, she could feel the form beginning to arrive. When the rest of the team went out three weeks before the Games to acclimatise, McGregor chose to stay at home until the very last minute, finally arriving at the British cycling base the week before, ready to 'do the business': 'Then Jason Queally won the gold which was a huge boost – and I was just waiting. I went out with the form of my life, the best power I'd been doing and mentally I knew it and I went knowing I could get a medal.'

Her sister, nine months pregnant, watched like the rest of the nation from the edge of her seat. A lot of her friends couldn't believe she'd done it, asked her how she'd won the race. It was the first cycling medal of any colour won by a British woman. McGregor opened the floodgates for the extraordinary success to follow, for the Victoria Pendletons and Laura Trotts and Joanna Rowsells who watched in wonder as a 39-and-a-half-year-old battled to that extraordinary bronze. She would joke afterwards that everybody in the world knew her age after Sydney, but age was never the important number – that was the power she was kicking out on her SRM Powermeter. The Sydney bronze was etched out of Bradford grit and the long hours of winter training, the times she was knocked off her bike and got back up again, the broken collarbones and cheekbone, the sheer mental toughness born out on the unforgiving Yorkshire roads. It is impossible to overestimate the enormity of what McGregor achieved in her few short years at the very top, the inspiration she gave to 39-year-old women everywhere.

Six weeks later she was back on the track again for what she knew would be her swansong – the World Track Championships on her home track at Manchester. And the numbers started coming again. McGregor was back in the zone, riding the best pursuit series of her life. 'I was so consistent, within half a second of my best time and I was getting faster every round and I've never done that.' She could travel from home, sleep in her own bed and know that she was riding in front of a home crowd. 'I was kind of in control of my surroundings.'

The day of her finals ride, Chris Boardman set the Athlete's Hour record – riding an ordinary road bike far removed from the specialised time trial bike on which he had smashed the best performance Hour record – at the Manchester track. The atmosphere that McGregor stepped into as she entered the velodrome was already electric, a seething cauldron of noise and excitement and anticipation as she entered the starting gate to ride off for the rainbow stripes against Germany's Judith Arndt. She knew she'd be slow out of the starting gate but that was the only similarity with her Olympic-medal-winning ride. 'In Sydney I felt I was in a silent tunnel, but in Manchester I set out and the crowd roars because it's your home track. But I knew when I'd gone ahead because I detected the difference in the noise, the roar of the crowd, when I went into the lead with probably a kilometre to go. I knew I wasn't going to slow down, it was hurting, but I just knew I had the strength, and I knew with a kilometre to go I was going to be the World Champion.'

This time she knew the gun had gone off on her side.

She rode one more season in the World Champion's jersey, just to show off the rainbow stripes. But it was finally time to climb off the bike, to ask the question 'Yvonne, what are you training for?' Realistically, there was nothing else to aim for or get motivated for. 'When you've been working to SRMs and heartrates and power plans for god knows how many years, it was a release from that, your life revolving around this box on your bike. It was good to let go of that.'

Fourteen years on from her *annus mirabilis*, Yvonne McGregor is a highly successful sports massage therapist, working from home in a purpose-built cabin in her back garden. She loves it, loves working with people – she says it's part of the caring side of her nature and that most of her clients are from the general public, some in their eighties. Some of them pull her leg when they realise who she is: 'They say "Oh, you used to cycle a bit did you?" It's a long time ago now, but I hold the memories.' Her work gives her the opportunity to give something back. Cycling had 10 years of her life – 10 extraordinary, unforgettable years – 'but elite sport is a very abnormal existence and I'm very much a grass roots person, coming from a working class background. It wouldn't serve or satisfy me to go back', she says. There is no hint of regret in her voice. 'I'm a giver,' she continues, 'which sounds bizarre when you have to be quite selfish to get on in sport. I follow cycling but 10 years was enough. It was time to experience something else.' She's considering doing Land's End to John O'Groats or running a marathon one day, but she simply doesn't have the time. Her life without cycling is all consuming and yet finally in balance.

She says she never needed inspiration beyond herself, because at 30 'I pretty much knew who I was.' But she does identify strongly with another great heroine of British cycling – who sat in the Manchester Velodrome and watched her set her Hour record – Beryl Burton. 'I really identified with her psyche, her mental toughness, her desire to do it all costs, to never give up, just keep going, going, going. She was a very unique athlete. McGregor says she was fortunate to have the opportunity to meet Burton on several occasions, even visiting her at home, 'and I think she could see herself in me, I could see that smile, I'd see that twinkle in her eye: "yup, she's going to do OK." She was just down to earth.'

It's the way McGregor likes to come across to the school kids she often gives presentations to. She tells them elite athletes are not that special, they're just human beings at the end of the day, and that anything is possible: 'I'm the biggest exponent of that – even when I got the Commonwealth gold I thought that was the pinnacle, that the Olympics would never happen. It wasn't even dreamt of them. But success breeds success. You have to dare to dream, decide on your stepping stones, set realistic goals.' She says the biggest thing for her is encouraging young people, especially girls, to never give up. 'It's as simple as that really.'

Talking to school kids makes her quite emotional, she says, 'because it all comes back to me, what I've achieved and that it actually happened'. She was painfully shy as a child: 'I wouldn't say boo to a goose, so sport brought me out of my shell.' She says of course you need a bit of talent to do what she did, but that 'what you put in is what you get out, it's very rare that doesn't happen'. She only earned that self-belief in her thirties, when she realised that 'the one who comes out on top is the one who just keeps keeping on. It took me a long time to realise, and that's what I try and instil in them –to have confidence in themselves, that I'm no-one special, I'm here with these medals because I learnt to believe.'

It's typical of McGregor – hewn from Yorkshire granite but with a warmth and passion in her strongly accented tones that is never far from laughter – that she wears her achievements lightly. The medals – including the MBE she was awarded in 2002 for services to cycling – are kept in their presentation boxes. Her bike, a Terry Dolan lightweight frame, is stored in the garage, unridden. Her

World Championship jersey is in the drawer. She lost most of her cycling photos when her computer crashed recently, but she doesn't need photos. 'It's a long time ago and the memories are there,' she says. But two remain – one in her downstairs toilet that she giggles about, and one at the top of her stairs. 'It's of me on the podium and it does sum it up; I've got a big grin on my face, a smile, a look of total self-satisfaction. It is nice to see that. I won't lose that.'

CHAPTER 13

CAROLINE STEWART

'My Cycling Might Not Be Your Cycling But It's Just as Valid'

Caroline Stewart is a fully qualified cycling mechanic who currently works in her local bike shop in Crowthorne, Berkshire, and has provided support for the Matrix Fitness team and worked in the pits at the Milton Keynes round of the Cyclocross World Cup. She also races cyclocross for the Royal Navy Royal Marines Cycling Association team as well as providing ride support for new cyclists.

🐦 @swordpanda
ᛒ http://pandaonabike.blogspot.co.uk
🏠 http://www.griffscyclelab.co.uk

Caroline Stewart has more than one string to her bow – or blade to her sword. I was intrigued by the woman behind the @swordpanda Twitter name and so, through many lengthy hours of Skype chats, I wanted to find out what made her – Navy veteran, cyclocross rider, historical martial artist and bicycle mechanic – tick. 'When you find out, could you explain it to me?' she asked with typical dry-as-dust humour. This is Caroline's story.

It all started with a desire to work with helicopters, and the Navy do that much better than the RAF. My grandfather had served in all three armed forces, but for him the Navy was key. He was part of the Royal Naval Patrol Service that did mine clearance from wooden hulled trawlers that didn't attract magnetic mines. They swept the English Channel before D-Day and were mentioned in dispatches – I stumbled across a letter in the Imperial War Museum a few years ago that made specific mention of them. So that was in the back of my mind when I first started looking into the services. But in the 1980s I couldn't fly – female air crew simply didn't exist. And at school I was a bizarre mix of heavy science and arts (strong at English, graphic art and drama), so I had no clear direction of where I might end up. I had the option of Glasgow School of Art, reading psychology at university – I'm fascinated by broken minds – or engineering, so I could fix inanimate objects. Engineering was something I knew I could do and the Navy did it best. So I followed in my grandfather's footsteps.

I joined as an aircraft engineering technician, an opportunity that was opening up for women as I entered the Navy. And I finally had the opportunity to fly in the early 1990s. When I joined up I was 17 and a half and I decided I wasn't mature enough to go into the Navy as an officer – the kicker being that it's probably one of the most mature decisions I ever made. Once I felt I was responsible enough I applied for, and was granted, a commission to train to be an officer and went to Dartmouth in 1992 as part of only the second-ever class of commissioned officers to include female air crew. I was lucky; at around this time the Women's Royal Navy Service disappeared and everything just became 'The Royal Navy'. Then I was sent back to the squadron with which I'd done my front-line engineering training – as a front-line squadron they were the last line of training before pilots went operational so we did a lot of sea training. In fact we were taking female engineering personnel to sea before the general fleet did. But I never fully qualified to fly.

Rewind to my first year in the Navy. I'd played hockey for the naval base as a goalie and was running cross country and cycling. But on this one occasion I agreed to play up front in a mixed team and someone on the opposing team was trying to score and instead hit my right ankle. The Achilles tendon stretched and buckled and put me out of action for quite a while. But I'd got back to full fitness and passed my air crew medical as a Category P1 – to put it in perspective, only Special Forces and Aircrew are ever P1 – and then my Achilles blew again on a routine exercise. I was downgraded and no longer considered fit to fly. Due to cuts from an ongoing defence review, they weren't recruiting in the engineering branch at officer level and I couldn't't go back to 'the ranks' in engineering so I was disabled out of the Navy. At 23, I was a retired, disabled pensioner.

My engineering background was in electronics, avionics and weapons so I ended up in quality engineering before blagging my way into IT, working my way up to business systems manager for a group of agricultural companies, which is exactly as exciting as it sounds. And I hated it – I was getting further and further away from being hands on and I loathed the corporate stuff, being in meetings when I could be actively doing things. And I started to identify the signs of depression – I'd had issues with it throughout my life and was then at the stage where I could identify when it was coming – and I knew that if I stayed it would be totally destructive. I needed to get out, to do something fulfilling and rewarding and that worked for me. I talked to my partner and we started looking at options and one of the things that had been floating around in the back of my head was from an interview I'd heard on a podcast, the Velocast, with Sean Lally from Cycle Systems Academy. They were discussing the fact that they had trained up several female mechanics and had placed one of them with a cycling team for a year. I remember listening to it and thinking 'that sounds like fun'.

Let's rewind again. In my teens, my dad had owned a drop handlebar, 10-speed bike that was quite impressive to a 14-year-old. It was a Holdsworth, orange and blue, full team colours, with a Brooks saddle, and it was the first geared bike I ever rode. I was 14, and I'd never been sporty at school, but I loved cycling. I saved up my pocket money and, for £45, bought a second-hand Elswick Mistral five speed. It was dark bronze and was so heavy that it may have been made from offcuts from the Titanic – but it was *my* bike. My grandfather had been a pretty good club cyclist in his youth, primarily as a time triallist – we're talking about the 1930s and 1940s when time trialling was *it* in the UK – and he was really proud and supportive of me. And my father had been to school with a guy called Billy Bilsland, who was an ex-pro with the Peugeot team and had ridden in the 1968 Mexico Olympics and owned a bike shop, Billy Bilsland Cycles, in Glasgow. So my dad would take me to see him and he'd sort me out with kit and advice. And in the shop, in a frame on the wall, was Robert Millar's polka dot skinsuit from the final time trial of the 1984 Tour de France when Robert won the King of the Mountains. Billy was Robert's coach. There was also a yellow jersey belonging to some Belgian. Eddy something, a rider almost as good as Marianne Vos, apparently. I never noticed it back then because it held no significance for me – but Robert's did.

I wanted to ride because it was my 'me' space, my way of getting away from the noise and the propensity for mental health issues which, along with my interest in psychology, were rooted in my teens. Being on the bike was freedom, I could be me in my head. I used to watch men's cycling, I'd go to the Kellogg's series in Glasgow and see the pros up close. Millar had resonance for me. I felt a connection. He'd trained in the hills north of Glasgow, he'd also not 'fitted in'. So that was my anchor. I was never going to be that powerful or fast climbing but I could fly down the hills.

Where I grew up, if I stood on a ridge and looked one way, I'd see the whole of the city of Glasgow laid out at my feet, and, when I turned 180 degrees, there was the green of the Campsie Fells and Ben Lomond in the distance. I used to go out alone into the hills – I wasn't interested in joining a local club because that way I controlled 'my' cycling. I've always enjoyed pretty positive experiences in the 'man's world' of the Navy and cycling – I was cossetted into that environment by very supportive people – but I also prefer to avoid conflict, so I stayed away from the blokey world of the club run. But one afternoon I was out in my black and white chequerboard Peugeot acrylic-wool blend jersey and tracksuit bottoms tucked in my socks – these were the pre-lycra days – and I was sitting at a roundabout when some slick looking cyclists whirred past. I waited a few minutes then jumped on my bike and caught them a few miles up the road. 'You were sitting at the roundabout?' Yes. 'You caught us?' Yes. 'Do you ride for a club?' No. 'Then you should.' And that was how I ended up riding with the Glasgow Nightingale Cycling Club, whose club colours are the same as the Belgian national champion's jersey. I remember my first ever race, the club hill climb. One of the riders lent me his bike and told me to get everything out and I did – I got to the top of the climb and promptly vomited. I was empty physically and mentally. I quite literally left it all on the road.

My grandparents bought me a steel-framed Bianchi, celeste blue, and that was my first proper bike. It had an Italian bottom bracket, threaded in such a way that it would undo as you rode, so I had to stop and tighten it periodically. My dad had some aluminium sheeting so I cut myself a bottom bracket spanner that was light enough to carry in my jersey pocket. So at 15 I was making my own tools and working on my own bike.

And that's what came back to me as I spiralled into darker places. I gave up my £40K job in IT and completed my Level 2 training at Cycle Systems and then started a voluntary work placement at Holdsworth of all places, tying together the threads. It was a brilliant experience, working in the workshop where the team were based and their frames were built. Holdsworth had taken over the premises of the Ashlone Cycle Works in Putney, south-west London, that had opened in 1911. The sense of heritage was deep.

I moved on to Cycle Surgery where I was expected to fold kid's fleeces as well as fix bikes – hardly ideal. But I'd texted Holdsworth and asked them to keep me in mind for the future and they replied offering me a job for the summer. So I completed my Level 3 at CSA and went back to the historic Holdsworth workshop where I learned so much. When I was offered a day's work a week at Cycle Systems I jumped at the chance, and with the ride support I was offering at weekends, I basically did nothing that didn't involve bicycles. I'd also qualified as a Sky Ride leader, so I was fitting in the local Go Sky Rides in any spare time I had. Which meant I had little time for my daughter and the complications of shared custody. Something had to give. So when an opportunity opened up at Cycle Systems for an instructor, I took it. I told Holdsworth and the next day the owners announced they had decided to close the shop as the other mechanic was also leaving. Rumours about selling the shop had been circulating for a while but it was still a huge guilt trip. But I had my escape route.

There are more women working as cycling mechanics than most people realise. When I completed my Level 3 course it was the first time that, of the six people on the course, there was a 50/50 split. It was a notable first. I've trained female shop staff and female instructors up to mechanics. There's a huge and developing market in cycling that needs to be tackled correctly – the old school 'local bike shop' has traditionally been a bit of a 'man-cave' and that model doesn't work anymore. But it's changing – I was approached by my local bike shop to work in their workshop and jumped at the chance. It gives me the flexibility to fit around parental responsibilities by replacing a four-hour commute with a 10-minute one and not working Saturdays. And I have the opportunity to develop my ideas about making 'local bike shops' female-friendly and leveraging links with the professional sport through my work with the Matrix Fitness team, for whom I have worked as mechanical support for events like the Nocturne and the Tour series. I was told by one of the Matrix riders Penny Rowson at the Nocturne that the UK men's continental NFTO Pro Cycling team liked the idea of Matrix having a female mechanic – it's a sign of the way that women are beginning to permeate through men's cycling at all levels. I'm not the first female mechanic at the Matrix team – they had a woman mechanic before, who had also qualified through the Cycle Systems programme, and that's part of what motivated me to get involved in the first place.

I was incredibly fortunate to be around for 4 out of 5 stages of the inaugural Women's Tour in 2014. It was a superb event, really well organised by Sweetspot whose logic for locating the race where they did was absolutely sound. East Anglia makes perfect sense because of the direct links to Belgium and Holland, where most of the women's teams are based. The route made a virtue out of the lack of money in the women's sport by concentrating on a small geographical area and setting up a series of almost 'Classics' type races. If you want to see women climb mountains, then support the Giro Rosa – or pressure the Tour de France to set up a proper women's Tour de France. The Women's Tour was an amazing advertisement for the sport, especially with Marianne Vos winning the overall. It was exactly the right narrative for the public who were eager to see a rematch of the 2012 Olympic road race, and I feel that was important for the development of the sport.

And the excitement around the race was palpable, both on the ground and through social media – the use of Twitter to co-ordinate fan response was fantastic. Sweetspot were genuinely surprised at just how successful it was. They'd sent riders round to local schools to talk about the event beforehand to build interest so the weekday stages were lined with excited schoolchildren. But they were scared that they wouldn't have such a big turnout for the weekend stages. I vividly remember driving out onto the race route on the Saturday and over the first few kilometres the crowd was already beginning to build and from then on it was non-stop. There's a photo taken down the finish straight at Welwyn that shows the crowd four deep. And the next day was even more extraordinary.

I was also lucky enough to be involved in the other huge cycling event in the UK in 2014, the Grand Depart of the Tour de France in Yorkshire. The Tour organisation asked the three armed forces to provide teams to test ride the first 2 stages in the week before the actual race start. I took time off work and offered my services as mechanic. It was fantastic to see the response that our riders got on the route and, for me, really rewarding to give a good level of mechanical support to the riders, whether it was working late into the night between stage one and two to prepare and fix bikes, jumping out of the support vehicle to pick up and help a crashed rider, change wheels, refit chains quickly or, on one notable occasion, adjust a rider's saddle while hanging out of the vehicle window on the move (which included negotiating a roundabout at the same time). I'm really proud of all of the riders, most of whom made it all the way round, and I'm sure the information we gathered as a group was of use to the Tour organisers.

But more than just a greater involvement in encouraging women to ride, for me, it's about developing cycling in the community and becoming the focus and the hub for that. My local bike shop LBS supported my partner and I when we did the Land's End to John O'Groats in 2012 and I want to give more people those kinds of opportunities. So shops need to be moving away from the old fashioned approach of the boy's club because it's not gendered – it puts everyone off equally. The MAMILs who have got into riding sportives because 'Geoff in accounts does them and says they're fun', or who were inspired by Wiggo in 2012, haven't grown up in that culture and they can find that attitude off-putting too. It's a developing market that's used to a different kind of service that the old school bike shop doesn't necessarily accommodate. Initiatives like 'Ladies Nights', where I can teach women the essentials they need to know for bike maintenance, open up the local bike shop as a community hub. I'm all for getting people out on their bikes more often by demystifying them and being approachable, so I'll answer technical questions on Twitter, I'll review pieces of kit because people seem to trust my opinion. I've done a couple of technical segments for a US-based podcast. And my partner invests in the best bikes he can afford because he knows he has someone on the spot that's qualified to look after them. And I race – badly – for the Royal Navy Royal Marines Cycling Association. As far as I know, I *am* their women's cyclocross team! I still get really nervous before each race, and try to do my best possible effort, though I race for nothing except my own amusement. But I love racing, especially when it's over!

I've been fascinated by the ideas of Dr Steve Peters, the sports psychiatrist who worked with Team Sky until 2014, for quite a while now – not only in my cycling but in my historical European martial arts practice. I'm known as @swordpanda on Twitter partially because of my involvement with the reconstruction and teaching of historical methods of swordplay. I've been teaching for over 16 years and find Steve Peters's ideas about the chimp, the human and the computer are really useful – I need to know when I'm talking to the chimp and when I'm talking to the human. In something with such a high level of calculated risk, you need to be able to control the chimp reaction and use the human reaction – which is what your rational self would do – or better yet the automatic response, the computer response. You need to be rational and dispassionate in high performance situations like armed combat, or a bike race, or even just motivation on a long training ride.

A good example would be in 2012. I had been off the bike for some years by that time, had bought a really cheap and nasty MTB just to get out and lose a bit of weight and really quickly felt that it was frustratingly slow, so I bought a new road bike. My partner decided to go out and buy one so that he could ride with me and soon after that we had a conversation that ended with 'OK, let's ride from Land's End to John O'Groats then'. A lot of planning later, including discussion with an ex-military disability charity and sports nutrition supplier and we set off from Land's End on a misty Saturday morning in August. Eight days later we arrived at the other end of the country, having cycled around 114 miles a day, having had 28 degree heat at Weston Super Mare on day 2, a serious 'stomach issue' overnight into day 3 (which nearly stopped me riding), biblical rain, some serious hills and a real mental battle on the last day. The second half of day 8 had two of the toughest climbs, with nearly 800 miles in our legs and promise of headwinds coming at us faster than we were riding. Having had to climb into the support vehicle for half an hour to warm up after the first of the climbs, Hemlsdale, which had been ridden in freezing rain, I wasn't sure that I could continue. Then came the final hard climb out of Berriedale (over 20% in places) where I had to go deep physically, but more importantly, mentally. Here is an extract from my blog entry for that day:

> *This was a vicious climb ... harder than anything I'd ridden ... but (and I'm still not sure of the actual mental process that got me up this) a combination of 'It's the last MAJOR barrier', 'why we are doing this?' (for the Project, for people who lose the ability to even walk again), 'just to this next corner, OK, just to the end of this wall' and 'we are over 800 miles into this now, we CAN'T not finish' managed to get me up this horror of a climb.*

The fact that I could almost step outside my head and analyse this process is testament to how important mental preparation can be to your success on a bike, or anywhere. Apparently eight days for Land's End to John O'Groats is pretty good going. I just know it was hard, but we did it.

My philosophy has always been 'my cycling might not be your cycling, but it's just as valid.' If you just watch the Tour de France once a year, that's fine, you're showing an interest in the sport. If you're out on the roads doing old school time trialling, that's valid. If you ride sportives because 'Geoff in accounts does', that's valid. Anyone who rides a bike is supporting the industry and, for me, they're a potential customer.

The women's sport will keep developing as long as it has perceived validity – when you're perceived as being equally valid then everything else works. That will take time, but with some really great advocates throughout the sport, it *is* changing.

And I like to fix things.

CHAPTER 14

EMMA O'REILLY

The Best of Times, The Worst of Times

Emma O'Reilly trained as an electrician before becoming a masseur for the Irish National Cycling Team. She was Lance Armstrong's personal soigneur for four years at the US Postal team before blowing the whistle on the team's doping activities. She currently runs the Body Clinic in Cheshire and is the author of *The Race to Truth*, her highly acclaimed account of her years at US Postal.

🐦 @Emma_OReilly
🏠 http://www.bodyclinichale.co.uk/

I first met Emma O'Reilly at the Change Cycling Now conference in London in 2012 and, for me, it was love at first sight. Her reputation as a fearless truth teller preceded her, but she was so much more – warm as a snuggly blanket, effortlessly funny and a natural storyteller. She was one of the first people I contacted for the book – and one of the most difficult to pin down after the success of The Race to Truth, *which was nominated for the Bord Gáis Energy Sports Book of the Year in Ireland in 2014. Eventually, through a series of emails and missed phone messages, we talked about her life as a soigneur, and her best – and worst – memories of her life at the heart of US Postal.*

Emma O'Reilly – for a woman who was at the very heart of the US Postal shitstorm and lived through what seemed like almost monthly subpoenas – is remarkably relaxed.

'I never really decided on a career in cycling,' she says. Born in Tallaght, near Dublin, and a teenage cycling fan, growing up in the era of Sean 'King' Kelly, she trained as an electrician. 'It stood me in good stead for being the only female soigneur in Europe,' she recalls, 'because at that time no other women were doing an apprenticeship in trades. So I never felt isolated.' She says one of the real advantages of being the only woman was that 'I didn't have to room share. I could go to my nice quiet room at night'.

Her love of the sport and an interest in sport therapy bought her into the sport 'by accident, really.' She spent three years with the Irish National team before a rider moving from Shaklee to the American US Postal team recommended her to the team management. 'The atmosphere was great,' she remembers, 'but it got more serious as the results improved.'

O'Reilly says she got into the sport because 'it was a role I enjoyed, I loved the work, the excitement, the travel. I was treated more like a little sister by all the lads on the team. Yet I felt I was like their big sister.' So what did being a soigneur (from the French 'to care') involve? 'I was feeding them, massaging them, cleaning them up after they crashed, making sure they had clean clothes, so it was a quite a caring relationship we had.' She describes the work as 'exhausting and frenetic', yet she clearly loved her job. What makes a good soigneur? 'You gotta like it and have a sense of humour,' she laughs 'and they're skills you can apply to any job.'

She describes a typical day on the Tour de France, professional cycling's biggest showcase, the race that US Postal's team leader Lance Armstrong 'won' seven times, before being stripped of his results in 2013. 'Early up, breakfast one hour before the riders. Two soigneurs would go to the race and two would go on the next hotel to set things up for the post-race massages. I'd usually go off to the race, prepare the musettes (the riders feed bags), get to the feed zone, hand out the musettes, finish on the race, get back to the hotel, give the riders their massage, have dinner and then bed.' Then repeat for the next 21 days. Nanny, nursemaid, mother hen, O'Reilly was so successful, Mark Gorski – the man who hired her for the US Postal team – called her 'the heart and soul of the team'. O'Reilly is modest: 'I played a part in what was a hugely stressful melting pot', she says.

'I remember, I asked one of my riders: "What are you most looking forward to about retiring?" He said: "Not being hungry."' O'Reilly says that dedication, that sheer hard work and self-discipline, is often forgotten when we talk about cycling in the light of the USADA Reasoned Decision, the American investigation into doping at the US Postal cycling team that finally brought down Lance Armstrong. She tells the story of driving a group of hungry riders to a race, how she turned them loose on a motorway service station with the team credit card and how they failed to bring anything for her. 'And how do you think *I* live?' she asked them, before sending them back to get her a can of Coke 'on principle'. Add moral conscience to the list of attributes Emma O'Reilly brought to a tough but often rewarding job.

There is an elephant in the room and it's a topic that O'Reilly feels she has exhausted in her book *The Race to Truth*. She wants, she says, to talk about her life on the road as a soigneur, a carer, about the best and worst of times during her years with Armstrong. 'Our relationship was based on a caring relationship,' she says, 'it was my job to care for him and in return he cared for me and he'd look out for me at times.' Armstrong even wrote the foreword for her book and compliments her for her ability to see the 'shades of grey' involved in a rider's decision to dope. She says she sees those riders as victims of the system, but that they were ultimately responsible for their choices. 'I have sympathy for the situation they were in but not the decision they made', she concludes. And Lance? 'How he behaved was horrendous. The machine got too big, too ugly and too corrupt.'

But this is the woman who gets a namecheck and a dedication in Freya North's *Cat* – one of the funniest and most truthful novels about cycling ever written – as the 'soigneur's soigneur' who always enjoyed the *craic*. O'Reilly laughs her generous, full-throated laugh. 'I could remember the good times as well as the bad times. I tried to focus on the good rather than bad,' she recalls, adding 'I feel the culture has really, really changed and I feel there have been so many steps in the right direction. It's moved on so much and they are doing their best to clean it up.' O'Reilly has spoken about her 'Catholic conscience', drummed into her in her upbringing, and it clearly informs her forgiving nature. 'We all have strengths and we all have weaknesses, and sometimes our strengths become our weaknesses', she concludes.

But for O'Reilly, her darkest memory of the Tour de France is not the gathering clouds of suspicion that hung over the US Postal team in the noughties, but the Tour that should have been the wake-up call for the sport – 1998, the year of the Festina Affair.

'For me the worst moment in the Tour was the 1998 from Albertville to Aix les Bain,' she says. 'It was the day the riders went on strike for the manner that they had been treated by the CRS [French police].' The Festina Team soigneur Willy Voet had been arrested with a car full of EPO and other performance-enhancing drugs on his way to the ferry for the start of the race in Ireland. 'The police had been all over the race and riders were getting pulled out of their rooms still in cycling clothes and out of the shower,' she recalls. 'We were all scared but for some reason it all got on top of me that day, I was scared going to bed that night and had my suitcase packed and dressed ready to be dragged out of my bed!'

O'Reilly had made the decision not to go to the race that day. 'I love Aix les Bains and the hotel we were staying in, and it meant I could hang out with one of my favourite people in the world, Julien.' She remembers how they got to the hotel and checked in. Julien (de Vries, one of the team's mechanics) busied himself with setting up his truck and the water and electricity supplies, while she went shopping for the riders. 'Julien was great, he had been around since Merckx's time and knew the ropes better than anyone else ever will,' she recalls. 'We worked well together, got everything done quickly, so once we'd finished we sat outside drinking our Perrier Menthes, enjoying the sun.' She remembers realising that the team were running late and should have been back at the hotel: 'so we spoke to a few staff members from the other teams and they said have a look on the TV – the riders are staging a sit-down protest. Initially my cynical thought was "gits, now we'll all have a late finish tonight!"'

But her thoughts quickly turned to sympathy with the riders. 'I thought – they are right, whatever has being going on, not everybody's involved and there are ways and means of doing anything including arresting athletes for their performing enhancing methods.' Finally the riders and race staff got back to Aix and everybody was 'stressed and wound up – after the treatment of the Dutch TVM team the previous night [6 TVM riders had been taken to a hospital in Albertville and had to give blood and hair samples for testing, after the police had searched all their belongings and even got interpreters to read their letters], the atmosphere had changed, it was no longer just a few riders and teams, everyone was involved and the fact that everyone could be brought to a jail cell was a very frightening thought.' She remembers the atmosphere at the dinner table being 'very subdued, but it was the fear felt going to bed that night that makes this my worst Tour day.'

She is quick to qualify that she has no sympathy for riders who were subsequently convicted of doping offences, but she does have a degree of empathy. 'This is from my perspective of when I was still in the sport,' she says, 'but I do see that people deserved to be arrested and shouldn't be given any special favours just because they are cyclists.' But it is her empathy, her ability to see the shades of grey, which must have made her so good at her job.

And the best moment? You sense there must have been many, but O'Reilly decides on recounting 'the nicest one, when Lance won the '99 Prologue in Puy de Fou.' She had been working with him through 1998, his comeback season after testicular cancer when a fourth place at the Vuelta a España had made the cycling world sit up and take notice. 'I'd seen first-hand how much hard work he put in, from the time at the end of the Vuelta the previous year when it was decided that he should go for the Tour the following year.' Once the decision was made 'everything was about the Tour. I went with him on his training camps in the Alps and Pyrenees, helped to get things organised in such a manner to help make sure things ran smoothly in the soigneurs section. Lance worked hard on every level and was great for being inclusive with those who could help him achieve his ambitions.'

What was it like, coming to the start line in 1999? 'The beginning of the Tour is a nightmare, everyone is nervous and anxious, sponsors are there, the big bosses are in town and everyone wants results.' She says she remembers the day as being 'gorgeous – at least in my mind, the sun was shining; in actual fact, it was an overcast day.' She says both she and the team knew that Armstrong would put in a big performance 'but were not expecting him to win it by 7 seconds – typical of Lance though; gets the jersey and now the poor lads might have to defend it for the three weeks!' But, as she points out, it was a huge achievement: 'he'd won the prologue and got the jersey, just two years after being declared cancer free.' Just as O'Reilly remembers sunshine on an overcast day, she remembers that 1999 Tour as 'such a lovely perfect time; he had worked hard, I was lucky enough to be a little part of something huge and inspiring. It was so nice to see hard work, dreams, ambition and dedication coupled with a refusal to give up in spite of all the odds.'

She remembers the sense of youth and optimism of that first Tour triumph: 'the team was still quite young, both as a team and in our ages. We were all in our early twenties, that time of your life when everything is possible and we think we can achieve all our dreams.' She talks about the aftermath of that victory, how the team had gone back to the hotel: 'all of us doing our jobs, riders showering, getting massages, seeing the mechanics, mechanics washing and prepping the bikes for tomorrow's stage, the Directors planning the next day and so on. I was late finishing and while in the shower I got a knock on the door.' She laughs as she remembers thinking 'for God's can I not have a shower in peace?', but it was Mark Gorski at the door, asking how long I'd be because they wanted to wait till I was down for dinner to pour the champagne. This was before the team became Lance Inc. and it was a somewhat intimate time as a team. That would have to be one of the best days of my career in cycling, we worked as a team – it was still an all-for-one-and-one-for-all time.

She says that, despite everything that has happened since, she chooses to remember the fact that Armstrong 'still had to work hard and make a lot of sacrifices to get that result'. And more than that, like the memory of a sun that never shon, 'It was also a day that I felt so lucky to be part of such a nice team.'

She says she had always planned to be out of the sport by the time she turned 30 and she duly left the team in 2000. She says it was 'a shock, even though I'd always planned to leave; change shocks the system.' But, she adds, 'I always knew the lifestyle was a temporary thing.' She now runs the Body Clinic in Hale, Cheshire, treating everyone from Olympic athletes and professional sports people to the general public. She has plans to open a spin and Wattbike studio. And she says she's finding cycling fun again: 'If it wasn't fun, I wouldn't do it!' she laughs, saying that for every woman she's ever met in the sport it is the sheer enjoyment, the sense of fun, the *craic* to be had that keeps them coming back for more. So what advice would she give her teenage self, on the brink of becoming involved with the biggest cycling team in the world? 'I'd tell myself to remember more about those days, focus on the good times and enjoy it. I've made so many mistakes I can't even remember what I should avoid!'

CHAPTER 15

HANNAH GRANT

'It's a Crazy Ride, It's a Cool Ride'

Hannah Grant is the chef for the Tinkoff-Saxo professional cycling team, where she provides the right meals for the pro riders to perform their best, which she calls 'performance cooking'. She graduated from the Copenhagen Culinary Institute in 2007, and has worked at The Fat Duck with Heston Blumenthal and NOMA with René Redzepi. Hannah is the author of *The Grand Tour Cookbook* and is working on another project with sports nutritionist Stacey Simms.

🐦 @dailystews
🏠 www.hannahgrantcooking.com http://dailystews.com/

Hannah Grant is funny and talkative, laughs often, and has a culinary CV some male chefs would die for, but this bright, beautiful woman has chosen to carve an extraordinary niche in the very masculine world of men's professional cycling. She took time out from planning next year's menus in her home town of Copenhagen to talk to me about her career in food and some of the memorable dishes she's cooked for the Tinkoff-Saxo team, one of the biggest men's professional teams in the world.

Hannah, you're currently the team chef for the Tinkoff-Saxo team, but you've worked at several top restaurants including NOMA, the best restaurant in the world. How did you come to be cooking for a cycling team?

I've always been interested in food. When I was a small child I'd pull out all the contents of the cupboards and drawers to make my own sauces! So I've always had an interest in cooking. In 9th grade, I decided I wanted to go into the restaurant business but my dear mum was under the impression that this was the slippery slope to becoming an alcoholic – in the old days, chefs were super-hard-working and they drank a lot; it was a very hard lifestyle. So my mum was reluctant to put me into chef school. She told me: 'When you're 18, you can decide, until then I'm in charge.' So when I left high school at 18, the chef thing was right at the back of my mind.

I was working full time, I went to fashion school – I tried a lot of things. But I realised I need to push myself in one direction, to give myself a big kick up the arse, as we say in Danish [laughs], and to figure out what I wanted to do, so I signed up for the Danish Royal Navy!

Why the Navy?

I'm really good at getting my own way and talking my way out of a lot of things but in there you can't talk your way out of anything. I wanted to learn discipline and to experience that. So I ended up on an inspection ship round Greenland and the Faroe Islands, doing fishing inspections – checking the quotas, making sure they hadn't overfished or fished the wrong things. On the boat I met a very dear friend, a guy named Karl, who had just graduated as a chef. And all of a sudden, on this boat in the middle of the ocean off the coast of Greenland, I'm standing in the galley with him making 200 litres of soup and it totally occurred to me 'this is what I wanted to do! I wanted to be a chef!' So I finished my time in the Navy and went straight off to sign up for chef school.

That was quite a change in direction!

It was weird – I'd taken the path away from it and then realised that this was the way I had to go. In Denmark you train for four years to be a chef and I'm glad I did it that way. Being a chef is a lot about accepting that you don't know anything and that you need to be taught. It's about saying 'yes, chef' constantly, about learning and failing and rising from the dust again and again. I don't think I could have done that without being a little older and having done the Navy thing as well – accepting the hierarchy, accepting that there's someone above you who tells you this is the way it goes.

You worked at one of the world's best restaurants, NOMA?

When I was an apprentice, NOMA had just opened. It was a small restaurant scene in Copenhagen and no one ate out at lunchtime because the Government had passed a law to stop meals out being deductible, so all these amazing chefs were forced to rethink things. NOMA was nothing – everyone laughed at them and called them 'field fuckers!' [laughs] But René was an amazing chef and his staff were really talented. Anyway, I kept an eye on it and two apprentices I knew started working there. But I took a different path.

Where I worked was super-classic French. During your training you're supposed to work at one restaurant – but then you don't develop, it becomes impossible to adapt and change to new things. So I worked at three places, but the last one was the super fine dining that I wanted to do. I was super happy. I never intended to work at NOMA. But the restaurant scene was so connected; I knew a girl apprentice at NOMA for whom René had arranged for her to work for three weeks at the Fat Duck, and I was unbelievably jealous. My chef said 'no' but René believed in sending people out to see what was going on, for ideas and inspiration, to learn to change and adapt and see that things are not the same everywhere.

So I got it stuck in my mind that I wanted to go to the Fat Duck when I graduated. NOMA was interesting, it was doing something different, but it didn't have the superstar appeal it has now and at that time the Fat Duck was the number two restaurant in the world. So when I graduated I applied to be a *stagiare* at the Fat Duck – I had to fill out a 10-page application form about my background and my motivation – and I got accepted. So I made as much money as I could in three months so I could go and work for free for Heston Blumenthal!

That's funny! How did you get the money together to get to the Fat Duck?
I applied for a lot of grants – I was going to be the biggest female Danish chef! The worst thing I could get would be a 'no'. I applied saying I was representing the female side of Danish culinary life, I was going to go out and get lots of inspiration, and come back and give back, and make Denmark a country with female chef power. And it worked out to my benefit and I got 10,000 Danish krone to go to the Fat Duck.

So I started working there and I met this amazing American guy who's now my husband. He was working in the development lab there. He has Norwegian heritage and he was into all things Scandinavian so I was telling him about NOMA. I ordered the book for him and I realised that what they were doing was super neat and I was kind of representing this! And I said to Lars, 'This is your dream scenario, you should develop dishes for this restaurant.' And that's what he does today.

So what happened when you left the Fat Duck? Where did you go next?
After the Fat Duck we didn't know where to go. There were visa issues and we weren't ready to get married, so I went to New York to visit him and try and figure out what we were going to do. And a chef friend of mine was in New York, working for the third-richest person in the world as a private chef on his yacht – and he had

Above: Former women's world cycle champion Beryl Burton in action, 1965. *Dan Morley/ EMPICS Sport. Courtesy of Press Association*

Right: Beryl Burton takes the bronze medal in the 3000 metres persuit during the World Cycling Championships in Leicester, 1970. *Nevill Chadwick/Getty Images*

Right: Portrait of Alfonsina Strada by Ilona Kamps. *Copyright Ilona Kamps*

Connie Carpenter-Phinney racing for gold in the Women's 79.2km Road Race during the 1984 Los Angeles Olympic Games. *Peter Brouillet/Getty Images*

Kathryn Bertine, racing for Wiggle Honda at the inaugural *La Course*, in the Tour de France. *Courtesy of Kathryn Bertine.*

Betsy Andreu, spouse of former cyclist Frankie Andreu, speaks during the World Anti-Doping Agency symposium in Switzerland, 2015. *AP Photo/Keystone, Jean-Christophe Bott. Courtesy of Press Association*

Hannah Grant, chef for the Tinkoff-Saxo professional cycling team. *Reproduced with kind permission from Hannah Grant*

Ottilie Quince, fastest female transplant cyclist on the planet, shown here with Marcel Kittle (L) and Bradley Wiggins (R). *Reproduced with kind permission from Ottilie Quince*

Portrait of Ashley Gruber taken by partner Jered Gruber. *Reproduced with kind permission from Ashley and Jered Gruber*

4.

5.

Joolze Dymond's Best Shots (see pages 188 – 190):

1: Nicki Harris,

2: Tour de France in Yorkshire,

3: Winter Fun,

4: Abby-Mae,

5: Women's Tour

All photos courtesy of Joolze Dymond

1.

2.

3.

Marianne Vos and the Rabo-Liv team race for the finish line during the Prudential RideLondon Grand Prix Pro Women's race in London, 2014. *Bryn Lennon/Getty Images*

(R–L) Penny Rowson, Jessie Walker and Lucy Shaw from the Matrix team take part in the 2015 British Cycling Women's Road Series round 1: Tour Of the Reservoir, at Derwent Reservoir in Northumberland. *Courtesy of Huw Williams.*

Black and white image of Fabio Aru, taken by Ashley and Jered Gruber at the 2014 Giro d'Italia. *Reproduced with kind permission from Ashley and Jered Gruber*

Clara Hughes leads the the way during the Women's Road Race at the London 2012 Olympic Games. *Pool/Getty Images*

Yvonne McGregor for Great Britain after winning bronze in the Women's Individual Track Cycling event at the 2000 Sydney Olympic Games. *Mark Dadswell/Getty Images*

Rochelle Gilmore celebrates with her gold medal at the Delhi Commonwealth Games, 2010. *Mark Kolbe/Getty Images*

plenty of free time and money and he said 'Hannah, work on a boat – you're in international waters, there are no visa issue and you can get to know each other better.' And I said, 'That sounds reasonable' [laughs]. I'd never thought about it before but the things we do for love [laughs]. So we signed up for boat crew and within three days we landed a job on a kiteboarding expedition boat travelling the world.

That sounds like an incredible job – where did that take you?
We flew to Panama City and started this crazy job on a catamaran sailboat that was meant to travel to the remotest places on earth. We did it for a year. We spent two months in the Galapagos Islands, sailed across the South Pacific to French Polynesia for six months, fishing and cooking everything we could get, and then on to the Cook Islands and Tonga. And it was a completely different world of cooking all of a sudden – every day we created new dishes for the guests and ourselves, it was very low key, there were only 10 of us on the boat so we all ate together.

After a year, Lars and I had got to know each other really well – we'd never been further apart than the 60 feet the boat allowed us to get away from each other [laughs]. It was a good time but we had to move on. I went to Denmark and he followed me. We were both broke – the boat was about the experience, not making money.

And after that you started working at NOMA, which was by this time the number one restaurant in the world. What was that experience like?
I was doing a full time job and full time study and I kind of snuck in from the side [laughs]. But I knew their style and I decided to quit my studies and work there. I was there for one season – 2009 to 2010, a year without a summer break, with very long days.

The sports nutrition idea was still lurking and I made a deal with the university to take chemistry at C-level and maths at A-level and they'd let me in. So I was working in a restaurant, getting up to go to class and working full time which was almost impossible. I moved away from NOMA and got a job at a place called David's Bistro – David had worked with René so I knew his way of thinking. I thought it would be more manageable but, surprisingly, it didn't work out that well [laughs]. It was super, super hard. I was still determined to get in but I couldn't work Wednesday night, get in at 1am and then be in class at 8am and get my head round complex maths problems – I hadn't done maths since I was 15, in high school!

Sounds like a tough life – how did you cope with everything?

I was determined to do it, so I called my old sous chef from NOMA and asked him if he had any contacts for jobs where you did a lot of work in a compressed space of time and then have time off for study – I was thinking about banquets and weddings where you work a lot at weekends but have weekdays free. He called me back in half an hour and said, 'You gotta talk to this guy Michael, it's a cycling team and they're looking for a chef.' And I thought 'this is interesting, but terrifying!' And he said, 'It's Bjarne Riis's team', and I was like: 'Oh, this is big – but I don't have the education.' And he said they had a nutritionist and I could talk to them.

So that was how you ended up working for Tinkoff-Saxo?

Basically, I met up with this guy from the team and asked 'what is this?' They'd had this idea that they wanted a Michelin-starred gourmet chef to do the job, but it's very hard to ask someone with a restaurant to do this job as well – it's extremely time-consuming and tiring, and you have to be in several places at once. And the chef they had wasn't happy because he wanted to do a 13-course meal for the riders every day and the riders didn't want that – they're tired, they're hungry and they don't have the mental capacity to enjoy delicately put together small, complex dishes. And the chef couldn't always be there, so he sent different apprentices to take his place and there were constant changes in the food and no one was happy. There was no routine and it was a big mess.

They told me I'd work four, maybe six days, then have some time off. And I had that weird feeling about doing something new and this being a once in a lifetime chance: you can't *not* take it. And they'd managed to get a chef who would start after the Tour de France in 2011, so I would do the job from January just until the end of the Tour, when he'd take over. So I thought 'I can do this – if I have time off I can study and it's a cool basis for sports nutrition.' And with the Tour de France ending in July I could, fingers crossed, start university on September 1st. So I said, 'Fuck it, let's do it!'

So you'd never done anything like this before! How did you start?

I was hooked up with the nutritionist and we spoke for hours and hours and hours, writing everything down, figuring out what do these guys *need*. It was so different from the kiteboarders (some of them were raw foodies, some were living on cookies) – but this was way more strict, an old-school, classic world where you can't just come in and change things. You can't start a revolution – that just doesn't happen in the cycling world!

So I spoke to the nutritionist and my ears were bleeding with all the information, and I was planning menus for the training camp in January when I had to meet them all and so I went to Majorca in January and I met 29 riders and 40 new staff members, none of whom I'd met before. And I was alone and I had to cook for two weeks for 30 guys eating like horses – it was freaking crazy!

But you'd spoken to the nutritionist so you had a good idea what you were doing?

In those two weeks I found out that what the nutritionist said versus what the riders want to eat doesn't correspond at all! [laughs] So it was two weeks of crazy fighting and trying to survive and being able to cook the food without passing out from being so tired. And the whole team were so sweet – they could see it was completely crazy and they helped me out as much as they could. So basically I survived the two weeks and called the nutritionist and said, 'this is insane because (a) I can't do this job alone and (b) what you dictate is not what the riders want. What you want them to eat is not what they want to eat.'

Anyway, I had a month off and then there was another training camp and I was very determined to succeed in this job. And at this camp I said, 'Listen, I need some extra hands.' So my cousin, who's a brilliant chef, came over from Scotland and, though it was still super tiring, we could manage, and I had someone to 'ping pong' ideas with.

The training camps are without doubt the hardest part of the year because you have all the riders at the same time.

Did life start getting easier when the team started the racing season?

That was crazy! It was super tough and I was alone, in my kitchen truck, trying to cook, clean and shop. And you're in a new place every day – it's completely overwhelming in a new job where no one can tell you how anything works. But I managed to get permission to have an assistant for the Grand Tours and halfway through the Giro the nutritionist told me the chef wasn't going to take the job and was I interested in continuing? My first thought was 'shit, this is really tough – we'll have to take this a few trips at a time' [laughs], but knowing they were interested in keeping me made negotiations easier. So I said yes to staying, on condition that I had an apprentice because the job was just too much for one person. The team were really in the shit with money but the Danish government had an apprenticeship scheme where they would pay the wages, so it was like getting a worker for free – the team's only costs were living expenses. They agreed and we graduated a chef from a cycling team!

What was that first year like?

That first year was crazy and extremely addictive, and it was very weird because – as hard and crazy as it was – it was also amazing, exciting, new and fulfilling. And then I got to really know the guys and we started on the negotiation of how we could find the middle way between the nutritionist's strict guidelines and helping them to eat better. So that was the foundation of really good team work between myself and the riders to figure out what worked and what didn't. But for the first couple of months they were super angry at me for coming in and changing everything! But, as each season went by, it got better and better and we got into a routine.

Do you think that had anything to do with you being a woman in a very male-dominated world?

It was a lot to do with that. Everyone was like 'No way! That's not how it works here.' A lot of my colleagues gave me a hard time in the beginning but I fought for my job and I earned my space. Next season will be my fifth with the team and I've been accepted in that world, I've gone through my fire baptism! [laughs] People were waiting for me to crack, saying, 'When is she going to leave?' But I didn't fold and the guys would say, 'Look at you, you're in it for the long run.'

Is it tough being a chef in cycling?

In a restaurant kitchen, everyone knows how everything works around you – in the cycling world, no one knows how anything works in my world. If I'm in the kitchen and I say 'we're going to do this and this', no one is going to doubt me because I'm female in the restaurant business. No one is going to say 'I won't take her seriously because she's a female.' I'm the chef because I'm capable of doing it.

Now it's much easier, but when I first started you had all these old-school types who had been in the cycling business for 20 years. All the teams are trying to have new ideas and funky plans. When

I first started some of the cyclists told me they thought I was just another crazy person trying to change things – but I'm not a crazy person and I'm not a nutritionist. But you learn from each race, each season, how to build up the menus.

This is now the job I've had for the longest, but it changes every day and that's the great thing about it and why you don't get tired of it. It's never the same – though sometimes you can get tired of that! There are a lot of unforeseen issues that can happen when you're in the middle of a race – you're dependent on generators and roads being open, there are a lot of other factors involved than just cooking for the riders and making sure it's the right stuff. I'm like the crazy logistics chef! But you get wrapped up in this cycling world and that's extremely addictive!

Were you interested in cycling before you took the job?

I knew *nothing* about cycling! [laughs] I knew my boss Bjarne Riis because he was the only Dane to win the Tour de France in 1996 and he's a hero where I come from. But I knew him and that's it. So at the beginning, at the dinner table with the staff, the *directeur sportif*s would entertain themselves asking me questions about cycling that I couldn't answer [laughs]. Like 'what colour is the mountains jersey?' or 'what does it mean to be dropped?' And I'd give some outrageous, hilarious answer because I had no idea. But it didn't take me that long to get super into it, so even when I'm not working I follow what's going on. When you're so wrapped up in this world if you don't get an interest in it, you shouldn't be there. I had a colleague at the team, a soigneur, and he said, 'Hannah, you can't be here if you care too much', and I said, 'Wait, if you don't care, you shouldn't be here.' He's not in the cycling world any more. Because if you *don't* care, if you don't enjoy it or see the fun in it, it's a really fucking hard job to do.

It's like having this extremely large, crazy family – like a weird circus family you travel around with – and you've really got to be into it because it's a really, really hard job, but it's a really, really fun job. It's super hard being away from family and friends but you create your family out on the road. It's like a whole little universe to itself.

So what's next for Hannah Grant? Will you stay with Tinkoff-Saxo?

I'm 32 now and at some point I'll want to have kids and this job is not well adapted for that! Every year after the Vuelta I ask myself where I'm going. I'm working on a book project with an American sports nutritionist, Stacey Simms, so while I'm doing that I want to stay in the business. And I think it's going to be hard to ever let it go completely. I can't see myself going back to a normal restaurant. But you can never plan for the future, you never know what doors are there.

Everything you do opens new opportunities. I said to my boss, 'If I say yes to next season, then I'm here for the year.' But if something interesting comes up, who knows? But I'll always be hooked on cycling – it's very addictive! It's a crazy ride, but it's a very cool ride!

I asked Hannah about some of the meals she's cooked for the Tinkoff-Saxo team over the years:

The first one – It was at Majorca at the training camp. I wanted to do a really kick-ass ratatouille and I was in the worst kitchen in Spain – it was so smashed up, with no equipment, and it occurred to me that you can't win the Tour de France on a rusty old bike and it's very hard to cook nice food for 30 guys when you're in a broken up kitchen! I remember being not completely satisfied, but I redeemed myself after that!

A celebration – The last couple of years it's turned into the tiramisu. I did it by accident when someone won a stage and everyone constantly asks for it, but you can't do it every day! It turned into 'if you win a stage, you get tiramisu' and they knew that all of a sudden. We'd always had the rule that if they did really well, a stage win or a podium, there'd be a dessert, but then it became every time there was a stage win, it was the tiramisu – and we've had a lot of stage wins this year! In the Giro and then in the Tour after Alberto broke his leg, the tiramisu just took over! So it's tiramisu for a stage win and a really good brownie for birthdays. But I also try and do a birthday cake from their country – I try and figure out what kind of cake they would normally celebrate with, to make it a little homey.

Alberto Contador's favourite – He absolutely loves (and it's very simple) potato frittata. He loves that! That and a really good paella.

Something you cook every day – That would be breakfast, and variation is the key to keep them eating and keep their appetites up. Because if you don't change it up they don't want to eat it. For dinner they *always* have chicken but I never cook the same recipe two days in a row. I mix it up a lot and keep it interesting because they get pretty sick of chicken! The thing is, you have to have something neutral for everyone to eat, so I do two types of protein – chicken as the safe option everyone can eat and then another option that could be lamb, fish, veal, pork, anything that's nice in the area. So if the guys don't like fish, there's always chicken to rely on so there's no crisis at the dinner table because, trust me, there will be if there's no chicken [laughs]. Some of the guys could eat plain chicken every day for a month, but they're in the minority, so I try and make sure everyone is happy with the selection of food I do.

A typical dinner after a race – We have two proteins, a lot of cooked vegetables, and then a vegetarian dish on the side, a light salad with cold cuts or goats cheese, and then a heavier salad of grains or root vegetables. So there's a constant variation and a way for them to mix and combine in a way they want. So they don't have to force feed themselves with pasta. They have to have so many carbohydrates and I know some guys could eat pasta every day and other guys are going to 'die' if they have to eat pasta every day! But there's always pasta and usually rice or another starch like roasted or crushed potatoes or sweet potatoes, something a little more adventurous. And it depends on the mood – sometimes they don't want to eat too much. But that's how I try and accommodate all their wishes – I know I can't make everyone 100% happy but at least you make sure they want to eat.

The team's favourite meal – Anything that resembles a day off, relaxed, something fast foodish. We have a rule that the day before the rest day in the Grand Tours, they get 'build your own' burgers with everything made from scratch, obviously. And then the next day before the rest day they get homemade pizzas, with a nice homemade sourdough crust – I'm very obsessed with bread. And those are the two things that, if you tell them they're on the menu, they're like 'yay!' And it means the rest day is coming.

On Kilimanjaro – I didn't cook on Kilimanjaro. I wasn't there to work, I was there to try and climb the mountain with the rest of the team. So the porters did the cooking. And I succeeded!

When you're off duty – I'm really into soups and stews all year round [laughs]. Yesterday I cooked a really nice sumo wrestler's hot pot, which is cool – in a way it's like making a sourdough, but with a soup. You have a broth and you add meats and vegetables on a daily basis so that flavours the broth, and then the next day you strain it and add more meat and vegetables and every day the flavour changes. I kind of like that [laughs]. Things that steep, and take flavour and marinade, I'm really into that. And fish, I eat fish as much as I can.

The best dish you ever cooked – The one I really nailed? That's such a difficult question [laughs]. People usually ask me what's my favourite thing to cook, my speciality – and my speciality is not having a speciality! Which is a lie because I do. But I've done so many different things and it's hard to find one dish that crosses them all. When you're in the South Pacific and you just pulled a giant yellowfin out of the water, then the most amazing dish is super-fresh fish with soy and ginger on the side of a boat. And there are different dishes for different moods – you need the perspective of the situation and the simplest things, the most rustic thing can be the very best thing in the right environment. And I don't cook to impress people – I love it when food looks amazing and you want to eat it and dive right into it, those delicate small plates, but that's completely different to what I do so I think the answer is I can't answer that! [laughs]

The fantasy meal – I think the team would want to go all in – I mean they like exclusive and delicate things, most of them really enjoy well-made classic food and they tell me about the great local restaurants they visit in the off season. And maybe a bit of an extravaganza – super fresh turbot and truffles. If I could, and I had the crew for it, I would love to cook them an amazing tasting menu, because I'm trained in classic French cuisine. So refined, small, light plates – not too heavy but with the mentality of how I think about food now – that would be fun to do. I'd like to show that I can do other things besides cooking huge portions of chicken and pasta, but rarely do you get the chance!

The most memorable meal you've cooked – In 2013 at the Vuelta we cooked a baby piglet, with the head and everything, and people went crazy on Twitter because I put up a picture of this suckling pig saying 'look what's for dinner' and it started a storm of people going crazy because there was a face on the food that I cooked! So it was kind of crazy but the riders loved that and they still ask if I can 'cook the baby piglet'! In Spain it's difficult to come across the fresh ones, they're usually super deep frozen, but that one was fresh and very nice. I remember everyone was so happy and thrilled, and we were sharing a hotel with Omega Pharma-Quickstep, and they only had four riders left. They were all looking and when our team was done eating, I said, 'You can taste if you want!' The other team was taking photos of it and I remember that often; it was very memorable. And the team still talk about it. The suckling pig. That was a big one.

And the most memorable meal you didn't have to cook – Oleg [Tinkoff, the owner and main sponsor of the team] is not high maintenance, he eats what the team eats, but he did bring caviar and vodka to the Giro this year – he flew in 2 kilos of Beluga caviar for the team to share, that was pretty crazy! And then Mick Rogers won a stage the day after and the team were saying: 'Apparently we have to have caviar more often because it helps us win stages!' And then we had tiramisu.

CHAPTER 16

KATHRYN BROWN

Tifosa

Kathryn Brown lives in Surrey with her partner Gavin and beagle Poppy. Having worked as administrator on four editions of the Tour of Britain and Tour Series she now runs her own cycling industry consultancy business, Tifosa Ltd.

🐦 @kathrynebrown
🏠 www.tifosa.co.uk

Kathryn is a self-confessed tifosa *– that lovely Italian word that describes the totally obsessed cycling fan. But Kathryn doesn't just stand by the roadside, she's managed to make a career out of her passion. In this piece, specially written for* Ride the Revolution, *she gives a behind-the-scenes look at the world of men's professional racing and what it's like to be a woman in a man's world.*

I have a confession to make: I love road racing. I admit it. Long before it was cool to like cycling, I would tune in to the Tour de France and listen for hours to the ramblings of David Duffield while the peloton snaked its way through some remote corner of France. I don't even know what it was that first got me hooked. But slowly and surely I went from a slightly confused, struggling to understand, TDF (Tour de France) widow to full-on race junkie displaying Pavlovian tendencies whenever the TDF theme tune started up. It became my crack and I was addicted!

And I don't just love the big races; the Grand Tours and the Monuments ... While it's true that I've been lucky enough to travel to watch numerous editions of Paris–Roubaix, RvV (Ronde van Vlaanderen, the tour of Flanders), Eneco Tour, TDF, Roma Maxima (The former Giro di Lazio), etc., I'm just as likely to be found sitting on the roadside of a semi-rural B road cheering on a Surrey League E12 race. Maybe even a 2/3 if I'm desperate. Come the winter I suffer with SAD but I'm sure that's mainly because for me, cyclocross can't fill the aching chasm that road racing leaves behind.

You get the picture. *Tifosa.*

Now, very few of us are ever lucky enough to work in the industry we love. Christ knows I plodded endlessly through lacklustre, menial jobs. I tried so hard to care when I just couldn't. Days dragged on, weeks seemed like eternities and I turned up just to get paid. It sucked. Big time.

But then I struck lucky. I landed a job working for SweetSpot Group working on the Tour of Britain and Tour Series. Bingo. I'd done it. My working life was looking up and I had a job I could care about and take pride in: race administrator across both events.

You may think you know what it takes to organise a bike race but I'm pretty sure you don't. You can take any preconceived images of what's required and treble them, quadruple them and you still won't get close. Multiply it by 10 and you'd be getting closer but you still wouldn't be there. A stage race takes on a life of its own. It becomes almost organic, constantly evolving from one form to the next and it takes an inordinate amount of managing and directing to mould it into a successful race. From gaining sponsors to fund the race, getting regions that want host stages, recruiting temporary staff, to booking hotels and just dealing with the day-to-day logistics of an event that moves, every day. It's immense.

The Tour of Britain is without doubt a great race. Having worked on it, I feel it is the best race it can be given the UCI-determined limited duration and restrictive geography of Britain. A team of hugely competent and highly committed individuals work long hours to make it so. My role in the build-up to the race was loosely titled 'administration' and it covered many aspects. I was responsible for recruiting the 200 or more temporary staff that the race required, overseeing the booking of the hotels for staff and teams, coordinating the ordering of staff clothing, recruiting volunteers and keeping them informed. I ordered the trophies, the race numbers, the presentation hostess dresses, etc., etc., etc. ...

Anyone who has ever worked in events will tell you about the endless hours of work needed just to bring an event to fruition and the Tour of Britain is no different. The pride the team took in their roles was only too evident by the number of people still sat at their desk at 8pm. The team was extremely close knit with many of us being friends outside of the office. If someone needed help, the team would rally around them and they would find the direction and support they needed. Everyone had their own area of responsibility and I was always amazed how seamlessly the roles would mesh together on race to become a whole which was almost certainly greater than the sum of its parts.

To help put some of this in to context, I should maybe take a moment to go through a few of the numbers involved. The race itself employs in excess of 250 personnel – including more than 60 NEG (National Escort Group) and police moto outriders. 17 teams of six riders plus at least six crew, each bring with them a team bus, lorry and several cars. There are over 50 official cars on race and over 30 vans are required to transport the technical kit around. There are seven types of personal accreditation and four types for vehicles. Typically the race would take over at least seven hotels for each stage. The race schedule for each stage runs in to hundreds of lines of minutely accurate detail. Each stage is planned, driven, driven again and then driven once more to make sure it is safe and suitable.

About a week out from the start of the race, staff would start shipping out to the 'permanence'; invariably a hotel which would act like our office and home in the lead-up to the race. Here the finishing touches would be put in place. Staff clothing would be delivered as would the race cars. Radios would be fitted and any remaining kinks would be ironed out. The day before the race, all race staff would pass through permanence to collect their clothing, race and hotel manuals and attend any staff briefing meetings that were pertinent to the role. Likewise, team managers would come to attend the team managers' meeting and to collect their manuals, numbers and rider cards and high-profile riders would come along to attend a press conference.

Just as the office staff work tirelessly to make the race the best it can be, the Tour of Britain also relies heavily on a large temporary staff base. Many of these temporary workers have been with the race since its inception and are practically irreplaceable. Temporary staff members are responsible for, among other things, making sure the race route is clearly signposted, setting up KOM (King of the Mountain) and Sprint hotspots, building the start and finish areas as well as helping run the press centre and helping me while on race. The temporary race staff also includes a panel of judges and *commissaires* from British Cycling who are instrumental in the smooth running of the event. Each race feels more like a family reunion at times.

My main responsibility on race was running the site office and ensuring that the podium presentations ran smoothly. This latter part of my role could be nerve wracking at times and certainly required a high level of organisation and coordination. Once the stage was finished the pressure was on to get the podium presentations under way – in accordance with UCI guidelines, the podium presentation needs to happen within 20 minutes of a stage finish, and while some results like sprints and KOMs could generally be decided before the race got in, the race leader and points leader were sometimes a little bit more complicated with the judges and results manager working meticulously in pressure-cooker corner.

Once the results were confirmed we could radio down to team parking to make sure the riders came to podium ASAP so we could get the ceremony under way.

Talking of which, there has been much debate of late about the role of 'podium girls' and for what it's worth here's my, fairly informed, opinion ... podium girls, or presentation hostesses as I personally prefer to call them, fulfil an absolutely essential role on race. The podium presentation is a high pressure, time critical and absolutely essential part of the race programme and requires careful directing from the podium itself. While I could make sure the back of podium was running smoothly I needed a safe and flappable pair of hands front of stage to make sure the presentation went off seamlessly. The riders are always unerringly professional and know exactly what is required of them but sometimes local dignitaries and sponsors can need a little more direction to get them in to the correct place for the photographers.

Presentation jerseys often have Velcro up the back for ease and speed of application and again aren't always the easiest things to handle especially on a breezy day so I just don't see a way around having the presentation hostesses. Many sponsors also provide prizes alongside the jerseys, flowers and trophies so the hostess is often having to juggle many handovers and needs to make it all flow smoothly and effortlessly, maneuvering dignitaries and riders into the correct position. Let's not forget that for the sponsors and teams alike that final photo of a rider in front of the race and sponsors logos is the proverbial money shot so it has to be right and you only get the one chance.

I have heard people moot suggestions of perhaps using local children for the presentation, but children carry their own set of limitations – there can be issues with the reproduction of a photograph of a child. They could also perhaps become a little stage-struck at just the wrong time and balancing a photo with a host or hostess of a correct height does always result in a better final product. During my time on the Tour of Britain I tried to move away from the stereotyped image of a podium presentation and did away with the kiss, which I personally felt was a little dated, and never asked any of my hostesses to wear anything I wouldn't have been prepared to wear myself. So please, let's not dumb down their vital role on the race.

Working on a race is not all a bed of roses. Working on a race alters your perception of races and can ruin your enjoyment of them forever. Let me explain. Mick Bennett and his team are perfectionists. His starts and finishes are things of beauty. You've probably always been too busy watching the final few hundred metres of racing, but trust me, they are. Take a look at any Tour of Britain stage finish replay. Check out the arrow straight barrier lines, the beautifully horizontal technical (metres to go) signage, the branding on the barriers, the podium back drop and flash interview background. All of it is stunning, pristine and just the way it should be. And remember that next time you watch another race. Not a biggie – a Grand Tour or a Monument – but something like the Eneco Tour or Three Days of De Panne. You'll see what I mean. Be careful though, if you look at it too much, you'll start noticing wonky barriers and shoddiness every way you turn, run-ins will look convoluted, scrappy maybe even dangerous, podiums presentation will look awkward, and you will almost certainly notice a badly stickered podium jersey.

My love affair for road racing is equalled only by that of my love for the riders. To be clear, that's not a lusting, sexual, 'rate them out of 10 for hotness' kind of love, but a deep admiration and unerring respect for athletes at the top of their game, competing in what I believe is one of the toughest sports going, throwing their leg over a crossbar day in and day out, and risking their personal safety every time they do so. I feel that at this juncture it is worth pointing out that the minimum wage for a neo pro in a pro tour team is €26,700 per annum. That's £20,826. (€23,000 or £17,940 for a pro continental level rider). Pretty piss poor for all those hours spent on the bike racing and training, living like a nomad, continually leaving your family and loved ones at home, being only as good as your last result ... No one who hasn't lived it can imagine the life of a pro cyclist; it's the absolute antithesis of glamour. Life on the road is tough. Hotels are of differing quality and riders have little or no privacy. Yes, they get paid to ride their bikes and I can imagine that for many readers that would seem like a wonderful way to earn a living but the reality is a little harsher. Long, post-race transfers and stage race pasta take their toll. Very few riders earn big bucks – perhaps the top 1 or 2%. One thing they all share is a finite career length with very few carrying on past their early 40s – and who can blame them, it's a hard life. The majority of riders will find themselves working tirelessly for their designated race leader, giving their all to see another succeed. I have been lucky enough to meet many riders and, in most instances, their absolute professionalism has been truly humbling. While I won't dwell on the more difficult, or perhaps I should say less obliging, riders I have met, it wouldn't be right for me not to mention some of the riders who over the years made my role on race an absolute pleasure.

My first year on race was 2010 and the riders made it an absolute joy to work on. Somewhere between Richie Porte chowing down on a post-race baguette, which we had to confiscate off him every time he ascended the steps to the podium, to Greg Henderson's genuine, Kiwi affableness and jokes I couldn't possible recount here, and Johnny Hoogerland's uber nonchalance and consummate getting to podium just in the nick of time, the back of podium was an absolute hoot and I loved every nerve-jangling minute of it. 2011 was the year of Lars Boom, who again was great to work with, and, of course, of Pieter Ghyllebert, who patiently corrected our mispronunciation of his name time and time again. And then 2012 where my highlights included Boy Van Poppel's taking of the points jersey, Kristian House winning the KOM and Sammy Sanchez's utter delight when teammate Pablo Urtasun won a hard-fought stage in to Dartmouth. Again, great riders and all of them absolute pleasure to work with. My standout rider from 2013 was Gerald Ciolek. He was delightful to work with and at the end of every podium took the time to ask if we needed him for anything else and then to thank us all. It may seem like a small thing and, it is, but he and his MTN Qhubeka support team were fantastic, as were the Movistar guys. I've just mentioned a few of the riders who really stood out for me over the four years. My experience is that 99% of them are fantastic to work with and I must admit that I only really dealt with the riders who podiummed, but it's amazing the difference a 'thank you' and a smile can make after a long and stressful day both for riders and race staff. There are some which are very firmly wedged in my head as my irreplaceable favourites and I will support them for many years to come.

So what does the future hold for road racing? While I cannot profess to having a crystal ball one thing is for sure, Stevie V was right: money talks. Sadly, I think we will see more races compromised for the sake of sponsorship. It's a sign of the times and a necessary evil: it's why races exist, to make money. Race organisers will take races to countries and regions that are prepared to pay for them over places with the right geography or the right politics. Grand Tours will perhaps continue to become harder and mountain stages more extreme. A trend which I feel will sadly see some riders tempted to turn nefarious means just to survive.

Too many times recently we have seen riders' safety compromised for the sake of the race. Surely no one can forget the 2013 Milan–San Remo, which saw riders who have a low, single-figure body fat percentage riding in near-zero degrees and white-out conditions? And stage 16 of this year's Giro d'Italia which yet again saw riders' being expected to perform like dancing ponies despite the difficult conditions. I'm just naming two. There have been many, many more. It's a trend I would like to see reversed. Rider safety has to be paramount at all times.

Much has been said about the UCI governance of road racing, and it wasn't that long ago there was talk of a breakaway movement to give teams more money and control. Personally I would like to see a future decided by riders, teams, race organisers and the UCI in conjunction. Where riders are treated with respect and where those in charge do not ride them to the finish like the proverbial cash cow.

But wherever it goes I will be there, roadside, cheering it along.

CHAPTER 17

ASHLEY GRUBER
Shooting the Peloton

Professional cycling has a tradition of epic photography and it's going through a golden age at the moment. Young photographers such as Kristof Ramon and Emily Maye have burst onto the scene in the last few years, bringing a reportage feel to their work. But none of this new generation does epic quite as powerfully as the duo behind Gruber Images: Jered and **Ashley Gruber**.

Their breakthrough image – a panoramic shot of the Passo di Giau, originally shot for a Castelli catalogue – was picked up as the brand image for the 2012 Giro d'Italia and their career has gone from strength to strength ever since. They spent last year embedded with the IAM Cycling and Garmin-Sharp teams, as well as shooting for Castelli, Focus Bikes and Cervelo and working with magazines such as Peloton, Bicycling and CycleSport.

This husband and wife team spend 10 months of the year chasing races, joking that they are of 'no fixed abode'. That might sound glamorous, but what does it really mean to be on the road day after day with just camera equipment and a rucksack of clothes?

Kathi Hall of VeloVoices talked to Ashley Gruber about how a 20-something woman from Louisiana found herself grafted into the European pro cycling race calendar and how she handles the challenge of often being the only woman on a busload of men.

🐦 @a_gruber @kittyfondue
🏠 http://www.gruberimages.pro http://velovoices.com

I've been a fan of Kathi's work for VeloVoices for some time and finally had the opportunity to meet her in Paris for the conclusion of the hundredth Tour de France. We bonded over a shared love of the 'sacred haunches' of Fabian Cancellara, great photography and the incredible spectacle that is the professional peloton in full flight. She was the obvious person to interview Ashley Gruber – one of the cohort of young women photographers who are capturing some of the outstanding images of male cycling.

When you were younger, what was your dream job? Does that dream and your professional life now have anything in common?

When I was young, I wanted to be a veterinarian. I've always loved animals and my dream job was getting to hang out with animals (outside) all day. Now, I do get to spend a lot of time outside, with sweaty people that smell an awful lot like animals, so I guess there are some similarities.

Take us through your journey to becoming a professional photographer.

I still don't think of myself as a professional photographer, but then again that partly depends on the day and situation. When I'm at a race, I'm working. When I'm on a mountainside, I'm working. When I describe what I do though, it doesn't sound so much like work. Maybe I haven't really admitted it to myself. It just feels like something I do – it just kind of happened.

The same is true of Jered. We started taking pictures of things we liked, and when we got home to look at them, we always talked about how we could make them cooler, what could have been better. Now, it's just part of the daily conversation: 'Oh! Let's go for a bike ride. Have you seen the light?!' Then we play.

When did you realise that you and Jered could actually make a living from your photography?

People kept telling us we should be making money and one day we started to believe them. I think that attitude shift to we should be getting paid was when I thought it could actually become a career. Up until that point, I think we were both playing, not necessarily making our future, but watching it happen.

Then Dan Patitucci, a very well-known outdoor photographer, reached out to us in 2012. He asked to compare rates and was shocked and angry at us when we admitted that we didn't invoice for a lot of our work. He really helped get us on our feet financially. I still email him with questions, and we're both huge fans of the work he and his wife, Janine, do.

No matter the profession, there are always people along the way who help you on your journey – mentors, friends, even those with a negative influence. Who gave you personal and professional support while you were establishing yourself?

In the beginning we borrowed money from my mom, interest free, to buy our equipment. We slowly paid her back, but knowing that we had that support if we needed it was huge. So first and foremost, we had a safety net. We were allowed to explore, because we knew that if it all fell apart, and we went totally broke (we already were), then our parents would be able to step in and make sure nothing too terrible happened.

To be honest, there are so many other people who have given us pushes and nudges along the way, it would be impossible to try to name them all.

Was there a negative experience that, in hindsight, actually was a transformative moment in a positive way?

In May 2012, our first-ever real day shooting the Giro d'Italia, our car was broken into and our computers and hard drives were stolen.

All of our archives were gone. At that moment, we had to start over completely. Luckily, we had our cameras to continue making new pictures, but it was pretty devastating to us.

They even stole my clothes! I don't think it would have bothered Jered as much if it had been his clothes, but it felt like they had taken a part of my dignity. I had to wash the only clothes I had – the ones on my back – in the hotel sink each night. As the race was on and we just kept working, we only had time to pick up the most basic of things.

Among the work that was stolen was a two-week project we'd been working on for our friend, Joao Correia of InGamba Tours. The guests that were on the trip that we had shot all stepped up and donated money to get us back on our feet. People we didn't even know sent us five euros via PayPal just to buy us a cup of coffee, because that's what they'd do if they were with us. It was very touching, and without that support we might have given up at that point, but the kind of kindness helped spur us on.

It's funny, I clearly remember Jered's tweet just after all your stuff got stolen and the outpouring of goodwill from your fans on Twitter. The role of social media certainly seems to have played a key part in getting the Gruber name out there.

We wouldn't be here without social media. I don't see how it would have worked otherwise. It's a lot of fun to share what we do. We both love the people we've been able to meet through all the different social media we use. Instagram, Twitter and Strava are the three most important platforms for us and we've made awesome friends through all of them. It is a lot to keep up with, though.

People know a lot about who we are and what we do via those accounts, but that degree of visibility can also put you under this weird pressure: maybe they think you're awesome because of your pictures, but then they meet you on a crap day and think you suck in real life. I know it sounds silly, but we both have this fear.

Your life is really one of a nomad – you and Jered seem to be travelling non-stop in the 10 months of the cycling season. Tell me what your typical season looks like.

In February, we fly to Europe and get back on our working feet. Our first big moment is taking our car out of storage in Belgium – after a few months idle, will it still start? So far, it has. Then we drive straight to Italy for Strade Bianche, Tirreno–Adriatico, and Milan–San Remo.

The evening that Sanremo finishes, we drive all night to get back to Belgium in time for Dwars door Vlaanderen (a Flanders Classics race), then it's full gas Classics time through to Liège–Bastogne–Liège. It seems like there really is a race every single day! May is the Giro and then June is the month we normally do commercial shoots, and try to catch up on everything. We normally fail at that.

July is now all Tour. We managed to escape it in previous years and ride bikes instead, but this year, because we were working for IAM and Garmin, we were committed. August was our first glimpse of free time this year, but that got hectic when we were lassoed back to the US for a family vacation. I'm so happy I went – it felt like the first breath of fresh air we got during the season – but I hate changing time zones!

The latter half of the year is more up to us. There are fewer races to attend, and that gives us free time for personal projects and riding bikes. So far, that means catching up on emails and photos that have been neglected up until this point. In late November, we head back to the US for our much beloved downtime in Athens, Georgia. We'll be there through February, and then the season begins anew!

When you're embedded in a team – like IAM Cycling – you are right in the very centre of an extremely masculine environment. At times you may be the only woman in a crowd of men. What are the particular challenges around that?

The guys on IAM are all great to be around, and everyone makes me feel welcome. I'm not very squeamish, and that probably helps. I have no problem walking into a hotel room and seeing most everything. I think the guys are more uncomfortable than I am at first! I don't care if I see a nasty cut, poo even, whatever. (A cyclist's hotel room can get a bit like a locker room.)

The times I do feel the difference between me and Jered is more around race finishes, or trying to get somewhere on a course. I find people don't take me as seriously as they do Jered. I can't think of specific examples, it's more a feeling – small gestures, like holding a hand up to me but not the men in a photo line.

I definitely have to fight for space, for my position, which is fine, but I've seen Japanese photographer Sonoko Tanaka get pushed out of the way as well. To be fair, I've seen men pushed as well, but maybe that's one area where I'd like a double standard to remain. You can't push girls! I honestly don't care that much about the finish shots, unless it's with one of the IAM riders, then I feel a little territorial.

Outside of races, when Jered and I are in meetings, the questions will often be addressed to Jered both verbally and in body language. They are totally looking at him, shoulders and toes squared to him, and sometimes even interrupting me when I have something to say on the matter.

That happens so frequently that we look at each other and laugh, but it's a bummer that it does happen at all. Jered is an amazing team partner, and has become a lot more sensitive to the issue, but there's only so much he can do, really.

How do you put the riders at their ease without compromising the emotional distance that a photographer needs in that situation?

I love working with people. My favourite part of working with the team is getting to know the riders and the staff as actual people – people you care about. Some people are obviously more photogenic than others, and handle being around the camera, but I feel like once you're around them long enough, they get to know you and they learn that you aren't trying to make them look bad.

I tend to shy away from people who love the camera too much – it's not really what I'm looking for in a picture. I think sticking a camera in someone's face can be an awkward thing. You can watch someone physically change in the presence of a camera. I act that way myself and that makes me extra sensitive to it happening.

The best thing I've learned is to keep taking pictures, maybe not all at once, until that person forgets you are there and becomes comfortable again. You are there a lot and the more normal it is, the less people care about you being there. That's when you get something special, because they are being themselves.

Are there any women on the pro circuit that you have become friends with – that you can hang out with when it all gets a bit much?

Laura is the team nutritionist on IAM, and she is truly sweet. We sit next to each other at dinner when we can, and talk about girl stuff. It's been really nice to have her as a friend. There aren't so many other women on the circuit that I hang out with. There are a few friendly faces that I see at the races, but it seems like everyone is always doing their own thing, and that's okay with me, as I usually am too! I've also made a few male friends on the circuit, and it's always fun to get a hello while out there.

Do you miss having a consistent home – one place that has all your stuff, not spread out around the world?

I do! We fit our world into a van and Jered and I only have one bag each when we're on the road. As we cycle ourselves, we have everything we need for four seasons of riding in our bags, as well as everything we need for four seasons existing as a human that works outdoors. Things that aren't very practical just get left behind. No extra shoes or dresses for me, unfortunately. It seems like a weird thing to complain about, but I get a little down sometimes and would just like to dress nicely. It can happen, but it has to be a special day.

I also miss cooking. This year I bought a big plastic container and filled it with a bunch of cooking stuff: juicer, rice cooker, blender, spices, and other ingredients, like vanilla extract, baking power, baking soda, and cumin. When I do get a place to settle for more than a few days, I pull everything out and cook up a storm. Baking is my favourite.

I've seen some amazing photographs that you and Jered have taken where, after the initial 'Wow!', I sit there and wonder how you got so close – or in the case of your panoramic shots of the peloton – how you got up so high yet then produced other photographs straight in the action. I assume that has a lot to do with how you and Jered can carve up a race. Tell me how that works.

It all depends on the race. Some of the areas we know really well, like Belgium and certain parts of Italy. Knowing your location is everything and we literally walk it out. We go for a walk together and talk about the shots we see, who likes what, we talk about how we're feeling, etc. Sometimes I feel more up for it and sometimes Jered does. Sometimes it's who feels 'lucky' or on edge that day.

On a more practical note, we've also got great shoes! We climb everywhere and don't have too much of a problem leaning out over an edge of a cliff to get a photo. We see it as part of our job, and good shoes make that a lot easier ... and safer.

During a race, you have to be absolutely in the moment to get the kind of photographs you get. Yet you also need to be thinking two or three steps ahead, where you need to go next, making sure you maximise your time and advantages to get as much material from the race as possible. How do you do that?

You have to be observant about what's going on around you, and you have to look at things objectively: what's special about what I'm seeing? Is there anything unusual? It's amazing how many times you'll see something so obvious and simple go right past you, but other people don't see it.

It's also kind of annoying, because once you see something and others notice what you're shooting, it can get a little crazy, especially at a finish. I always have an advantage in that Jered and I are pretty complementary shooters. If one covers the finish, the other will shoot a different part of the finish, or go directly to the bus. We're a good team.

What's the difference between shooting a Grand Tour and a one-day Classic? Which is your favourite – or what parts are your favourites in each?

I think it's probably the same answer that the riders would tell you: when shooting a one-day race, it's all-out, and much more intense. You aim for more locations on course, and the pressure you put yourself under is much higher. It's also more likely that Jered and I will split up on those days to maximise locations, giving us a better chance of getting something good.

During a Grand Tour, you have to take it a little easier. It's three weeks. You try to get something – one thing – that you're proud of every day, but you have to take it easy. For example, during Gent–Wevelgem two years ago, we saw the race 22 times. 22! During an average Tour or Giro stage, we hope to see the race three or four times in a day.

The photographs that you and Jered create are all under the 'Gruber Images' byline, but a few years ago, there was often your name or Jered's on the images as well. Why have you changed that?

In the beginning, I wasn't taking as many photos. When I started to have a go at it, I still wasn't getting credit because people assumed it was all Jered, so we changed the name to Gruber Images to include me, whether people knew it was me or not.

I noticed that, before all your photographs were branded as Gruber Images, the 'race portraiture' that I really loved, where you focused right on a rider's face during the action, came from your camera. Is that true or did I imagine that?

It is true that I tended to take a lot of portraits at that time. I still do, but to a lesser extent. I think the two of us definitely influence each other in all aspects of our lives, and that's certainly true with the photos. I used to hate shooting wide, now it's something I've started to really enjoy, thanks to Jered.

Is there a particular aspect of pro cycling that interests you most when you're shooting? Are you able to do enough of that?

The best part of pro cycling for me is that it takes place in so many different venues, and I love to explore new places and meet new people. My favourite moments from the races have been chatting with people on the side of the road before or after the race goes by.

The peloton is so fast, but the people on the side of the road are very real. Sometimes being a foreigner in this landscape causes people to let you in a lot more readily than they would otherwise. All kinds of people have invited me into their homes, told me about their families, fed me, and even given Jered a proper shave! I feel like I'm always looking for those connections and it's hard to get enough of that.

In what little spare time you seem to have, do you try to get completely away from cycling and photography?

I love to ride my bike in my spare time: mountain or road bikes. I take fewer pictures when I ride, but that's mainly because I'm always the slow one compared to Jered. We always have a camera with us, and will sometimes go on camera dates – shooting something completely different for fun. Unfortunately, those pictures don't see the light of day very often, as we've been so busy, but I like taking them anyway. I also really enjoy hiking – I like to experience the world a little slower, and I feel like I stumble upon some of the things I'm most excited about pursuing when hiking.

Everyone has certain goals as they climb their own professional ladder: what have been some of yours and how did you accomplish them? What's the goal for next year?

We accomplished several goals this past year: working for a team the whole season – we work with both IAM and Garmin – and shooting the entire Tour de France. We've worked on new relationships within the industry as well, and hopefully that will continue for the foreseeable future.

The other goals are more personal. As we live on the road roughly 10 months a year, personal and professional goals are often mixed. I would say our personal goals are the ones that are always left until last. They are pretty simple goals in a 'normal' life, but for us they often feel impossible. Things like cooking dinner together, taking time away from the bike to enjoy other aspects of the outdoors, working on our language skills, reading, etc. Sometimes the smallest things like having a blender to make a smoothie can make me happy!

And in five years' time?

We just got our visas renewed for another two years, and that's pretty much as far in the future as I can think at the moment. We're both interested in branching out to other aspects of photography. In November [of 2014] we had our first chance at that: we were able to photograph the Swedish National cross-country ski team before their World Cup season opening in northern Sweden. It was fun and presented a whole new set of challenges – namely, cold fingers and toes!

CHAPTER 18

JOOLZE DYMOND

My Best Shots

Joolze Dymond is equally at home in damp ditches, muddy pits, warm, dry studios, back of motorbikes and exposed sections of tarmac as she waits to grab those action-packed, evocative images of every aspect of cycling. A lifetime of being immersed in the world of cycling has led Joolze to carve out an impressive career and, after a decade of honing her craft racking up a portfolio of passionate and expressive images, she is now regarded as the UK's premier female professional cycling photographer.

 @joolzephoto
 www.joolzedymond.com

I got in touch with Joolze when I was researching the piece on Beryl Burton. Joolze had ridden against Burton at the end of her long and illustrious career and remembered what a bittersweet moment it was to stand on the start line with the mighty BB. Born into the sport, Joolze has found her true métier behind the lens and her shots of cycling in all its glory are superb. I asked her to select some of her favourite shots for Ride the Revolution *and we finally decided on the following five. They showcase Joolze's wonderful eye for the sport and each comes with its own story.*

Nikki Harris

An amazing day at Milton Keynes watching the best riders in the world of cyclocross (CX) battle it out on British soil. UK hasn't held such a prestigious event since 1992 when Leeds held host to the World CX champs. Nikki Harris is a rider I have supported ever since she was a youngster fighting it out on mountain bikes. A brief dabble on the track and the road saw her make the huge decision to follow her heart and return to her love of mud and dedicate her career to CX racing. She is regularly in the mix in the top 10 of the world's best and to see her fighting for a well-earned podium position on home soil was pretty special. Support for her from the crowds was amazing and this sums up Nikki's determined outlook on a difficult race while supporters cheer her on.

Tour de France in Yorkshire

The day the Grand Depart came to my home soil. What can I say? It was emotional. The entire route was lined with spectators, I've never seen anything like it, the world's best fighting it out in the rural stone-wall-lined roads. The rest of Yorkshire was deserted. My training roads will never be the same again. I was delighted that Yorkshire did us proud. This image was taken at the Cote de Cray. People had been camped out there since the day before hoping to get the best position to grab that fleeting image as the world's hardest race fly's past. They crowd around the riders, cheering them on. It's hard to distinguish riders from spectators.

Winter Fun

A cold winter's night. A well-attended women's night ride run by the affable Sarah Shaw otherwise known as Mrs Garage Bikes. She regularly organises women's rides throughout the year. All abilities welcome and they are all very well attended, encouraging everyone she meets to come along and give it a go! Even on the coldest, wettest days, these ladies can't stop smiling.

Abby-Mae

Abby-Mae Parkinson is the incredibly talented and photogenic daughter of Lisa Brambani. Currently on the Olympic Development Plan with British Cycling, the 17-year-old already has a trophy cabinet bursting to the seams along with a national title. The image was part of a series of images I shot of Abby riding; this turned out to be my favourite, taken from the back of a moto as Abby descended behind me.

Women's Tour

2014 saw the inaugural Women's Tour get under way in the UK. Ranked a 2.1, this put the British stage race instantly on the calendar for the world's top riders, resulting in widespread coverage for the women at a time when women's cycling was starting to gain momentum in its efforts to be granted equal status in regards to pay and media coverage. This image shows the young riders of the GB team warming up before the start of stage 3 in the seafront of Felixstowe.

CHAPTER 19

LAURA MESEGUER
A New Perspective

Laura Meseguer is a Spanish cycling journalist who works for the magazine *Pedalier Pro*, the Festina cycling site and the cyclotourist race Mallorca 312. Laura is familiar to viewers of Eurosport as the 'face of cycling', interviewing riders and team staff at the Grand Tours.

🐦 @Laura_Meseguer

Laura Meseguer is one of the new generation of women cycling journalists who are becoming increasingly visible on our screens. I had the opportunity to talk to Laura about her career in the sport and how it feels to be the 'female face of cycling'. The following profile is based on a series of email interviews conducted after she had made a big impact on Eurosport's coverage of the 2014 Tour de France.

Laura Meseguer is far more than a pretty face – though she is that as well. Arriving on our screens as Eurosport's roving reporter at the 2014 Tour de France, she bought some much-needed colour and perspective to an event that can seem sometimes dour and overwhelmingly masculine. I was interested to know what had motivated her to storm the Bastille of men's professional cycling, so I contacted her – first on Twitter, then by email – to give me her thoughts on being a cycling groundbreaker.

Journalism runs in the Mesegueur family – her father had worked for Agencia EFE, the Spanish speaking world's foremost press agency for 35 years. It was he that suggested that his 22-year-old media studies graduate daughter should apply for the summer internship programme. It was Laura's first taste of professional journalism and she wanted more: 'so much that, when I heard my university ran a nine month internship with Agencia EFE, I focused for months on getting the opportunity.' Though the internship was intended for students with strong academic records – 'and mine was not that brilliant' notes Laura – she was determined to win the prize: 'so I started my particular fight by nagging teachers and former bosses I had in the agency to get some recommendation letters!' She was successful and the internship started in her final year of university. She says it was the first time she 'fought with such determination for something – to be successful gave me a lot of confidence for the future'.

After learning from the best – journalists Laura describes as 'great professionals who gave us the freedom and responsibility to learn on our own in different scenarios' – she graduated and started work at a construction company in Spain. 'That was a real man's world!' she exclaims. Though not as dynamic as her work for Agencia EFE, she learnt vital communication and content creation skills that were to stand her in good stead when she discovered the company had signed a last minute deal to sponsor the Vuelta a España, one of cycling's three Grand Tours. 'My boss told me we had to be at the event and, to be honest, I had never watched a cycling race in my life', Laura confesses. Her only knowledge of the sport was of something that played out in the background during family holidays in Spain or during her childhood in Argentina and Chile.

'The first time I heard about the Vuelta a España was in that meeting, and I just thought it was a popular race, not high performance elite sport,' she says. She joined the race in Lagos de Covadonga 'and I didn't have a clue what to expect!' She took photos of the race leader Vladimir Efimkin on the podium in his gold jersey and found herself more and more fascinated by the sport. She remembers talking to a 'sympathetic Italian cyclist, not very old, called Bettini'. Paolo Bettini, double World Champion and Olympic road race gold medallist, was happy to answer Laura's questions, even though he would laugh at them. 'I would ask basic, maybe silly questions – like 'you race every day?!' and 'how can you race today if you crashed yesterday?!' – the kinds of questions someone who doesn't know the sport would ask.' But Bettini would patiently answer them all and Laura felt a growing attraction to the sport 'to its hardness, the daily fight, the sacrifice, the way riders overcome so many obstacles – it's a metaphor for life!' she says.

She was soon attending more races, learning about the sport and finding opportunities coming her way. She says she is in the position she is in 'because of the confidence of many people who trusted me and allowed me to become part of this sport.' Does she find it hard working in a 'man's world'? 'I have no complaints because it was men who gave me the opportunity and opened the doors for me and they still remind me every day that what I do, I do professionally.'

I ask Laura to talk me through a typical day on the Tour de France as Eurosport's roving reporter. It's an early start 'no later than 8am', she tells me, followed by a drive from her hotel to the 'Village Depart' – the crazy cluster of tents and media events that mark the start of each day's stage during the race. There she would meet with fellow Eurosport reporter Vincent Renault to decide who would be interviewed that morning, based on the situation in the race and the profile of the day's stage. Laura says she takes time the evening before to go over the general classification and the route of the race – the *parcours* – 'to make our meetings and the time we spend going from team bus to team bus more efficient'. Having spoken to the day's main contenders and sent their interviews via satellite, Laura and Vincent head for the stage finish 'and every day we had to stop at a gas station to buy a sandwich or grab some fast food – we had 21 days of that!' she recalls, noting that the free buffet offered by the race organisers 'only lasts until 3pm so we never made it on time!'

At the finish line, Laura meets up with the rest of the team in the Eurosport tent 'nearly 30 of us, and the ever smiling Greg and Kathy LeMond,' she remembers. The legendary American three-time winner of the race was introducing his own daily show *LeMond on Tour* from each day's finish line. But Laura had no time to socialise – for her the rest of the day will be spent 'in the mix zone doing live interviews with the winner and the leaders of the different classifications'. Then back to the hotel to prepare to do it all again in the morning.

The Tour is without doubt the highest-profile cycling event in the world so I was interested to know how Laura's experiences at the Vuelta a España compared. 'Of the 30 people who are at the Tour, only two were at the Vuelta – just Pedro the cameraman and I', she says. In addition to the daily interviews, Laura also prepares the kind of special reports and 'backstage' stories that are handled by her colleague Philippe Celieres at the Tour. So the Vuelta is a much tougher race for you? 'Despite the Vuelta finishing at midnight and the Tour at 8pm, the French race is much more demanding,' she tells me, 'you feel far more tired there than after a day in Spain.' I'm interested to know which teams she enjoys working with and she tells me there's a 'very good atmosphere' at the German Giant-Alpecin team, though she's quick to point out all the World Tour teams are easy to work with. She says the British Sky team is 'a little more inaccessible', adding that she had no problems at the Vuelta; 'less media, less stress, more access, I guess' she says.

Laura also works for *Pedalier* magazine – an online and print magazine that is the Spanish equivalent of the UK's *Rouleur* – covering a range of cycling related topics and producing thoughtful, in-depth profiles of cycling's stars. She hopes the magazine will available in English soon and is clearly very proud of the work that takes her 'deeper into the lives of our protagonists'. The opportunity to establish stronger relationships with riders also has a positive impact on her work for Eurosport. She tells me a race day working for *Pedalier* is similar to any other 'but the objectives are different': 'I don't chase news stories, I look for the stories that are deeper and more personal.' Her magazine work usually takes place in hotels, in a relaxed atmosphere where she can take her time to interview riders 'and over 40 minutes to an hour we can really talk about a rider's life.' She says the best thing about writing for *Pedalier* is that she can take her time and get to know the riders well, citing interviews with Jens Voigt, Mark Cavendish and Dan Martin among the best and most revealing work she has done. But her favourite interview was with the Spanish rider Joaquim 'Purito' Rodríguez in 2014: 'We managed to find a moment of intimacy in the middle of the chaos at the San Luis race in Argentina and we talked for an hour.' What surprised her most, Laura says, is that Rodríguez subsequently mentioned it as one of the best interviews he had ever given and the one where he felt most comfortable. It's her ability to create the calm amid the chaos that produces such memorable results.

Despite the glamour of covering the biggest races in the cycling calendar with such a high profile, her favourite race takes place far away from the spotlight of mainland Europe. 'I really enjoy the Tour of San Luis in January,' she tells me, 'because I grew up in Argentina so I feel like I'm at home. I have a lot of friends at that race.' Friends that she sits down to dinner with every evening after a stage to discuss the day's events on the road. 'It's a very special connection,' she says, 'the Tour is the complete opposite.' In what way? 'It's very demanding and everybody is so professional – I learned a lot in my first year with Eurosport in 2014.' But Laura's most memorable cycling experience took place in Spain, at the 2011 Vuelta a España. It was stage three of the Spanish Grand Tour, with the race destined to end that day in Totana, in the hot and arid south. The next day's stage was set to be the first tough test of the race with a finish in the Sierra Nevada. Xavier Tondo, a close friend of Laura's and Spanish rider Pablo Lastras, had died nearby that May – killed in a freak accident when he was crushed to death between his car and his garage door when preparing to go for a training ride. It later emerged that 'Xavi' had tipped off police about a doping ring . His death had come as a terrible shock. 'Those were tough days', Laura says simply.

Not yet a part of the Eurosport team, Laura had hitched a ride in a race car with Spanish ex-professional Serafin Martinez. After 10km of racing they had watched a breakaway form in the race – a breakaway that included Pablo Lastras. 'I had goosebumps – I knew Penka's intentions'. She asked Martinez to drive up to the breakaway riders, so she could cheer Lastras on: 'I'd never seen him riding that way, with anger and determination. It was as if he wasn't riding alone, as if someone else was pushing him. He looked at me and I said no more.' Sensing that Lastras was riding for victory – 'I *knew* he was going to win that stage' – she arrived at the stage finish just in time to see him launch his stage-winning attack. 'I could hardly contain my emotions,' she recalls, 'after the podium and a big hug to the memory of our friend, Pablo gave me the flowers and told me 'you know where you have to leave them.' And that's exactly what I did, next day in the Sierra Nevada.'

For all its new-found popularity, cycling remains one of the toughest and most complex of sports – and one of the most fiercely masculine. What advice would Laura give to other women journalists hoping to follow in her footsteps? 'I think it's important to try and start working in "big" media so that you learn from the best professionals. You'll always have time to become more professional yourself later.' She says it's crucial that aspiring cycling journalists not only have a good knowledge of the sport, but 'they need to take time to know more about the world of work – it gives what you do some coherence.' Most importantly, Laura feels the need for clarity 'to be clear about the difference if you're a fan or you're a journalist':

'in my case I wanted to get into cycling because of the reasons I've explained, but I'm not a fan and I hardly ever go to a race if I'm not working.' She has one more piece of advice for wannabes: 'It's important not to work for free – it's a right! And the more you work, the more you learn and the more success you get. There's no special secret, I guess.'

But what about the macho culture of cycling – has she had any difficulty fitting into that world as a woman? She says it's a question people always ask her and that she always gives the same answer: 'I never have the feeling of working in a man's world. I feel valued and respected and I'm treated very well.' She values that good working environment – particularly in a job in which 'you spend so much time from home, with hundreds of people, some of whom you don't know'. But far from feeling homesick or lonely, 'people are always open to help you with whatever you need' she says, 'if you're hungry, thirsty, sick or suffer from knee problems as I do – even if you have more serious problems in your life – you never feel alone.' Which is why, she tells me, she feels so fortunate to work in the sport.

Beyond her journalism, Laura also works as head of communications for a mass participation *sportive* event, the Mallorca 312, a one day race open to amateur riders. Covering 312km around Mallorca, the event has grown hugely in its short life: 'While five years ago there were only 200 riders, for the fifth edition we had 2000.' It's clear she's proud of this exponential growth but is aware of the increased demands that come with popularity. 'It's a new challenge for our team to keep giving the same service and attention to every single participant, whether there are 10 or 10,000', she notes.

In addition, Laura has recently become the communications officer for City Mountainbike, a Belgian organisation that organises city-centre cross-country eliminator races over a 400m track. That seems like it's out of her comfort zone and she agrees. 'It's something completely knew for me,' she replies, adding that she was motivated to take the job because she was impressed by the team – headed by Kristof Bruyneel and ex-basketball player Caroline de Roose – and the competition itself. 'And it was a new challenge, in a very different discipline to the one I'm used to working in.'

And what does Laura Meseguer do to get away from cycling and relax? She replies that, thanks to her various commitments she's working most of the time, whether she's at a cycling event or not. But when she's home in Madrid she looks forward to settling into some kind of routine, 'training in the gym every day and doing some yoga'. Then she'll work from home on one of her many projects before meetings friends in the afternoon: 'we all live very close and in Madrid there are plenty of plans to make and things to do!'

So how does it feel to be the 'female face of cycling' for the UK cycling audience? I wonder whether she feels she's breaking down barriers for other women or whether there's still a long way to go before more women's voices – and faces – are prevalent in the sport. 'I hadn't thought about that until you asked me!' she exclaims. 'I think it's something that's becoming more natural, or at least should be.' She got her break with Eurosport, she says, because they were keen to introduce more women into their sports coverage. 'That's a sign of a new perspective,' she says, noting that she owes a debt to Nieves Moya, a Spanish journalist who was a pioneer of sports journalism in her home country 30 years ago. 'Those were hard times for women!' says Laura, 'they weren't even allowed to ride in a team car during a race! Now you see more and more women working with teams as *soigneurs*, bus drivers, communications officers and so on.'

She says that men and women may work differently but that both perspectives are equally valid, be they 'a different way to treat and take care of a rider, or a different view point for a story or solution to a problem'. There are, she points out, different skills for different jobs and different ways of communicating 'and I wouldn't like to think I'm breaking down barriers – because we're in the 21st century! But

I would like to think this is becoming more natural, just as society is developing and changing.'

I thank Laura for her time then spend some time reading through the links she sends me to examples of her work. I remember a comment that she made in our email exchanges, that she would like to express herself in English as she does in Spanish, 'but it's quite difficult!' She writes beautifully, in a tone and rhythm that is quite different to English-language, male-dominated cycling reportage. It is a new perspective, with each one enhancing and complementing the other, giving a complete picture of a complex, fascinating sport.

CHAPTER 20

OTTILIE QUINCE
Poppet's Tale

Ottilie Quince is a rising star in the world of women's cycling commentary, having commentated for Eurosport on the inaugural edition of La Course. She is also the fastest female transplant cyclist on the planet, having won multiple national and world titles in the road and time trial disciplines.

🐦 @OttilieQ

It took a little while for Ottilie and me to be (a) free at the same time and (b) in the same geographical space at the same time. We share a lot in common – we both grew up in Luton, a town that has been the butt of so many jokes, attended the local sixth-form college, drank in the same pubs (though not at the same time). But I have never needed a kidney transplant or been a World Champion on the bike, as Ottilie has. This is her – or rather Poppet's – extraordinary tale.

Ottilie and I are finally catching up in what she affectionately refers to as her 'little house' in Luton, and there are bikes everywhere – on rollers, on the walls, on bike stands around the room. She cuddles her cat Cav – she has two, the other is Wiggo – and tells me how cycling, and a kidney she nicknames 'Poppet' 'because they popped it in', saved her life.

'Where to begin? I was born in 1982 with kidney disease but I didn't find out until I was 24. I'd gone for my six month check-up at the doctors for the pill and they discovered my blood pressure was really high. I was teaching A-level PE and coaching studies at the time and I'd just nipped out in my lunch break and I can still remember the nurse who took my blood pressure. She was called Mary, a really chubby West Indian lady, and she was kissing her teeth at the sphygmomanometer, shaking her head and saying "goddamn machine!", and she said it must be wrong because it was recording 220 over 100 something. So she sent for the doctor, an Australian lady called Dr Campbell, and she checked it again. It was still really high so they sent me for a blood test and she assured me it was nothing, probably just the pill. She told me "at worst you'll be on medication for the rest of your life" and I thought, "what a ballache, I'm fit and healthy!"' She laughs at the memory, at the irony. Ottilie laughs a lot, her lofty peroxide quiff shaking.

Two days later she had a phone call while in class. It was her doctor, asking her to come into the surgery as soon as possible and to have a think whether there was anyone in her family who had had heart or kidney disease. She didn't have to think long – her father had donated a kidney to his brother when Ottilie was four.

'She asked what he'd needed a transplant for. I said I didn't know, I was only four and I just thought that's what you do, your dad saves your uncle. It turns out it was more than likely a hereditary disease called reflux nephropathy where the urine from your bladder basically passes back up to your kidneys and destroys them. My mum said when I was two or three I used to have loads of infections like cystitis. I remember in my old house that I'd sit on the toilet and scream with pain when I had a wee; whereas nowadays I'd have been scanned straight away and checked for the disease.'

She tells the tale with absolute honesty – the fastest woman transplant cyclist in the world doesn't believe in filters. She is utterly natural and direct as she tells me about the bleak diagnosis and limited options she was faced with.

'We went to the Luton and Dunstable Hospital to see Dr Farringdon, this really wise old chap, who said, "You've got less than 20 per cent kidney function. You were born with less and you'll never have any more, so you've basically got two options: dialysis and transplant." To me dialysis is three times a week, seven or eight hours a day, restricted diet and fluid intake and I thought that's no way to live, that's not an option. My dad was my uncle's donor, why can't I do that? So just before Christmas in 2006 I spoke to my brothers and my mum and said, "On a serious note, I'm really ill, who wants to be my donor?" They all stepped forward and said "Of course we will; we'll all be tested and we'll see who wins."'

'They' are mother Lesley, and brothers Benedict, Elliott and Maxwell. As time wore on, the pressure became as much psychological as physiological – she was tired all the time, got thinner, turned yellow like a Simpsons character, felt itchy. But she continued to work at Luton Sixth Form College, right up until her transplant.

'I had all these symptoms I'd never had before but I guess until your brain notices what's going on you're pretty resilient and can get on with most things. All my family had the tests – obviously my dad was out of the running because he'd already donated a kidney. We found out Max the youngest was only born with one kidney which was a surprise to him. Elliott's really scared of needles and stuff but Max turned out to be the worst. The transplant specialist was beautiful – really eloquent and soft and kind – and she sat down with all my brothers, all over six foot, and she's tiny, and she's explaining it all and Max started hyperventilating. His mouth got so small and we were all pissing ourselves and I was really ill, laughing at him. Ben had the wrong blood group, so he was out, so it was between my mum and Elliott. Elliott has two daughters now and [the hospital staff] said if the girls had a problem, he'd be their donor, so they said "We'll go with your mum and keep him on the bench staying warm."'

The football metaphor belies the other great love of her life – football. More specifically Luton Town Football Club. She played in defence for Luton Town Ladies, owns a straw boater (the team are known as the Hatters for the industry that used to dominate the town) from their 1959 FA Cup appearance, and went crazy on Twitter when the team won promotion to the Football League in 2014. But she likens the transplant process to a very different pop culture phenomenon: 'My mum had to go to Addenbrooke's Hospital (in Cambridge). It was like going to boot camp, we called it the "Kidney Factor". She got through to Judge's Houses in Cambridge. We tried to make it quite comical.'

We fall about laughing at the mental image of Simon Cowell deciding whose kidney Ottilie would get. But not everything about the experience was funny. Her husband at the time developed a drink problem, and friends and family would have to give her lifts to the hospital because he was drunk and incapable of driving her. The relationship broke down under the strain and she lost her house.

'I went through a lot of crap. I was six months away from the transplant – on dialysis – but I was doing an FA course to train as a therapist [she now runs her own sports therapy business]. I did a sports science degree in 2003 then graduated as a teacher in 2006, so I was taking this diploma and really wanted to finish it so I asked if they could hold off [the surgery]. It finished in July and the transplant was set for May. But they told me I was really ill and didn't know how much recovery I would need. But I can get really headstrong, and driven and determined, so they said, "OK, we'll plan it for August."'

Meanwhile, she was on the national transplant waiting list. In cases where a living donor is available, surgeons prefer to go down the cadaveric donor route first, if possible, rather than put the living donor at risk. But Ottilie was not one of the over 2,000 people who benefit from kidney transplants in the UK every year, and Lesley went under the knife.

'My mum was focused on saving me. She said at the time she created me and she wanted to save me. And that's why she didn't want my brother to be my donor, because she didn't want two of her children in hospital. In her words she just wanted to fix me. Which is incredible – it's the most altruistic act ever isn't it?'

I nod and agree. We both blink back tears. I wonder if I would have Lesley's extraordinary strength of character in the same situation, and agree that what she did for her bright, feisty, articulate daughter was indeed incredible.

'My mum saved me and sometimes I sometimes step outside it all and think both of my parents have saved someone, what an amazing thing to do. Not many kids can say both their parents have saved someone in a way that no one else can. People think a transplant is done, you get on with it; people don't realise you can reject, it can fail at any time, you're on loads of tablets – I'm on 14 tablets a day, I was on 36 to stop the kidney rejecting.' She jokes that she would never make an Olympian, she's on too many drugs.

But the drugs did their job. Ottilie's kidney didn't reject. Others are not so lucky. A friend she made in hospital rejected her transplanted kidney and died of heart failure in her mid-twenties. Ottilie has nicknamed one of the hills on her regular training rides after her lost friend. 'Sam's Hill' is a bitch, she says, but riding hard up that hill is guaranteed to motivate her.

She was out of hospital in 10 days, her mother after six. She was back driving three months after the surgery, so determined was she to get back to fitness. But she was still back in Cambridge twice a week to check that all was well with the transplant.

'You always take an overnight bag with you in case you have to stay in, but my rule was I never took it in with me. I left it in the car and I'd only get it if they told me I had to stay, but my reasoning was if it stayed in the car then I'd never have to stay in overnight. I tell people that only other transplant patients can really feel empathy with me, but what I've never spoken about it how guilty you feel. It's quite a burden to know my mum has saved me – it sounds really weird, but when she's ill, I always worry if it's because she has one less kidney. She's 64 and I see her getting older and it's kind of hard and sometimes it's just weird having someone else's body part in you. It's a headfuck, to be honest. It's weird to say the least. My parents don't get on particularly well – they're divorced – but they're both heroes in my eyes.'

It is clear she's fiercely proud of coming from a family where saving each other is just what you do. She talks more about her marriage, saying that she was never a wedding person, and that her ex-husband had blamed her for his alcoholism, something she has never understood. After freeing herself from what she describes as a really shit relationship, she has her little house, her bikes, her medals and her cats. The best thing to come out of the marriage, however, was her first bike.

'When I got married, I needed to get fit again. I'd been doing voluntary work for Luton Town FC because I'd had three weeks holiday and couldn't go abroad, so I'd written to the manager, Kevin Blackwell, and told him I wasn't allowed to play football anymore because if my kidney got hit or kicked, it could rupture, so my playing days were over; and after the transplant they offered me a full-time job, so I left my teaching job and started working in football. But for a wedding present, my dad bought me a bike; he had a friend who ran a shop over in Hunstanton (in Norfolk) called "Fat Birds Don't Fly" and he got a bike from them – it's my turbo bike now, an Italian Ambrosio Solaro – so I started cycling.'

'I heard about the British Transplant Games so I did my first one in Bath in 2010 – it was my very first race – and I won my age group in the road race and the time trial and it went from there.'

'There' took her to Sweden in 2011 where she won the road race and time trial in her age group again, then repeated the feat at the British Games the following year. Finally, at the European Transplant and Dialysis Games in Zagreb in 2012, she won both races outright. That's when she decided she would become the fastest female transplant cyclist in the world.

'Which I did, in South Africa, in the Worlds last year. Then I did it again in Krakow in Poland at the Europeans. And last year I started track cycling against 'normal' people in the national omniums and I wasn't finishing last! I didn't even know what the omnium was so I bought a track bike, because I fancied doing some track racing, and entered an omnium. My friend said, "Do you know what an omnium is?" and I said, "Not a fucking clue."'

She wants to go sub-25 minutes for a 10-mile time trial – I confess to her that the esoteric world of the British road time trial is lost on me and she laughs – and get the handful of points she needs to earn her Cat 3 licence. She tells me no female transplant cyclist has ever ridden a season above a fourth category licence. Then she'll aim for her second category licence next season by doing as much racing as she can.

But there is another Ottilie Quince besides the transplant rider: the willowy, tattooed woman with one of the most recognisable coiffures in the sport; the woman who had the ability to make the cycling world laugh with her, not at her, when she failed to recognise the great Belgian rider Eddy Merckx; the woman who was the voice of La Course and who hopes to be out in the deserts of Qatar again covering the men's and women's Tours on the back of a motorbike from the heart of the peloton.

'I'd like to do more commentary. The La Course gig came about because Rochelle Gilmore was offered the job and she was already working for ITV4 so she emailed Eurosport and recommended me. I'd met her in Qatar and interviewed her a few times, and she's done loads to develop the women's sport and a lot of commentary. I'm new to it all and it's a bit of a catch-22 because you only get better by actually doing it. People tell me to practise by turning down the volume on the TV and commentating on something but I think, for fuck's sake, I talk to myself all day anyway! Why would I want to do that?!'

She says that it doesn't replicate the experience of being live on TV anyway where you have to be in the moment and ready to react at a moment's notice to something that's been pre-recorded but that you haven't seen.

'It's not the same as being in some sweaty little commentary booth in South London or on the back of a motorbike, trying to see what number a rider's wearing or identify them from their riding style. You don't have graphics on a motorbike. You've got your team list stuck on the back of your moto pilot and that's all you've got.'

She tells me it was sheer fluke that she got the Tour of Qatar job in the first place, when she got a text from old family friend Stef Wyman, manager of the Matrix Fitness team, saying 'Poppet, get Otts to wake up.' He told her to expect a call about some commentary work on the grounds that she was used to talking in public as a teacher, which was what she told Marty MacDonald, who would become her commentary partner.

'Marty talked to the guys at Qatar who said there might be an issue because I'm a woman, and I said "It's a woman's Tour" and I asked why there might be a problem, and he said it was because of the state it is, how all the women are covered from head to toe but with killer heels and flirty eye make-up! And I said "But the women are all racing in Lycra!" But it was go and he called me Thursday to fly out on Sunday, so I said, "Yup, no worries", and then I thought "Fuck! I've got to learn how to commentate in three days!" I mainly watch men's cycling because women's cycling isn't often on TV, and I've only been involved in it for three years, and I've only been racing against 'normal' people for a year, so it's really new to me – whereas if it was football … So I had to learn a whole new sport, new etiquette, word terminology, and then I got a phone call on Friday telling me they wanted the same commentary team for the men's race and "are you in?" And I said, "In for a penny, in for a pound – let's do it."'

It was, she says, an awesome experience – long, tiring days and the steepest of learning curves. 'My pilot was Portuguese and didn't speak English and I don't speak Portuguese so I had him practising English and taught him the numbers from one to ten, but with riders' numbers he'd use his hands to show me the numbers – like one-zero-one – and I'm going "No, Tony, hands on the motorbike!" With La Course it was different – I was trying to make it more like a conversation, to communicate what was going on by putting the viewer in the moment.'

She hopes to keep building her public profile and works with a series of companies as an ambassador. She'd like to have more opportunities to hone her commentary skills. She's already quite a personality in the relatively small cycling community with her own poster designed by cycling artist Mark Fairhurst and she's still bowled over when people recognise her and ask for her autograph. But through it all, she refuses to lose sight of why she cycles.

'First to keep fit, but also to promote organ donation. I'm on a board, a 2020 stakeholder group for the NHS who are aiming to raise the number of organ donors by 2020 because three people a day still die waiting for an organ transplant. I work for them on a voluntary basis because I think it's important to have someone who has had a transplant who is visible and active rather than mopey – you see so many mopey people about. So I'm doing that. I'd also like to win the Worlds in Argentina to get the triple, and then it's the Europeans in Helsinki. And I try to do as well as I can against "normal" people – they're bloody hard though and too fast!'

But it's not all plain sailing. In August 2013, just after the Worlds in South Africa, she had surgery to remove a cancerous tumour on her kidney caused, the doctors believe, by the immuno-suppressant drugs she takes.

'I was facing dialysis and another transplant, but they saved Poppet, and it was the catalyst for me to give up my full-time job and set up my own business and try to capitalise on all the opportunities coming up in cycling. The tumour gave me the kick up the arse I needed to say life really is too fucking short: "You've had the transplant, now this – when are you going to do what you want to do?"'

She said she got Jens Voigt – known for his personal mantra 'Shut up legs!' – to sign a poster for her with the words 'Shut up, Otts!' to remind herself just to be quiet sometimes. To stay in the zone and keep focused, especially when cycling. 'I've been knocked so many times it's psychologically difficult to do that, and it's easy to fall back and say "I'm just a transplant cyclist" when I want to take myself more seriously as *a* cyclist, not just a transplant one.'

She is absolutely clear about how central cycling has become to her life now: 'I don't know what my life was like without cycling. Pre-transplant was football, post-transplant is cycling. All the good things that have happened in my life have been cycling. I can't say 24 years of my life have been wasted, but the last seven years have been amazing, even though I had so many hurdles to get over, so many things to get through. But cycling has always been the key, the foundation of it. If I've had a really bad day, I get on my bike. If I've had a good day, I get on my bike. If I feel indifferent, I get on my bike. And every single time I never think to myself "that was really shit, why did I do that?" I always set off and think "yeah, that was brilliant, amazing!" That's why I have all the bikes hanging up everywhere, because that's my post-transplant life. It's telling me that this is what I've got to do, this is what I'm getting good at. It's what I'm meant to do and I love it.'

She says she lives with the knowledge that it could all go wrong. She shows me the intricately beautiful tattoo around the scar where they popped Poppet in – 'Scars heal and fade, but tattoos will always be there to remind me of what I've been through and what my mum has done for me.' She also shows me the heart-shaped note her mum slipped into her dressing gown pocket before they took her down to surgery, and a photo of her in her pre-transplant, pre-bike life. It's almost impossible to recognise the plumply pretty, smiling face as that of the honed and cheekboned beauty she has become. She tells me that having a transplant is not like cancer, where you have the chance of remission, and that the worry is there all the time – of knowing her brother might one day have to be her donor, how scary it is and how guilty she feels. How she'll rub his back and ask him if he's taking care of the kidney for her, how she buys him Merino base layers for Christmas to keep him warm. She urges me to get out on my bike and go riding with my son because, well, you never know.

'You don't like to put on people but someone's going to have to save me again. My mum did say that she'll knit me a kidney, but whether that'll help or not, I don't know.'

That big infectious laugh again. The sun is sinking past the windows in a technicolour flare as we say our goodbyes. And then the fastest woman transplant cyclist in the world puts on her cleats and gets ready to ride off into the amazing sunset.

CHAPTER 21

SARAH CONNOLLY
The Voice of Women's Cycling

Sarah Connolly is one of the UK's best-known voices in the field of women's cycling. She is a prolific writer, providing content for a huge number of cycling websites, including translating for Marijn de Vries, and is – alongside co-host Dan Wright – one of the voices you'll hear on the unashamedly enthusiastic and unapologetically sweary podcast, 'The Unofficial Unsanctioned Women's UCI Cycling Show'. Sarah is the communications director for the Friends Life Women's Tour, staged annually in Britain. Tremendously well informed and passionate about her sport, Sarah tweets, blogs, podcasts and campaigns on every aspect and discipline of women's cycling.

🐦 @_pigeons_
🏠 prowomenscycling.com womenscycling.tumblr.com

For many fans, Sarah Connolly is women's cycling. She is the 'go-to gal' during any event – an equal opportunities, cross-discipline fan, whose passionate enthusiasm informs every tweet, interview and blog post. She was the first person I spoke to about this project and it's true to say that, without her enthusiasm and knowledge, it would never have got off the ground. She has built a network of contacts in women's cycling that are second to none and enjoys relationships with riders that allow her to ask questions many other cycling journalists wouldn't think to ask. Her direct, refreshing, incisive style informs the following interviews with riders from across the disciplines of track, road, Paracycling and cyclocross.

Alex Green is a highly talented athlete in a diverse range of sports – the Sydney native trains and has competed in rowing and cycling. Competing in the 3000m individual pursuit C4 category, Alex is a prolific medallist at Olympic and World Championships level, who owns the full set of gold, silver and bronze medals. She was World Champion in 2012 after a meteoric rise through a sport she only started in 2010. A fully qualified mechanical engineer, she hopes to ride to Rio and beyond. She talked to Sarah about how her career in Paracycling began.

Sarah: You're in the middle of the Paralympic cycle, getting ready to aim for Rio – how does that feel?

Alex: Time has gone very quickly from London – it's been a blur, and there's been no downtime really, and suddenly it's two years and I'll blink and it'll be one year, and I'll blink again and we'll be there – hopefully! Hopefully I'll be there! It's going and it's gone and it's a whirlwind and there's barely time to breathe.

Like all the Paracyclists, you ride on the road and on the track – and you've only been riding since 2010, so when you won your bronze medal in the London Olympics, that was after two years of racing. Can you tell us a little bit about yourself and how you got into cycling?

Alex: It's a weird kind of thing. I grew up being told I don't have a disability, 'just get on with it', so I spent my teenage years just being an able-bodied person with a limp, and then one day in 2007, I was watching a documentary about this girl trying to make the Para-equestrian team for Beijing, and it got me thinking – is my

Cerebral Palsy enough to qualify me to go to a Paralympics? And I googled the Australian Paralympic Committee, they had a talent search day, I went, I was eligible, and I got into rowing, because I lived by the water and I loved the water, and I'd always wanted to learn to row. By this stage I was 21. I started rowing, and six months later I was on my first World Championship team for rowing, so that was amazing, and I loved it, but then some stuff happened where they weren't going to take a boat to London as they didn't have the depth within the team they were looking for. I was cycling for cross training, and I had a local coach helping me out, and he said, 'Come to the velodrome'. He spoke to the Paracycling coach who came out and saw me ride on the track, and he said, 'She's got to come to Paracycling', and that was it, basically. I jumped over and then another six months later I was on a track bike at a World Championships. It's crazy, amazing, but intense. It's a pressure situation, but at least with cycling it's pretty easy-ish to ride a bike – with rowing it's so technique-based, so it takes years to build up that technique. But with cycling it's about specific power and endurance, and I have that endurance from the rowing side, so it was an easier switch. If I hadn't come from rowing, I don't know if it would have been as quick.

Was it weird then, making that adaptation from thinking of yourself as able-bodied-with-a-limp to thinking of yourself as someone with a disability – did you have to make a head-switch there?

Alex: Yeah, and now I consider myself disabled, but I'm almost apologetic about it sometimes – 'yeah I'm disabled enough to compete for my country, but it's mild, so, yeah ...' I don't know where I fit in, necessarily. To all my friends and family I'm just me, it's not necessarily that there's a tag attached that says 'disabled', so I don't qualify for a disabled parking permit, I'm on the very mild scale – but I still have a disability. Getting my head around that is pretty ridiculous sometimes.

I read that you're the youngest director on the board of the Cerebral Palsy Alliance (CPA).

Alex: I am, yes, that's another crazy, amazing thing that happened to me. I was asked to join a pool of people they were looking for to become board directors, to bring a youth perspective, and part of the constitution of our board is that at least two members have a disability, so they have to create a pool of potentials, so if anything happens they have people to fill the places. I got asked, and said yes, did some due diligence of looking in terms of what I needed to do for the board, and they asked me to join pretty much straight away, and it's been an intense and crazy ride. The pressure that's on you in a board environment is amazing, and I love it! I am the youngest, but we have a very diverse board, and it's something brilliant to be part of, and I'm learning so much.

Did that come about through the Paracycling, or was it from somewhere else?

Alex: Cerebral Palsy Alliance is formerly the Spastics Centre, they deal with children and adults with Cerebral Palsy (CP), and I saw them when I was young and first diagnosed with CP and did some treatments through the Centre, so my name's been on the books my whole life. I did another induction programme after London with the CPA, and I think that reintroduced me to the Association – and paracycling brought that about.

It must be quite frustrating that you don't have many Track World Championships – do you look at it and think you want to beat Sue Powell [another Aussie Paracyclist in the C4 category] on the track, but there's not many chances to race?

Alex: I guess I'm lucky with Sue, one of my main rivals, being another Australian. We see each other a bit more often, we have State races and Nationals, and things like that, but Worlds is the pinnacle, it's what we aim for, and build up for, and I want those World Champs stripes back. I need another opportunity, I'm desperate for another opportunity. It's tough when the UCI have not announced the next Track Worlds, and I hope they're working on it; I'm sure they're working on it, and there's stuff going on behind the scenes that I'm aware of, but at the moment there's no announcement. I'm building up as if there's a World Champs, it's all we can do, but mentally it's really hard when you jump on the bike and you know that there's nothing there. It's the mental side of it that get to you. I can prepare physically, but mentally my visualisations are off because there's no location.

One of the things I find interesting is that the Aussie Paracyling team seems so close, like a family, very close-knit.
Alex: It's pretty awesome. Not that I've had experience with the Great Britain or USA cycling teams, but in terms of my perspective, and seeing other teams out there, we're a pretty cool team if I do say so myself! The staff and mechanics and soigneurs and coaches, and the staff back in Australia helping us with the sports side, the nutrition, everything. Everyone gets along really well and it's pretty relaxed and chilled, as most Australian team environments are – and then race day comes and race faces go on! Behind the scenes it's an amazing bunch of people, we ride together and have fun together and I love it.

So if you had any tips for another 15-year-old Alex sitting out there, what would you advise her about getting into Paracycling?
Alex: Save up your money for a good carbon bike first! No ... If it's really what you want to do, go for it. Don't let anything hold you back if it's your dream, and don't be afraid. I'm still working on that, I have a lot of fear, and if I'd been more focused when I was

younger, on getting past that, that would have been nice. Try not to be scared.

Lisa Brennauer is still only 23 but she has already risen to the very top of her favourite discipline, time trialling. Following her brother into competitive cycling at the age of 13, she rapidly found success when she became Junior World Time Trial Champion in 2005. She realised her dream of becoming World Time Trial Champion in Ponferrada, Spain in 2014. Sarah caught up with her after her triumphant performance at the Worlds to find out what it's like to be the best time trialler in the women's sport.

Sarah: You were obviously amazing at Road World Champs, and I wanted to start off by asking about that. You started off winning the team time trial, which is not that surprising, because Specialized-Lululemon (now Velocio-SRAM Pro Cycling) have won for all three years.

Lisa: Yeah, it was obviously a big goal for us to win it again, but our competition was not sleeping. They worked really hard at it, so in the end it was a lot of hard work to make it happen, and we were all so happy afterwards.

When you win the Team Time Trial World Championships for the third year in a row, does it still feel as exciting?

Lisa: Yes, definitely. For me, personally, it was the second time – I wasn't part of the team in Valkenburg. But it's an event where you go out with the whole team, and everyone has to stick together, you all work towards the same goal, you have to be ready to all do it on the same day, and for me it's always a very special discipline, it's so much fun to stand on the podium and have achieved something as a whole team.

I was wondering, when you have the team time trial and the individual time trial so close, and you're an individual time trial star, are you able to go full gas in the team time trial, or do you worry about the individual time trial coming up?

Lisa: You actually can't worry about the individual time trial. It's a bit shitty that it's so close, compared to the guys who have one more day in between, which would be a lot better, but that's just the case, and if you want to win the team time trial, you all have to give everything, not think about your individual time trial. And the past few years have shown that every individual time trial Champion has taken part in the team time trial. It's probably not the very best, but it's still good to manage, and you definitely can't worry about your individual time trial.

When it was your individual time trial, I was shouting at the television, because you were behind at the third checkpoint, weren't you?

Lisa: Yes I was! The key point is not to stress about it, but I had no idea that I was getting closer and closer and closer at the finish, and that the time gap was getting smaller. I had no idea, because the last time check I got was when I was still in second place, and that was the last thing I heard, and then I went full gas on the last part, as hard as I could.

There was that moment on the video where you can see where you suddenly knew that you won, and you were jumping up and down. When you finished, and there were still riders like Villumsen and Van Dijk on the road, did you know you had won, or were you just waiting?

Lisa: I knew that they were so much behind that it would be crazy if they beat me, but I'm still the kind of person who wants to wait until the last one is finished, just to be sure, just to know it's the truth, that it's not something wrong on the television and I could see the intermediate times. So I wanted to wait, and really be clear that it was true, and that was the moment when Ellen crossed the finishline, and I can't describe it, it was amazing. I still get goosebumps when I think about that moment because I worked so hard, so when you achieve something [like that], it's great.

It was so beautiful to watch. Obviously you've got a lot of fans, and you're a former Junior individual time trial World Champion, it felt so good to see you win.

Lisa: It was my biggest goal of the season, the individual time trial World Championships, and it's still unbelievable somehow. I think I will still need some time, and I'm *so* looking forward to getting my individual time trial suit, the feeling of the first time I put it on – I'll have the feeling that I'm really the World Champion. That is still the thing I'm waiting for, to put the skinsuit on and really be the WC.

Putting it on and going training in it in winter is really not the same!

Lisa: No it's not! And I don't have it yet, I only have the jersey I got at the ceremony. I'm so happy, but to really realise it completely – the piece that's missing – will be putting the skinsuit on to go out and race.

You also had the road race, and you nearly won that as well!

Lisa: To be honest it was very hard after two gold medals to get my mindset back, to realise it's not over yet, that there's still competition to come, which you want to give everything for. It took me some days, to be honest, and I didn't expect the German team to race for me, because I thought that the course was a little bit too hard for me. But when I heard that I was going to be the first choice, I thought 'Ok, Lisa, get your shit together, go out there and ride a good race.'

With Pauline Ferrand-Prévot (also a former Junior World Champion) winning the road race, it was good to see young riders who'd been so good as juniors develop. You've had a strong career ever since, developing and then coming into your own like that – what's your journey been like?

Lisa: It's obvious to everyone that I've needed more time to develop than riders like Marianne Vos or Ellen van Dijk – we're all almost the same age, and they had their breakthrough a bit earlier than me – but it also has to do with the fact that I've wanted to be good on the track as well, and go to the Olympic Games.

I'm a person who needs some more time to develop to be able to get everything out of her body, and to perform on the highest level, with everything that goes with that – lifestyle as well. To become a world champion you need a good set-up for your whole life; that plays a really big part.

My journey has always been going up and down, but always going slightly uphill, but I needed some more time than maybe others did.

I think we saw that with Pauline as well. It's very hard coming from juniors into seniors (and unless you're Marianne Vos, it must be very difficult), knowing you won a lot of things as a junior, to suddenly be at the back of the pack, having to learn all over again. How do you manage that?
It's definitely hard. I have, let's call it, a strong character. I was patient enough. Some were not, some stopped on their way to becoming a very good cyclist, but you have to be patient and wait for your time to come, and that for me was 2014. I am very close to my family, and they support me a lot, and that's important to me to have people around me who also support me in the bad times. If you have people around you supporting you in the days that are not so good, then you're able to be patient enough to wait for your time to come.

One of the reasons I was so happy for you was because you are always such a good team player. I don't know if it's a German thing, but it seems both you and Trixi are really happy to work for other people as for yourself. I thought about the Thüringen Rundfahrt stage race in Germany, where you were leading, and then there was that stage when Evelyn Stevens got away, and immediately you were working for Evelyn, and it didn't matter which one of you won.
Lisa: Maybe that's my nature, I don't know if it's a German thing, but that's how I learned cycling, how I grew into the sport. I always

had to work really hard to achieve certain goals. You all know me as a worker for the others, and suddenly I have my own opportunities, and I try to grab them, to fulfil them, and with every little success I grow a little bit more, and I get more self-assured. And that's the thing about me. I love to work for the others, and sometimes I can work harder than if I'm working for myself, that's the funny thing about it. You will still see me back as a hard worker for other people next year!

So next year, how are you going to top two gold medals and a silver, and two national champions jerseys?
Lisa: I'm looking forward to 2015, I feel very good in the team, I like our staff and everyone, so I decided that this is going be the surroundings I want to be in. I'm looking forward to it – I want to ride as many TTs as possible of course, to wear my World Champion skinsuit. For the rest, my biggest goal will still be World Championships and National Championships, and I hope I can still develop.

Helen Wyman was born in Hertfordshire in England but spends most of her professional racing life in Belgium, where she is one of the stars of women's cyclocross. Helen has competed in cycling since the age of 14 and has represented her country at World Championship level. She is the dominant rider in cyclocross in the UK, having been national champion eight times, winning seven in a row between 2006 and 2012. Here she talks to Sarah about the work she is doing to bring equality to the sport they both love – cyclocross.

Sarah: The Koppenbergcross will be the first elite European race to pay equal prize money for the men and the women thanks to a sponsor from the USA, Maryland-based Twenty20 Cycling. As a Koppenbergcross champion, what does this news mean to you?

Helen: This is more than just money, this is *huge*. This really is something special. I know in the USA they have had equal prize money at races for years now, but Europe have never taken the initiative before. It's so exciting because Koppenberg is such an iconic 'cross race, not just here in Belgium, but across the world too.

The guys at Koppenberg were open to changes. They're a pretty young, progressive committee and see there is a proper opportunity to do something big for women's 'cross. They were the first race to listen to us, to see there was good publicity in it for them, and that it was the right thing to do.

The committee are really proactive about equality – so we've said that they should do things like have the same parking for the men and women, so the best riders are seen when the press come along. When you're opposite Sven Nys [one of the greatest cyclocross racers of all time], you get seen, you get the same publicity, and that's really important too. They're also going to do thing like getting as many women as possible on the start, and paying start contracts. They want to take their race and elevate it even higher than the races around them, and this is one of the best ways they can do that. They were so keen to have equal prize money, so when Stef [Wyman, Helen's husband] and I said 'why don't you do this?' and they told us they wanted to but they needed a bit more money, we said we'd find someone to sponsor the women for them.

Kris Auer from Twenty20 was really keen to get involved. It's such a huge thing too, because an American company is standing up and saying: 'Hey, you guys need to do this right and we want to make it right – let's do it together.' I think it makes a really huge impact, an American company sponsoring a Belgian cyclocross race – but it's not just any Belgian race, it's Koppenberg, the most iconic race in Belgium outside the World Championships! It's such a huge race – and they were the first people to listen to us and it's so important that they want to make a change with us.

And you've been working with Twenty20 for a while, haven't you?

Helen: Yes, they've supported me for the last three years – they hooked us up when we first went to America. Kris, and Adam Myerson [a professional cyclist and coach, and organiser of the Cycle-Smart International Cyclocross], got us together with all the right people. Kris puts on an amazing weekend of racing in Baltimore, the C2-ranked Charm City Cyclocross, and his bike shop Twenty20 Cycling are the main sponsors of that event. Having Kris step in as an American sponsor is important as well, because it says 'Why is there no one in Belgium doing this?'

I was wondering about that – they've had races over in the US where the women get more prize money than the men. It really shows the impact the USA is having on the sport, especially for the women when Katie Compton is one of the very best riders in the world, and there are established stars like Meredith Miller, and up-and-coming riders like Elle Anderson and Kaitie Antonneau. It's so cool to see the Americans changing the sport over here too.

Helen: It has an even bigger impact because it's coming from outside of Belgium. It's guys saying: 'We do it right in our country, let's start doing it right in yours.' The response has been brilliant but we're trying to get people involved in Belgium to promote it as well, because as soon as people see the publicity that's driven from it, other sponsors will realise they're missing out on something here too. We are having discussions about increasing TV time for the women's races, and other viewing platforms that could be available to us, and the Bpost Bank Trophy series is announcing something big about the women's race on Monday, so everything's going in the right direction, but this should kick a few people into saying 'we need to do this too'.

What surprised me, though, was seeing that the prize money isn't even a huge amount – the winning prize has gone up from €350 to €1,667 for first place.

Helen: It's the point of it, isn't it? But it still does make a big difference, €350 to €1,700 for first place, and just under €5,000 added to the prize purse.

It must make it actually worth winning – you make real money after everything you spend getting yourself and your bikes there. It must make it worthwhile racing, and not just for the winner, but for the riders coming 5th and 10th and so on.

Helen: It makes a difference to everyone. A lot of women rely on prize money to race, which is a shame, but it takes time and progress to build that too, but this is a good step in that direction as well. With all the publicity around it, riders will want to race this race, racing for more prize money which helps them live and survive, but other teams will be looking at it and thinking 'Hold on a minute, this race is getting big as well – why don't we have women in there? Why don't we have a women's team?' So when you start having more teams, you start having more money for more riders, and everything grows.

It's so important, too, because, say some Marianne Vos of the future, some 16-year-old girl, comes twentieth and gets a real prize, she can use that to persuade her family to support her to come into the sport as a pro. You've said before that you want young riders to see a career in the sport, and it says to that young girl that it's possible; and changes will keep happening, so by the time she's 20, she can be making real money from this.

Helen: And it's not just seeing that there's prize money, it's seeing that there's progression. This will be remembered as the first European cyclocross race that has equal prize money!

I understand this is small, and I understand the stuff on the UCI Cyclo-Cross Commission is political, where you need to do things in different ways because you need to please everybody across generations, from race organisers to the people who run all the series, to the 16-year-old who's just turning elite, and I understand they all have different issues. But I just love what we do – I love our sport, and it's so exciting. I've been in races this year that I've been excited to be racing it, so I can't imagine how exciting it is to watch! A race like Hasselt, where the crowds go wild for Sanne [Cant, the Belgian racer] and then wild for me, and then wild for Sanne, and it all comes down to a final sprint – that kind of thing just enthuses me. And every step I try to make to make it even more exciting, and to bring even more people into that battle, is a step in the right direction for me.

That's what I want to do, I want to get progress before the end of my career. People are now saying 'what can we do to help you?', and I've never been in that position before, and I hope that I can help progress what we have, and more people like Kris come along. For me, working with the UCI Commission to try to get equal prize money is a long process, and in some respects it's actually easier to work like this. You know you have a problem, that it's not equal, and you know you have people that are prepared to make a solution: it's just mixing the two together. That's a quicker process than changing stuff at the Commission! In some ways, connecting the right people is easier than making a rule – although that obviously still has a place.

And it also shows the Commission, and other race organisers, that this is possible – it's good to work on both paths at the same time, especially to show people who think it's not possible that it is already happening.
Helen: It's the best way to do it – everyone should work together as a community, to further our sport for men and women. There are 6 million Belgians that watch 'cross, but the people who are racing, who are organising, who are proactive in making it happen are a small community, and we need to work together to make things happen.

This is one step showing how we can work together. The Commission are doing a fantastic job, they're really using everything they have to progress the sport, and that's exciting too. It's just good that this comes alongside it – it shows how we can work together.

Marianne Vos and you are both on UCI commissions, going crazy in your wonderful ways! Is that part of cyclocross, trying to make it better?

Helen: I think everyone wants to make it better. It's our job and when there's so much work that can be done and you see these flashes of brilliance, like the Women's Tour or equal prize money, it inspires you to do more because you know there's no excuse not to. To me, it's not about 'women want this' or 'women want more'; it's about everybody having the same opportunities. So if the opportunity is that more women can race 'cross and there are more and better and faster women at the top of the sport because the prize money is equal, then that should be the inspiration for the prize money to be equal. If by doing that, it means races have to get a better return for the sponsor by being televised then that's the way it should be. Everyone should have the opportunity to be as successful as they possibly can.

I was interested in how you've been talking with the fan community too – you were saying to people that in a way the fans are more important to reach than the cycling media to get this news out.

Helen: Well, you guys are. The fans are the people that want to see change, that come to the races. I was speaking to the guy who was in charge of the World Championships at Hoogerheide [in the Netherlands], and he said that ticket sales on Saturday were between 17,500 and 20,000 sales – that's a lot of people who came to watch the women's race on Saturday afternoon. On Sunday it was between 35,000 and 40,000, so Sunday's men's race was around double what we got. And there were more people at the elite women's race than the U23 men. And that, in my eyes, is progress too, that we got to race in the prime afternoon slot rather than in the morning before the men, and so many people came and saw us.

Women's races not being at stupid o'clock but being raced before the men's events are giving you parity?

Helen: Yeah, it's those 'silly little things' that people don't think make a difference, but actually do. Like the announcer saying: 'Now we have the two elite races of the day; first up the women, then the men.' I don't think I've heard a Belgian commentator put it like that before and it does make a difference because suddenly he's saying *these* are the elite races. There's no separation. And people won't even realise it's been said, but somewhere in the back of their minds they'll think 'ah, it's the elite women!' It's those small steps in attitude, the changing of minds. It'll take a long time and there's still a long way to go, but every time something good happens, it's worth saying 'thanks, guys, that's pretty damned cool'.

We can now watch all the women's World Cup races, streamed for free, with English commentary! And getting to talk about the races with people all over the world, who love cyclocross, or love Marianne Vos, or love riders like you, that's brilliant too!

Helen: We have fanatical fans! The people who support us know all about us and follow us as much as they can, and are so excited about it, and that's really, really exciting! Even in those races that are on so early in the morning, we're seeing people come specifically to watch us, and that's really exciting too. There are obviously still big steps to get full equality, but every time we make this progress, we're going in the right direction, and people are hearing us still – and that means such a lot to me.

CHAPTER 22

ROCHELLE GILMORE
Raising the Level

Australian **Rochelle Gilmore** is the owner and manager of the Wiggle-Honda cycling team. She has been an elite road rider for over 10 years for teams including Safi–Pasta Zara–Manhattan, Menikini–Selle Italia–Gysko, Lotto Ladies Team and Faren-Honda Team. She also rides for her Wiggle-Honda team. Rochelle has recorded a string of top 10 and podium places during her career and won Commonwealth Games gold in Delhi after two silver medals. Rochelle is also the voice of women's cycling for EuroSport, ITV4 and the BBC, covering the Olympics, Women's World Cup and the World Championships.

🐦 @RochelleGilmore
🏠 www.rochellegilmore.com

🥇 **Major palmarès:**
Gold medal – Commonwealth Games Road Race (2010)

Rochelle Gilmore is one of the formidable women who is finally bringing the sport of women's cycling into the 21st century. With her compatriot Tracey Gaudry, she is part of a strong group of women who are developing a sport that is not only attractive to sponsors but which provides equality for women riders. I spoke to Rochelle about her life in the sport and about her transition into full-time management and sports media.

Growing up with two older brothers honed Rochelle Gilmore's competitive streak from an early age. 'I started racing BMX at three, in boy's races. I knew if I was going to go riding with my brothers, I had to keep up with them, but even from a young age I wanted to outride them,' she says. Rochelle grew up in Sydney's Royal National Park in New South Wales, Australia, a breathtaking area of cliff-top walks and perfect surf, ideal for a girl who loved to bike and run and surf. Identified at 13 as a potential Olympic athlete, within three months she was in the top 1 per cent and offered a place on a government-funded programme to pursue either cycling, rowing, triathlon or mountain biking. Rochelle had fallen in love with BMX as a child but it wasn't an Olympic sport at the time. '[But] I had this dream of being an Olympian, so I took the opportunity to start pursuing a career as a road cyclist. At 13, the Institute of Sport came to my house and showed me what a road bike was like, the bib shorts and jersey, cleats, all that stuff.' She was offered a weekend trip to see what road racing involved: 'it was a 7km road race, out and back, and I said, "I have to have a go". I finished second.' Success came thick and fast – within two months she was the New South Wales champion in the criterium and the road race. Six months later, she won the National Championship.

Talent spotted by the Australian Institute of Sport, at 16 she was taken over to Europe by the AIS and raced in the Junior Worlds: 'So by the time I was 18, I had already been in Europe for six months, just racing.' Rochelle spent three years with the AIS in Italy at their training base near Pistoia in Tuscany (they now have a purpose built facility in Varese, northern Italy), training on roads ideal for young cyclists preparing for a career in Europe. She turned pro in 2001, aged 20 – a huge leap for a young woman rider at that time. 'Now they don't take over riders at such a young age,' she recalls, 'but in my time there was a lot of talent that came out of that pool of athletes.'

In 2006 she bought a house in Italy and settled in the heart of the Dolomites, where she says she feels at home. It's where she retreats to work on her bikes – she says she has a toolbox many professional teams would be envious of – and from where she manages her Wiggle-Honda team and her cycling clothing brand rmgsport.com. Her desire to run a team stemmed from the time she spent riding with Nicole Cooke. 'We spoke back then about how ridiculous the situation was and how we could do it better. We went to different teams, then came back together and I said I was still going to do it.' The catalyst came in 2012 when Rochelle was injured six months before the Olympics and wasn't selected for the Australian team. Instead she commentated on the Olympic cycling events for Eurosport and had an epiphany while watching the women's road race when Marianne Vos beat Lizzie Armitstead on a rain-soaked Mall and arguably ignited interest in the women's sport worldwide. 'At that moment, during that race, I decided "I'm going to do this now" because I realised the roads were lined with people and Lizzie came second and the UK was going crazy and I just decided to myself that this was the right time. If I wanted to capitalise on a sponsor from the UK, now was the time because cycling in London was huge.' She says women's cycling gained 'a huge amount of respect from that race and showed a lot of potential'. Having worked with Honda from 2009 to 2012 and gained a lot of experience, she approached them and said, 'If I'm going to do this, and make all these things better, will you be behind me?' And they said, 'Of course.'

Rochelle had been coached by Gary Sutton from the age of 13. His brother Shane was at the heart of British Cycling's extraordinarily successful operation to rebuild the sport of cycling in the UK. It was a match made in heaven. 'Shane wanted to give young UK riders a chance on the road and trusted me to do the job – it was great for the profile of the team.' With the cream of young British women's talent on her roster – Laura Trott, Dani King, Joanna Rowsell and Elinor Barker, who had shone so brightly on the track at the 2012 Olympics – the team was an instant success. 'I guess I didn't realise how big it would be so quickly, we had a lot of success right from the start.' But that success had been a long time in the planning: 'I'm not tempted to rush things, I have to be completely on top of something before I do it. And I was, I felt like I had everything I needed, had enough experience and was at the place in my own career to make that step – I had enough contacts and relationships with athletes. People had faith in me and they signed with me.' Rochelle is also giving something back to the Australian system that supported her, announcing at the start of 2015 the development of the High5 Dream Team, which aims to prepare Australian riders for the European peloton.

It helped that she had been a highly successful rider in her own right and knew exactly what she was looking for in a rider. She has good advice for other women who would like to follow in her footsteps: 'As a rider, talk to other athletes, be clear about what environment you want to be in and really know what it's going to be like. Do your research. Find out about people who are running the team – always ask what a team expects of you and express what you expect from them.' She believes women riders need better education in how to make decisions about their careers. 'A lot of riders negotiate with me but they make demands without telling me what they can offer to the team. They assume I know what they have to offer but an athlete needs to know what *they* can offer, where the team is going long term, where *they* are going long term, what are the synergies.' She feels athletes should not be scared to say what they want.

For other women aspiring to be team mangers she has similar advice, but admits that, however well prepared you are, and however sustainable your business model, it's scary: 'When I was going to start a team, in 2012, I called Kristy [Scrymegeour, manager of Specialized-Lululemon], who I was with in my AIS days and I said, "I think I'm going to do this and I'm really scared, and there's so much stuff I don't know like registration documents and this and that", and Kristy said you do need to follow your nose as there's so much unknown in running a women's cycling team. But she gave me the confidence – 'If I can do it, you can do it.'" Gilmore's approach is to be thoroughly prepared and totally methodical: 'Just start step by step. Tick the boxes off one by one. Have a grand plan, but be open – when challenges come up, think creatively about how to deal with them.'

Rochelle says she has been lucky enough not to meet any particularly tough challenges since the team launched, but she has found management of staff to be more difficult than she anticipated. 'I'm a control freak,' she laughs, 'so I want things done my way, and my staff would like more communication with me.' With so many irons in the fire and constantly on the move between projects, she says it's difficult to find the time at the end of the day to find the time to discuss the day-to-day running of the team and to ensure things are going the way she wants them to. She'd like to get to more races in the future: 'I was only at the Giro one day for dinner and people like their boss around. A manager needs to realise the staff are the most important thing in an organisation. I thought it was the athletes in our team, and for the first year it was, but you need to invest time in your staff and their training.'

Gilmore has shown that same steely determination and attention to detail throughout her lengthy career, identifying the Commonwealth gold in Delhi as her career high point: 'I'd been second twice before and I didn't want to come home with silver again. And it was towards the end of my career. I had to not make sacrifices exactly, but challenge myself – I turned off the phone and the computer a week before the race and so I missed out on some business opportunities. But if I hadn't come away with gold, I'd have been really disappointed so it feels really satisfying.' In the gold and green of Australia, Rochelle beat Great Britain's Lizzie Armitstead at the end of the hotly contested 112km race. 'You have other wins where you're underprepared or you didn't sleep the night before or you didn't eat right, but I really switched on for that gold medal and it means a lot to me.'

Rochelle also considers the creation of the Wiggle-Honda team to be one of the greatest achievements of her career. 'The impact the team had in its first year and the fact that all the athletes were extremely satisfied, it's an achievement – it's even difficult for me to comprehend sometimes that the team is only a couple of years old.' But it's not only the string of victories that she considers to be an achievement: 'It's the little things that make it a success for me. This year I had a real success with a Japanese rider Mayuko Hagiwara. It's a significant achievement in my career because I brought her into the team not speaking English or knowing anything about the European peloton and bike racing, and the staff didn't want me to re-sign her after the first year because she was time consuming, you had to spend time with her, she didn't even understand what a puncture is.' Gilmore went out riding with her and put her in groups with male riders and soon realised they couldn't drop her on the climbs. Gilmore believed the Japanese rider had the core values of determination and commitment to become an elite rider, saying that leaving your home and country to pursue your career says something about a rider. 'This year by the beginning of the season the other riders wanted her in the team because she became reliable, they liked her personality, she'd learned to speak English, and she finished third in a Giro stage in a hilltop finish. So for me that's what I'm in it for, that one's a real highlight for me.' Hagiwara repaid Gilmore's faith in her by becoming Japanese National Road Race and Time Trial Champion and taking the Best Asian Rider classification at the Tour of Zhoushan Island. 'Now she's picked as one of the first people on the team because she's strong, reliable and fun.'

But she isn't just looking for results in a rider – far from it. 'A lot of athletes think they'll be selected on results but I'm looking for potential. I'm not interested in what you *have* done but what you *will* do in the next three years.' Personality is also important to her: 'your potential as a person, to have a good career, to be a bike rider.' New riders signing for the team are presented with a contract that contains clauses about the team's ambition to pave the way for the next generation of riders and Rochelle believes 'if they're not in line with those core values, they don't have a place on the team.' She selects riders who she believes are open to education and advice about developing the sport for future athletes: 'If they're not willing to invest the time, then this isn't the team for them. If they just want to win bike races, it's not the place for them because it's bigger than that.'

Rochelle has a clear long range plan for the team. 'I want to make a difference in women's cycling,' she states, 'I want to give as much of my time as possible to education, to giving advice and opinions.' Keen to raise the professional standards in the sport and to improve the working conditions of women cyclists, she believes that improved TV coverage of women's races will make the sport far more attractive to potential sponsors and hopes that her insightful commentary can help with that. 'It wasn't something I thought of doing,' she recalls, 'I was just helping out in the first year of coverage so that there was a female voice with experience of being in the peloton – not a lot of people have the confidence to do that, and I happened to be one of the best options.' She says she's starting to enjoy her time in the commentary booth and hopes to continue to do more 'for the benefit of the sport'. But she's clear that the sport needs to do more to enable a range of voices to be heard and to get the positive, good news stories about the women's sport to the general public. 'Before Brian [Cookson, President of the UCI] and Tracey [Gaudry, the first female Vice President of the UCI], there was nothing, so we're playing catch-up on social media and TV – but it's catching up at a rate of knots. They've realised that the demand from the public is such that it needs a strong presence on Twitter and Facebook. Social media is so powerful.'

If Wiggle-Honda launched with a bang in 2013, recording 22 victories including wins at the Milk Race for Dani King and 17 stage successes for their sprinter Georgia Bronzhini, there was more to follow in 2014, with Bronzhini continuing her rich run of form. But the Italian went into the inaugural Friend's Life Women's Tour not feeling in her best shape after the team were struck down by flu forcing the withdrawal of Olympic team pursuit champion Joanna Rowsell. Despite being off form, Bronzhini still managed a top 10 finish on every stage and just missed the podium, finishing fourth overall. Rochelle remembers what a special event the Women's Tour was, calling the race 'overwhelming'. 'The men's Giro was taking place in the UK at the same time,' she recalls, 'however, the event and athletes were surrounded by mainstream media.' Acknowledging that her 'British Wiggle-Honda athletes are quite famous and they're used to having a lot of attention from media and fans at home', she and the team were still amazed at the response, recalling: 'The attention was barely manageable for all involved ... in a good way!'

The Women's Tour clearly struck a chord with fans eager for a repeat of that thrilling 'Mall moment' and a rematch between Marianne Vos and Lizzie Armitstead. Vos went on to dominate the race and ran out the deserved winner, but the public gave the race overwhelming support. 'The streets were lined with spectators every day and after each race. Our athletes would have needed a few hours if they were to sign autographs for all of their fans waiting around the team's set-up', Gilmore says. She is also quick to praise the organisers, Sweetspot, for their achievement. 'The event organisers did a wonderful job with promotion,' she enthuses, adding 'the Women's Tour had a huge impact on the profile of women's cycling in the UK and globally.'

2014 was a huge year for women's cycling with another event capturing hearts and minds and showcasing the women on one of the biggest stages in cycling – the Champs-Élysées in Paris. La Course was the response by the Amaury Sport Organisation, who organise the biggest men's race the Tour de France, to the pressure group Le Tour Entier. One of the movers and shakers behind that group is

Kathryn Bertine, who pulled on the distinctive black and orange jersey of Wiggle Honda to line up on the Champs-Élysées on 27 July 2014. Writing on her blog, Bertine said, 'I will never forget: Crowds lining the course, cheering for our race (with as much passion as they cheer for the men), the fantastic and aggressive racing, an exciting sprint finish, and an understanding that even though Vos took the podium, we all shared in the win that day. We made history. And at the same time, we're creating the future.'

Gilmore is equally enthusiastic about the event. 'It's such an honour to be able to say to people that women now have a TDF event on the Champs-Élysées,' she says. 'It's something that gives our sport recognition and something that people can relate to.' Did she regret that she didn't have one last turn of the pedals in such an historic event? 'I would have loved to be able to say that I've raced on the Champs-Élysées at the TDF,' Rochelle responds, 'however, as a consolation, I do get a lot of satisfaction out of saying that I commentated the race and had a team participating.' She is absolutely clear about the impact that the race has had on the women's sport: 'The La Course event has put women's cycling on the map and has contributed significantly to the status of our sport now being considered 'professional'.'

It's clear that the pull of the road is still strong: 'My heart wants to race, but I'm a bit too educated to go back to that. I've achieved a huge amount and it would be too much of a sacrifice for the future of women's cycling if I went back to racing, so I'm just coming to terms with the fact that that's it.' She hasn't formally announced her retirement, she says: 'I might choose to race a club race in Australia and I don't want to be criticised for that so I just need to finish the transition period into cycling for exercise not competition.' So is she finding that transition from active athlete to retired athlete difficult? 'It is difficult because in the business I'm in now, there's no real definitive measure of success so you don't get that real high. You accomplish things and sign good riders but in sport you get a win or a lose, you achieve your target, you're satisfied. In business you don't get that and that's what I miss.' She accepts that, by any standards, her career has been a successful one, but needs to develop a way of measuring that for herself. 'You don't have the proof that you went for that and got that, so I think that's an unspoken difficulty for athletes retiring. It's not easy.' But she considers herself lucky to have so many things happening in her life, particularly her 'burning desire to help develop women's cycling.' She says her involvement in the sport goes beyond her team. 'Wiggle-Honda is there for a reason and I want to give as many people as possible an opportunity to work with me through that team, move through it and see how it functions and how it should be done.' She is passionate about lifting the level of the women's sport: 'That's what I want to do. I pass on sponsors to other teams – anything to lift the level. And I give our girls good contracts to do that.'

But the ambition that drove a three-year-old Australian girl to try and outride her brothers on a BMX bike still burns brightly. 'I can say I've achieved a lot over 10 years. I've been a part of a lot of the successes in the sport, but I'd never say I've succeeded. I know where I want women's cycling to be in 10 years, in 20 years, but I'll never sit there and say job done. There are always more doors to open, more opportunities to develop.'

CHAPTER 23

TRACEY GAUDRY
Challenging History

Tracey Gaudry is an elite Australian cyclist who was elected President of the Oceania Cycling Confederation in 2012 and became the first ever woman Vice-President of the UCI in 2013. She is also the CEO of the Amy Gillett Foundation, which campaigns for better road safety in Australia.

🐦 @gaudryt
🏠 www.amygillett.org.au www.uci.ch

🥇 **Major palmarès:**
Australian National Road Race Champion (1995, 1999)
Australian National Individual Time Trial Champion (2000)
Winner – Trophée d'Or Feminin (1999)
Winner – Tour de Snowy (2000)

When Tracey Gaudry challenged 114 years of history to become the first ever woman Vice-President of the UCI, it felt like change had finally arrived. Here was a woman who could, and would, make changes at the very highest levels of the sport, after her meteoric rise through the administration of the sport when she defeated long term incumbent Mike Turtur to become President of the Oceania Cycling Confederation in 2012. I talked to Tracey via Skype – alas, there was no possibility of a trip to Melbourne where she is based – and so I sat in my office as the rain lashed down outside and she remained in Australia where the temperature was hitting 30°C. We talked not only about the UCI but her work with the Amy Gillett Foundation – Amy was a professional Australian cyclist who was killed in a tragic accident when a teenage driver smashed into the Australian women's cycling squad as they trained on the open road in Germany. The Foundation is a cause close to Tracey's heart.

Tracey Gaudry has – quite literally and by her own admission – been there and done that. She's a multiple national champion, has ranked third in the world, won World Cups, the Tour de Snowy in New South Wales, Australia, and the French stage race, the Trophée d'Or Feminin, where her name is written in the *palmarès* alongside the likes of Johansson, Vos and Borghini. She's a successful businesswoman and CEO of the Amy Gillett Foundation, Head of the Oceania Cycling Confederation (OCC) and Vice-President of the Union Cycliste Internationale (UCI), the international body that governs cycling. She is the definition of doing it all. 'I have experienced a great ride in cycling over 20 years', she says, experiencing the highs and lows of an elite cyclist, the lifestyle that we know so much more about thanks to what Gaudry describes as the 'grand year of cycling' in 2014. From the high of being ranked top three in the world to the low of crashing in an Olympic Games road race, Gaudry saw life as a top-flight pro from the inside before moving into cycling advocacy with the Amy Gillett Foundation and becoming the first ever woman President of the OCC in 2012. 'I am fortunate to bring a wide range of professional skills as well as cycling experience into the space,' she says of her election.

Then another first – Gaudry was elected as one of president Brian Cookson's three vice-presidents at an ill-tempered Congress in September 2013. Gaudry is part of a dynamic group of women – alongside the likes of Kristy Scrymgeour, who sits on the UCI's

Professional Cycling Council, Wiggle-Honda team owner Rochelle Gilmore and Le Tour Entier co-founder Emma Pooley – who, with the support of Cookson, are finally dragging women's cycling into the 21st century.

So are women's voices finally being heard at the UCI? Gaudry thinks they are but concedes there is a long way to go. But, as she points out, her presence at the heart of the UCI is challenging '114 years of history where there has not been a female voice – that's a lot of history to start and think about how we might adapt the culture, adapt the conversation, bring a new perspective into an existing conversation.' But Gaudry is equally clear that lobbying for action on the women's sport shouldn't come from women alone. 'It's about bringing everyone along for the journey,' she states, 'and for me it's about lining up alongside my Management Committee colleagues and encouraging a conversation across the UCI and looking at elevating women in positions of significance and influence.' The really great news, Gaudry says, is that this approach is beginning to take root and bear fruit: 'It's not only Gaudry and the women on the commissions putting forward proposals and opportunities to develop women in cycling, it's the blokes as well.'

Gaudry is keen to point out that all the UCI commissions have people of great experience, expertise and knowledge: 'And guess what? More of those people are women these days.' She says that women have 'a lot to offer, not just the women's side of cycling but cycling as a sport, to grow it as a way of life and a great activity for everybody'. She points out that the UCI is at the head of a complex and worldwide system of 179 National Federations that represent hundreds and hundreds of clubs around the world, across five continents. 'There are many ways to foster the involvement of women and to promote the role of women, and to achieve great outcomes all the way up and down the spectrum of cycling', she points out.

I'm keen to know more about the role of the Women's Commission, the much-vaunted body set up by Cookson on his election and Gaudry is just as keen to outline its role in strategic development and facilitation. It does not, she tells me, 'decide everything that happens for women in cycling'. Instead the commission takes proposals from other parts of the UCI – every commission is tasked with providing updates to the Women's Commission, be that cycling disciplines, ethics, governance of anti-doping – and works transversally 'to understand what they're striving to achieve, to bring that together and build an argument and a proposal for some of the more significant changes and investments we'd like to make in women's cycling'.

I wonder whether one of those 'significant changes' is the much debated minimum wage for professional women cyclists. With Brian Cookson admitting he has failed in his manifesto pledge to deliver the minimum wage, and still clearly entertaining doubts about levels of remuneration for women riders, I'm interested to know Gaudry's opinion on this thorniest of issues. Does she agree with the commonly voiced opinion that a minimum wage will simply see teams collapse or re-register as amateur teams? Or is the minimum wage even the most important issue the women's sport needs to tackle? Gaudry takes time over her answer, again contextualising the issue in terms of her presence on the Management Committee as a rider who has 'lived and breathed the environment we are campaigning internally and externally to improve'. She points out that it is this whole environment that needs to change, and that some teams are making great steps to achieve that change, but that there are still 'some conditions that haven't improved a hell of a lot since [she] retired, so there's an absolute personal commitment to moving forward'.

She talks about the need to look at the medium and long term, while recognising that urgent action needs to be taken in the short term 'to demonstrate the commitment is there and to make changes that are well overdue.' For Gaudry, the picture is very much bigger than a minimum wage – it's about the environment that professional women cyclists find themselves in, about making that environment as supportive and protective and challenging as possible – 'because road cycling's not for the faint hearted, I think it's fair to say'. The wage equation is simply one part of the whole platform – it's up to the UCI to determine that events are prepared and delivered and promoted well 'so that the stage women are racing on is set for them to perform at their very best'. Gaudry talks about 'professionalising the duty of care' to women riders – ensuring that races are safe as well as spectacular – and looking closely at the team environment 'so that women are not only protected but challenged so they can be tested to the extent of their capability'. Gaudry is pushing to raise the standards and conditions that make up a well-organised team: 'pay and remuneration is of course one element, but it also includes housing and transport'. She uses the example of non-European athletes who can't just go home on a weekend or between races. She wants teams to ensure that their medical and coaching environment is sound, that equipment is properly maintained, that athletes have robust contracts with their teams. Gaudry is quite clear that all these factors need to be taken into account so that 'when we're raising the bar we're looking at the key elements that are important in women's cycling'.

The expectation seems to be that weaker teams will fold if equal pay structures are created but doesn't that run the risk of sacrificing the opportunities of women who are involved in the sport now for their potential opportunities in the future? Gaudry says this is 'exactly right' and that the UCI are looking very carefully at the step change that they are implementing 'to raise the bar in a way that is substantial and real, not undercooked and token'. She says that talks have been under way for some time with teams to determine just what that bar looks like 'so we don't throw the baby out with the bathwater, so we don't set the bar so high that the system breaks, because if you set it so high that all the teams folded you wouldn't have an environment or system'. In order to ensure that the top women's teams appear in the top women's races, the UCI are working with team managers, owners and event organisers to 'develop a model, so that when we do put it into the marketplace it has been socialised and tested with the teams, so that everyone knows what's coming and can prepare for that'.

That model will take the form of a two tier system – not dissimilar to the World Tour/Pro-Continental structure that exists in men's professional cycling – and work on its implementation has been going on all year. 'The serious work started in July when the Women's Commission met in the afterglow of La Course,' Gaudry says, referencing the historic one-day race that saw women compete on one of the most iconic stages in cycling, the Champs-Élysées. The two-tier model will be implemented over the next two to three years developing a series of top-tier and second-tier events, all at UCI Level, including one-day events and stage races. The top-tier events will be raced by the top-tier teams with possibilities for development teams to race by invitation. 'It's been tested in concept, the management team has approved it and now we're going back to work with the race organisers,' Gaudry says, mentioning the race organisers' meeting in early December where the model will be further developed. Then it's over to the teams to 'look at what team structures need to be like to truly set out a professional road series'.

I want to switch the focus from the UCI towards the work of the Amy Gillett Foundation (AGF), set up by Gillett's husband after her untimely death in 2005. Gillett and five of her Australian teammates were out on a training ride in Germany when tragedy struck – a young driver piled headlong into the group of riders. Five were injured, Gillett was killed. Her death sent shockwaves through Australia, and the AGF, born out of the tragedy, advocates for safe cycling in Australia. With a stated intention to be 'a catalyst for change, focused on what should be, rather than what is', they're a good fit for Gaudry. The day before we speak, the AGF's Cycle Safe Communities programme has just been awarded the prestigious 3M-ACRS Diamond Road Safety Award and Gaudry's tone brightens when she talks about her work with the Foundation. 'The AGF is a relatively small organisation that enables us to be agile and nimble,' she enthuses, before drawing some parallels with the UCI: 'It's really important to be principled, to be robust in your mission and what you're striving to achieve, to have strong governance so that structures underpinning your work are sound.' She says that both organisations 'are well and truly focused on their community and the stakeholders who are important to achieving their respective missions and visions'. But she highlights an important, and telling, difference between the two organisations and one that she says is really healthy for her role at the UCI: 'The AGF advocates for a lot of change, so if you think about that from the UCI's perspective, it's a little bit like the Le Tour Entier group who are advocating change and calling out to the UCI to take up the task and the challenge and deliver that change.' As a member of the Management Committee, she says, it's good to know what it's like being on the 'other side of the fence': 'I respect advocacy and I respect the power and good intent, when it's well directed, of organisations and groups advocating for better outcomes where the current situation has room for improvement.'

So has that involvement in 'hearts and minds' culture change helped with the pressure to change the culture around women's cycling at the UCI – has Gaudry been able to build a 'culture of mutual respect' as she has with the AGF? 'Oh, absolutely!' she enthuses, 'because it could be conceived by the broader community of people who love bike riding and everything bike that the UCI is an untouchable organisation that sits out there making its decisions and not listening and not caring'. The AGF, she explains, builds strength in the community – the award was '100 per cent because of the way the AGF collaborates with the community, engages them and has the community as partners in bike rider safety' – an approach she brings to the UCI, to ensure that 'wherever we can, the UCI engages with the community we are trying to support and with whom we're trying to engage great outcomes'.

But that approach seems to have failed the Paracycling community. I'm interested to know Gaudry's opinion on the recent debacle when the UCI failed to file paperwork on time that would have guaranteed paracycling's participation in the 2020 Tokyo Paralympics. Gaudry is open about the UCI's failure to submit the application in a 'timely fashion' saying there were 'unfortunate reasons' behind it. She accepts that the UCI 'didn't deliver to the standard that we expect of ourselves in every part of the work we do in cycling' saying that the situation 'is not a demonstration of a lack of commitment and that we're working very hard in our dialogue with the IPC to ensure cycling plays a big part in the Paralympic Games'. Indeed since we spoke the International Paralympic Committee (IPC) has confirmed paracycling's inclusion in the 2020 Tokyo programme after the UCI provided additional information.

If paracycling seems to be assuming the outsider's role in the 'great cycling family' that women's cycling once assumed, there's no denying that 2014 was a great year for the women's sport – and not just on the road. And Gaudry is keen to reflect on and celebrate that success. 'Let's reflect on the fact that women's cycling didn't start [in 2014],' she points out 'it has been growing in various forms for four decades now.' She points to the abolition of the maximum age, and the fact that all the women's World Cup races were televised 'and [in 2014] there was a different winner in every single race just showing the depth of talent in the women's field'. The World Cup also introduced new categories to showcase different styles of racing, and different stories from the women's peloton. Then came the Women's Tour in Britain and La Course, races she calls 'great outcomes' for the sport. Finally she highlights the fact that 'significant' investment from the UCI ensured that all the broadcast events actually happened. 'So the thing that high achievers – and people who get involved in cycling are generally pretty high achievers – is to say "how do we keep raising the bar by that amount every single year?"' The trick is to be able to celebrate what the sport has achieved, then ensure that each year 'we can raise the profile of more events on the women's road calendar'. The calendar for 2015, Gaudry says, was approved at the end of September and the 2015 World Cup series consists of some 'amazing' existing and new one day races, as well as stage races that are growing in profile. The UCI is also working hard to ensure that all major Women's UCI road events receive significant TV broadcasting so women's cycling is profiled around the world. The work with key stakeholders to underpin that strong platform is already under way and there is, she assures me 'a sense of urgency inside the UCI because of how important that is for the sport, for women's cycling and for the movement of cycling worldwide'.

But just how robust is the current state of women's cycling, bearing in mind that a big team like Lululemon is struggling, that Specialized are pulling back on their investment in the sport, that some teams have not been paying wages and a rider like Anna Solovey, who won the silver medal in the World Championships time trial, has just returned from a doping ban and seems like a doping case waiting to happen? Gaudry makes an excellent point when she says, 'Gee, that sounds like the men's team environment – they sound like problems that you might see at Pro-continental level or continental level on the men's circuit.' She says these are challenges the sport has to face 'across the board – let's not try and badge every problem because it's in the women's environment – we're working to improve the standard all around'.

Gaudry is aware of the things that need to improve and the need to improve them, but she says those improvements lie in working conditions for women's teams and the profile of events, the whole platform which she is working so hard to improve. 'But that's not pointing the finger at parts of the system or stakeholders in the system at present – teams, women, organisers – we as a collective need to do that.' But she agrees that, where racing is concerned, I am 'dead right': 'If you look at the elite men's and women's road races, the elite men have a field of nine riders per country, the women have six per country, so your tactics are going to be different because your team make-up is different.' Women's teams don't have, as she points out, 'four, five, six pieces of ammunition, if you can call it that, to shoot out early in the race and have three or four riders left at the back end of the race'. Women's teams have to think very carefully about how they use their resources, when the race gets to the business end 'and that's what you saw, and what really excited those who were truly looking at how the race was run and won'. With five World Championship time trials and road races under her belt, Gaudry speaks with her usual knowledge and authority and I pity Tan if he ever makes that call.

Our time is nearly up and I ask Gaudry one final question – just what does the road map for the future of women's cycling look like? And when will we see it delivered? Gaudry talks first about the future for women's road cycling, pointing out the work that is being done across all the cycling disciplines, including coaching and development programmes worldwide. The timing looks like this: in December 2014 there was a women's World Cup seminar, which took place in Switzerland bringing together World Cup race organisers with organisers of other major races 'to plan to maximise the profile of all the major women's events throughout 2015, to build on the great work that was done [in 2014].' The seminar examined the programme of the concept for a professional women's road series and how to develop its structure, possibly in two tiers, to be ratified in terms of rules, regulations and protocols during 2015, for implementation in 2016. Beyond that, Gaudry says, 'we're also continuing the conversations we're already having with women's team owners, organisers and selectors to look at the structure of women's teams in the top tier of women's races and to set the arrangements for those teams during 2015 so that we can implement an improved structure in 2016.' The women's and road commissions within the UCI are working 'intensively' with event organisers and team owners 'to establish a platform which literally – in the space of one season – will truly raise the standard'.

Across the broader spectrum, Gaudry points out, 'one of the great benefits we have in place is that some of the newer disciplines of cycling – mountain biking, BMX, cyclocross – we have a greater level of equity in place already because those disciplines are very largely built around a stage and a platform where men's and women's events are conducted together.' For those disciplines, Gaudry wants to continue build a higher profile so that all events benefit. It's also about extending the length of women's races 'if that's feasible and it's what the women want.' Looking outside the racing environment it's about 'how we can bring more women into cycling – as directors, as coaches'. To that end, Gaudry says, 'we hope to be making some announcements pretty soon about facilitating the involvement of women in team director courses.' Since I spoke to her, the UCI have announced a revamped Women's World Cup calendar that sees racing return to the United States, a stronger commitment to promoting the sport across all platforms including television and social media and the introduction, from 2016, of a new team structure that aims to properly professionalise the women's sport. It seems that Gaudry might finally be effecting the changes the sport so desperately needs to build on the success of 2014.

I've seen it said of Gaudry that when she enters a room, she owns it. I reflect on the fact that changing that 114 years of history must be like turning the proverbial supertanker – but if there's a woman who can take the helm and force through the changes that she, the stakeholders and the fans so desperately want to see in the sport, it is Tracey Gaudry, the woman who has been there, done it and got a drawer full of T-shirts.

CHAPTER 24

BETSY ANDREU

Breaking the Silence

Betsy Andreu is married to Frankie Andreu, who rode on the infamous US Postal team alongside Lance Armstrong between 1998 and 2000. Betsy and Frankie were both present in a hospital room in Indiana in 1996 when Armstrong admitted to doctors that he had taken a number of performance-enhancing drugs. Betsy later weathered a sustained campaign of intimidation when she chose to speak out about Armstrong's doping, culminating in him characterising her as a 'fat, ugly liar'. Betsy and Frankie currently live near Detroit, Michigan with their three children.

I feel as if Betsy Andreu is an old friend, though we've never actually met. But we are both veterans of the protracted battle to expose Lance Armstrong – a battle that was fought through online cycling forums and the exchange of hundreds of emails. Through it all, Betsy impressed me with her commitment to telling the truth and facing down with dignity the slurs and insults the Armstrong camp threw in her direction. I was determined that Betsy's honesty and integrity be a part of this book and so, late one night, I picked up the phone and dialled her number and finally spoke to her directly for the first time. I could sense her life going on in that different time zone – her children engaging in their different pursuits, her husband Frankie moving through the house just out of

earshot. What follows is a transcript of that conversation: this is Betsy's
story in Betsy's voice.

Tell me how you first met Frankie.

A mutual friend asked me if I wanted to go out for pizza with a few
of her friends. Frankie was one of the guys there. He'd just come back
from racing Paris–Roubaix that April 1994.

So you talked about cycling?

We didn't talk about cycling at all; I didn't know anything about it for
me to bring it up. The only name in cycling I knew was Greg LeMond
and that was because he was the only American to win the Tour de
France. Frankie said he was trying to shake off the jet lag which
prompted questions from me about where he was and why. The only
thing he said about cycling that entire night was that he rode a bike
for a living and that's only because I asked him why he was in Europe.

So when did you first meet Lance?

I met Lance at the US National Championships in Philadelphia
six weeks after I met Frankie. I thought he was fun, he was full of
energy. He was completely different than Frankie, who is naturally
more reserved. Lance had a lot of energy and we had fun.

People always asked him how he was like back then: my answer
was he was always nice to me but he was so crass with others. I liked
him but the more I got to know him I got to see the rude, arrogant,
cocky side. Honestly, I chided him so many times for being so rude.
He wasn't like that with me, however, since I'd call him out on it. I
never had a problem with him because we both spoke our minds to
each other.

I'll give you an example. We'd all go out to eat when they lived
in Como [Italy]. In Europe, service is slow for an American. Lance
didn't like that. He wanted it fast. I remember the first time we all
went out to a pizza place he was so loud, just like the stereotypical

Texan. He complained loudly, 'These fucking Italians take so fucking long to give you the damn drink ...' He'd didn't care they heard or understood him. Lance and I are so opposite in so many ways but we both enjoyed getting under each other's skin if that makes sense. He'd like to engage me in dialogue on topics he knew I was passionate about just to get me going and we'd go back and forth on whatever issue it was. He used to tease Frankie about being cheap all the time. He was on my side on that issue.

I have some nice memories of him but that's because we were friends – or so I thought. As time went on, it just became apparent he wasn't the type of guy you'd want your husband hanging out with. It wasn't a matter of trust with Frankie; believe me, if Frankie had cheated on me, the Lance Mafia would've made sure that got out. As you get older and you have kids you tend to hang out with people who share your ideals. Frankie and Lance were bound to go their separate ways even if none of this had happened. Frankie's a family man and prefers to spend his time at home with his family instead of going to bars of any kind. His idea of partying is getting an ice cream with the kids after their sporting event – that's a treat. Frankie really is a homebody. I'm the one who likes to go out, and when I say go out, I mean to dinner – I don't go to bars or clubs. Frankie prefers to stay at home seemingly all the time. But even Frankie has said, had there been none of this stuff with Lance, he and Lance would've gone their separate ways, remaining friendly, but not close like before. They're just too different.

I've learned through this whole thing that money, fame and power don't change someone; it just brings out who the person really is.

When did it all start to go wrong with your friendship?
The straw that broke the camel's back was idiotic and stupid. I told his then-wife Kristin that I'd read on an internet forum that she was going to a get a nanny. This was something we both talked

about and were both against. Why have a nanny when you're a stay-at-home mom, right? I told her I chimed in anonymously and vouched that she wouldn't have a nanny since that's not the type of person she was, i.e. [she] wanted to be a hands-on mom since she wouldn't be working. She cried and got very upset that a stranger would say something that wasn't true about her. Lance went crazy and became very angry with me, blaming me for Kristin getting so upset. He blamed me for telling her about the cycling forum because he didn't want her to know about it because there was a lot of negative stuff about him on there. The irony was they had a nanny anyway – even before the baby was born.

But it was all so stupid. I wonder if he was looking for a reason, an excuse to break the friendship. He knew from the beginning I was absolutely adamantly against doping from my reaction to the hospital room when he asked Frankie what my reaction was to his admission of using PEDs. I had flipped when I heard him say he was doing performance-enhancing drugs. I can't help but think that Lance knew I'd be an impediment to any doping at all.

You knew he'd been doping back in 1996, when you were in that hospital room ...

You want me to talk about it again? The detail of that is out there – we visited him when he was receiving cancer treatment and we were in the room when he told two doctors he had taken performance-enhancing drugs. Given it was a research hospital, there were different doctors coming in and out of his room all the time. One of the doctors asked all these banal questions and then boom! He asked Lance if he'd ever taken any performing-enhancing drugs. Lance reeled off the names EPO, cortisone, growth hormone. I got really upset. To me it was a no-brainer. My immediate reaction was, 'My God, he got his cancer from doing this shit!' And that was how I found out about doping in cycling. Frankie had no idea Lance was doing all that stuff.

But Frankie became involved in doping too, when he rode with Lance on the US Postal team from 1998–2000. How did you feel when you found out, given your anti-doping stance?

How did I feel? It was not a mistake. He made a conscious decision to do wrong. I will never justify what he did but will try to explain it. You have to remember that at the time there was zero support from USAC [USA Cycling] and the UCI. Doping was tolerated, accepted, expected. I don't buy the bunk that 'you had to do it to compete', but I believe you had to do it to be on Lance's Tour de France teams and if you wanted to make millions. Frankie did say no [to] Ferrari and the doping that came along with that – in his mind he did the bare minimum and sparingly. But he knew it was wrong nevertheless. In 1999 after I found out he had used EPO, we had a serious discussion. He promised me he'd never use it again and he stayed true to his word. I believe he was fired for not getting on the full-blown doping programme with Ferrari. He rode the rest of his career clean but it doesn't pay to finish the Tour 111th on Lance's team.

Frankie didn't even know the full extent of the doping programme until the Hamilton book [*The Secret Race*]. Frankie righted his wrong on his own volition. He put his reputation and his livelihood on the line by admitting to doping, even though it paled into comparison with what was going on.

What motivated him to take EPO do you think?

Frankie was almost 30 years old before he used EPO. He was a bona fide pro getting there clean via hard work, discipline and determination with no performance-enhancing drugs in his body. The guys talked about what was going on in the peloton because the speed was increasing like never before. Refusing to see Ferrari, Frankie was treated with trepidation as regards to doping in that he couldn't be completely trusted because he wasn't on board with it.

So why did he step over that line?

He believed the BS that 'everyone was doing it' from the shift he saw in the peloton. He said on record he got tired of seeing riders who went from donkeys to racehorses. He really thought 'If I want to keep my job, I have to do it.' The UCI didn't care at all, furthering the problem by making a rule not to have one's haematocrit [level] going over 50%.

How did you feel when you found out? This was something you were absolutely opposed to.

I found out in 1999 – he knew my stance. I didn't drink in high school and I didn't do illegal drugs, never, ever. I flipped out, I *flipped,* so he promised me he would stop, but told me that meant he probably wouldn't have a spot on Lance's team. My take was 'Good!' That team was nothing but trouble. In 2000, he'd had two other offers from other teams but Lance and Johan Bruyneel [the sports director at US Postal] put a stop to that.

Lance had already threatened Frankie the year before – they got into an argument at the Amstel Gold Race in 1999 (about the nanny incident and how I'd made Kristin cry). Frankie told him he couldn't believe he was so bent out of shape about it, that he was being idiotic. Kristin had apologised to me, saying she was hormonal from being pregnant. We cleared it up but Lance wouldn't let it go – he was making a mountain out of a molehill. Lance went into a tirade and told him, 'I have the power to stop you from ever riding the Tour ever again.' It's all in the USADA Reasoned Decision [the evidence gathered by the US anti-doping agency of the use of performing-enhancing drugs at US Postal].

It's extraordinary that Armstrong was allowed to have that level of influence in the peloton and at the UCI ...

Hein Verbruggen [President of the UCI from 1991 to 2005] didn't care enough about the integrity of reputation of the sport – he was only interested in money, money, money and power, and his position on the International Olympic Committee in my ever-so-humble opinion. It was a money and power grab, and cyclists were the pawns. With Lance he saw the dream story, and we know now it wasn't like that at all. Lance perpetuated the myth of the poor white boy growing up without a father, but his mother yanked him away from his biological father (who turned out to be a dud) and eventually from his paternal grandmother who was very involved in his upbringing, looking after him when Linda was at work. His mom married Terry Armstrong, his stepdad, who was a dad in every sense of the word: he gave them a good, stable and solidly middle-class life. He supported Lance more than Lance's own mother did when it came to Lance's racing as a teenager. He was not poor at all and not without a father. Another lie. But the rags to riches and the recovery from cancer was an incredible story – cancer touches all of our lives and from it comes that emotional connection. People really connected with Lance. Not only did he survive but he went on to win the most gruelling sporting event in the world.

So you didn't trust Lance. What were those years like at US Postal?

We didn't know what Lance was doing but we knew he was doing *something* – I figured he'd gone back to all the stuff he was doing in 1996. The mere fact he was seeing Ferrari was a huge red flag; he's there for one reason – doping. He was using riders as guinea pigs. He made tons of money off them. It's funny, I remember talking to the other wives, just to see what they knew and where they stood. And I think some were deeply involved, some knew just a little, but I don't know to what extent. I was just trying to find out 'what's going on here?'

Did you ever meet Ferrari?

Yes, in 1999. I was with Frankie, Lance and Kristin on the way to Milan–San Remo. We had to stop off on the way for Lance to do some testing with him, so we dropped him off in a gas station car park. Ferrari was travelling around in his little camper van. When we picked him up again, Ferrari came over to the car and my first thought was 'that guy needs braces'. We Americans are a very orthodontic nation! Really, I didn't think anything. Frankie introduced him, said 'Michele, this is my wife Betsy'. For the minute or two he was at the car, he seemed like a friendly guy.

So what was life like being married to a professional cyclist based in Europe?
We were six months in Europe, six months in the US. Before I had the baby, life was fun. We lived in downtown Nice and I had no car. I didn't travel a lot to the races either. There was camaraderie with the other wives. Looking back you realise they were not true friends. Friendly, yes, but not more than that. We found out who our true friends were when the going got rough.

We'd go out to lunch, sometimes dinner with other couples. We'd go to the beach a lot, to Italy for the markets, to Monaco – it was a totally different way of life. And there weren't the amenities of life in America. And I remember there was dog shit everywhere in France and found that disgusting. The food was fantastic, however.

But if you're going to marry a cyclist, especially if he rides in Europe, and if you're going to have that marriage work, you have to give up any aspirations of what you want to do with your life. I'm not whining or complaining because I'm blessed with being able to raise my own children. After our first baby was born it was much more difficult, we couldn't just pick up and go here or there because everything revolves around the baby. And being on your own with an infant and then a toddler is tiring – tiring but rewarding.

You'd been living this, some would say, glamorous life – what happened when Frankie lost his job on the team?
We had just bought a bigger house and I was pregnant with our second child when he lost his job. And I thought 'holy shit, what are we going to do?' We were a bit nervous. Then Johan Bruyneel

called and offered him a job [at US Postal]. And the funny thing was, about that time, Lance also called Stephanie McIllvain [who was also present in the hospital room and told Greg LeMond in a phone call that Armstrong had admitted to doping; she later denied having said this and contacted Betsy Andreu to call her a 'bitch'] and asked her to be his personal liaison. Looking back, we thought these offers were to shut them up because of what they knew regarding Lance's doping. If they relied on Lance for work, they'd be less likely to talk about what they knew. Lance had won his second Tour and was getting more popular and famous. So Frankie took the job of American sports director for the 2001 season. But we didn't know what we know now. We had no idea. And Frankie liked the guys, liked being a tactician – he's very passionate about the sport.

We'd talked before about what he'd do when cycling would be over and he wanted to stay in the sport because he liked it so much. Johan offered him the job and he took it because he wanted to be a sports director.

Let's fast forward to the USADA Reasoned Decision, Travis Tygart's investigation into doping at US Postal and what happened with that. How did that play out?

We obviously cooperated with the federal agents for the criminal investigation and years before that Frankie had told Travis about his own doping. Because Travis and his board, which are comprised of people of integrity in my opinion, worked hard and diligently, they were able to bring charges against Lance just a few months after the AUSA [Assistant US Attorney] Andre Birotte shut down the criminal case against him.

How did it feel to watch the Oprah interview in January 2013, to hear Lance finally admit what you'd known all along?

I was in New York City and I was getting bombarded with calls and texts, so I wasn't able to watch the whole thing in peace. I missed the last 30 minutes because I was on my way to the Anderson Cooper show. He answered 'yes' to those first questions posed by Oprah. That was nothing new to me, but it was amazing he finally admitted it. However, he dropped the ball on the hospital room – he was supposed to be coming clean, yet he refused to talk about the hospital room because of the legal situation ... So, he's supposed to be coming clean, but he won't talk about the hospital room which is the foundation for all this mess? If he's not going to admit to the hospital room, then he's not going to tell the truth about a whole lot of other things.

You did a lot of press as a result of the Oprah confession. You made a very strong, emotional appearance on the Anderson Cooper show, full of righteous anger.

If I look back, I wouldn't have done it again right after the interview aired because I was really emotional. I was so sick and tired of hearing over and over again 'you can't be angry, you have to take the anger out of you'. Are you kidding me? You try doing that when you've been publicly smeared for eight years. All these people telling me that I shouldn't let it affect me – let their husband's career be derailed because of it, let their husband be blackballed and blacklisted because of it, and them suffer financially because of it, let them suffer in the press, let them be lied about relentlessly by journalists who buy into a lie. Tell me how would you react if that had happened to you? Would you say 'oh, it's OK, let them continue to do it'? So I was very emotional and I was very angry he wouldn't admit to the hospital room incident because in that phone call he made to us the night before he taped with Oprah I told him I wanted him to admit that it happened because it did indeed happen. I had every single right to be emotional and angry. See if you can handle it with the grace and dignity I handled it. Give me a break.

Now I can take the emotion out of it and laugh about some of it. Thank goodness he's let the world know that he's never called me fat! It's Lance, he's never going to change. He'll be a lying snake for the rest of his life. And I do believe he called me fat. He's lying about that too.

Lance famously called you to apologise. He also talked to Emma O'Reilly [his soigneur at US Postal, who talked to David Walsh about his doping] and Christophe Bassons [the self-styled 'Mr Clean' who was writing articles for the press while riding the 1999 Tour de France, reporting that the sport was still dirty, and who Armstrong forced out of the race]. How did that go?

Well, he spoke to Christophe and Emma *months* afterwards. When he called me the day before he was taping with Oprah, I told him his timing was suspect. But I was very gracious for the 23 minutes that we spoke. I really thought he might be sorry. He said he wanted to meet me and Frankie and I looked forward to it. I wanted to meet him and wanted him to see that, even though he had tried to destroy our lives, he didn't succeed. Even though he wanted my head on a platter for telling the truth, I was showing him grace and humanity. I didn't want to be buddies with him, but it would have been cathartic.

There was always the fact that he told me he wasn't going to admit to the hospital room – so then I knew this was no more than damage control. It was a very good conversation but I think the old Lance came back right away after he saw that Oprah didn't go the way he was hoping. He quickly went back to the same ole Lance right away – trying to call the narrative as well as rewrite history.

Where are you now – in a good place?

Yeah, I extended an olive branch – I went to Austin, Texas, as part of an anti-doping panel. We agreed to meet with each other but at the eleventh hour he cancelled. After everything he'd done to me, I was willing to bury the hatchet with him and he said 'no'. Instead, he's launched his smear campaign 2.0 with his loyal lieutenant Hincapie doing some of his dirty work for him. I was like 'Oh, OK, here we go again – nothing, absolutely nothing has changed with this guy.'

He relies on some of his sycophantic fans on social media to do his smearing for him. So here we are almost 2 years later and nothing's changed in that aspect. He's still at it – sometimes I get agitated and sometimes I feel sorry for him because I do truly wonder if he's a sociopath and a narcissist to be like that.

The Tyler Hamilton book ends with the quote 'the truth will set you free'. But you told the truth all along and instead of freedom it gave you eight years of hell.

That's true. Does doping pay? Look at the financial rewards it has given Lance and his teammates who doped under Ferrari's guidance. It's the American way – profit from your crime. If you've grown up to be the kind of guy who doped his entire career and have weak morals and ethics, then you really don't care if it comes out that you doped. Frankie and I had to make a choice: lie and be financially set or tell the truth and have peace within.

It's a paradox – we have peace within, but you still have to make a living and pay the bills. We were never in a position to be financially set for the rest of our lives like the teammates who made millions. I don't know how some of these guys do it – do they never wonder what their children are going to think when they find out the truth of their careers? Kids don't stay kids forever – when they're adults and they see not just the doping their dads did but their complicity in their silence of evil when Armstrong was trying to destroy people, will these men who were involved in the 'most sophisticated doping conspiracy in the history of sport' care? Maybe, maybe not. I don't know.

How have you handled it with your children?

Our youngest doesn't know, but the older two do. They know dad did wrong, he caved in to peer pressure – something we tell the kids not to do. However, he knew it was wrong and without anybody telling him, he stopped using a PED. He didn't just refuse to see a doctor and get on a doping programme, but he refused to take even one drug ever again and that cost him his career as a pro cyclist. There was a bit of a catharsis and a relief in Frankie saying: 'I took one drug, EPO, but it didn't define my career. I was a strong professional cyclist way before I ever took anything. I ended up doing the right thing, but it cost me my career.' The kids have asked 'If you would have doped like George or Lance, would we have millions?' And the answer is: 'Most likely yes.'

The issue that came out was: 'Imagine the worst thing you've ever done in your life is going to be on the front page on one of the most powerful newspapers in the United States and people around the world are going to hear about it. That's what happend with Dad. He knew there was a problem in the sport and that the sport of cycling was in trouble. Dad thought that by talking about what he did he could help the sport, but instead the sport turned its back on him.'

The lesson to our kids is twofold: standing up to the bully and redemption. Frankie did wrong, but I really, truly believe he redeemed himself. You can be given second chances, but a second chance *means* a second chance. You have to right your wrong by action. Words alone are not enough.

So will any of your children follow their father into the sport?

Absolutely not! We've seriously turned them from getting involved in the sport. We are so cynical and sceptical when it comes to pro sports; we really, truly, stress education. Education is the way to go. You have to have common sense and, if you really want to do well in life, you have to take risks, but sport is not the way to go from my perspective.

Sports is good for so many reasons. Our kids are involved in sport. It's great for physical wellbeing, for learning to be a gracious winner and a gracious loser, it offers camaraderie – but to make a living? Get that out of your head! It's not even an option for our kids. You want to get somewhere in life? Be smart. Be honest.

CHAPTER 25

CLARA HUGHES
The Big Ride

Clara Hughes is one of the most decorated athletes in Canadian Olympic history, winning medals in both the Winter and Summer Games in speed skating and cycling. Now retired, she is an active campaigner for the humanitarian organisation Right to Play, which seeks to empower young people, and is a spokeswoman for the 'Let's Talk' campaign, which is designed to break the silence around mental health issues. By sharing her own struggles with depression, Clara has helped to break down the stigma associated with mental illness and, in 2014, she undertook the Big Ride around Canada, covering 11,000km and raising awareness of mental health issues.

Clara has been honoured both in her homeland and by the International Olympic Committee, who awarded her the prestigious 'Sport and the Community' award. She carried the Canadian flag at the 2010 Vancouver Winter Olympics, proudly leading her nation to a historic medal winning performance.

🐦 @clarahughes_
🏠 http://clara-hughes.com

🎖 **Major palmarès:**
Gold medal – Olympic Speed Skating 5000 metres (2006)
World Champion Speed Skating 5000 metres (2004)
Gold medal – Commonwealth Games Time Trial (2002)

Silver medal – World Championships Time Trial (1995)
Bronze medal – Olympic Road Race (1996)
Bronze medal – Olympic Time Trial (1996)

I've had a long-term, semi-professional interest in the issue of mental health and sport, particularly cycling, and had previously written about Clara's issues with depression in a piece about cycling and the Black Dog (Winston Churchill's name for it). I followed her Big Ride with huge interest and really wanted her contribution to this book, knowing what an issue depression is for many recreational cyclists and how much a ride can help put things in perspective. Clara was kind enough to open her online archive to me and, with her help, I selected a number of pieces that trace her life in women's cycling. The article on the Big Ride itself captures beautifully the enormous undertaking that riding across Canada was – not only physically, but emotionally.

In these extracts from her online journal, Clara talks about her progression from skates to bikes, the risks all athletes run in pursuit of their dreams, riding the 2012 Giro Donne and her final transition from professional athlete to active retirement.

Monday, 16 June 2003, Glen Sutton, Quebec

Light years have passed since the final weekend of the speed skating season. At least that's how it feels. For me, the dual-sport athlete (that's what I am labelled lately), it was only the beginning of another season, another sport. From skating to cycling, it was time to shift the focus to the bike. Many have asked how I do it; how the transition is made. From the outside it looks, in all its complexity, a rather simple step. That it is one of the most difficult and humbling changes to make is something I try not to show. Perhaps more to not let the enormity of the task set in to myself than the façade it creates for others. This year marks my third attempt at such. It has been, in many ways, the most challenging.

After two weeks of rest (which seemed to lack of the definition of the term 'rest') my husband Peter and I boarded a sunshine-bound plane to California. A vacation of sorts, taking us to the glorious Eastern Sierra Nevada to visit the spectacular mountain vistas, spend quality time with friends in the desert landscape, and cleanse our lungs with the thin air. We did not stop for a moment as if desperately attempting to get in as much 'mountain time' as possible. Before we knew it our rental car headed south to our destination/departure point for round two of the 'vacation'. Our destination was the desert place of Baja California, Mexico. The mountainous peninsula, nearly 2000 kilometres in length, was waiting for us, the bike tourists.

To simplify this story I'll make our intentions clear: we planned to ride the peninsula, in its entirety. Bike touring is a great way to get in the training miles necessary to make the transition after a gruelling season of skating, or cycling. Now you may wonder why I need to ride 2000 kilometres to get fit. As sad as it may seem, fitness is lost in the most important parts of the competitive seasons. When peaking for competitions it is necessary to cut back on training volume. Thus endurance is lost and must be built back by miles, miles and more miles.

On average we covered 90 kilometres a day on our mountain bikes rigged for the road with semi-slick tires. That we can make these distances by the power of our legs is liberating. When the roads were quiet and we moved through a land so diverse, it was magical. The jungle of cactus lining the man-made vein of concrete running the length of Baja captured my imagination. Camping in that tangle of cactus was something intense yet peaceful, filling me each night with energy that will carry me through the next phase of racing and training; through life.

Knowing I can have the freedom to travel in virtual anonymity for a month here, a month there, is powerful fuel. The August prior I went from winning cycling gold in the Manchester Commonwealth

Games individual time trial to cycling the Dempster Highway, a rugged dirt route running north through the Yukon and Northwest Territories, beyond the Arctic Circle up to Inuvik. I had my best speed skating season ever after that trip, and I suppose I expect the same from this one.

What I did not expect was the return of a back injury I was plagued with the last two weeks of the skating season. It's been four weeks since hurting my back again, and what a roller-coaster it has been. So many people have helped me through this, with advice or just plain kindness. Everyone kept saying 'You'll be fine, you know how to listen to your body. If anyone can get through this, it's you.' Inside I felt insane. Only thing missing was the straight jacket. There have been many occasions I am sure Peter wished for one, to use on me. I have been through a lot of pain and discomfort in the past, but there is nothing that compares to the incessant pain of an injured back.

I hid the struggle from all but those closest to me. Pain is something incomprehensible save for the person experiencing it, so I figured why say anything at all. It was difficult to answer when people began to ask 'Are you on form? How is the form? Are you racing?' What to say, except that things were okay, I would be racing soon, just finished my longest speed skating season and was, well, human ... leave me alone! But all of that is behind me now. It took a good four weeks and, finally, I am happily on my bike again. Even on a day like today, in the pouring rain, doing intervals I could not dream to have attempted two weeks ago, I love it. Sunday I will go and do one of my favourite mountain rides, Jay Peak, in Vermont. Last summer I would ride it three, sometimes four, times per week. Now I am happy to ride. Period.

Which leads me to the points of great introspection which are understanding through a period of excruciating pain: first, don't ever lose a day, no matter how bad things seem, they can always be worse; second, listen to those who love most you when you are in pain, they are not trying to make you feel worse, they only want to help; and finally, don't, under any circumstances, try to move boulders because you have nothing else to do after being laid up with a bum back for 10 days, in the pouring rain, by yourself. But I didn't do something as stupid as that ...

○ ○ ○

Wednesday, 1 February 2012, Mt. Aire Canyon, Utah

The reality of the risk of a sport like mine, an 'extreme' sport, became clear once again a few weeks ago. The event making these daily risks real was on a famous and sometimes infamous training ride/race in Tucson called 'the Shootout'. With the usual early start and the typical all-out pace for a good 45 minutes, I stopped with a few other Canucks to wait for one of the SpiderTech boys who had flatted. A bunch of us planned on racing up Madera Canyon after the Shootout proper and I didn't want to lose the guys I was supposed to be riding with.

Guillaume Boivin, the SpiderTech-er with the flat, and the rest of us started riding again at a good pace to catch the others. Just up the road we saw a number of the 70 or so cyclists on the ride standing on the side of the road with their bikes. A sheriff's SUV blocked both lanes of desert roadway. My first thought was a car had run into the pack of riders. Second thought was more hopeful, one of 'maybe they all got pulled over for taking up the lane of traffic'. Still, a bad feeling in my gut increased as we rolled closer. After the sheriff's SUV, a handful of riders crouched on the ground. Sticking out from these athletes was a set of tanned, long and lean legs, feet hanging side to side. I saw one of the guys holding the downed rider in his arms and turned away. Others said they saw blood all over the roadway.

What had happened? It was a young athlete from the Garmin development team. An ambulance came swiftly to the scene. We all rolled away, re-grouping at the usual Shootout gas station to refuel for the rest of the five or so hour ride. Of course, everyone was talking about the crash. Turns out the rider was trying to take off his shoe cover while riding, and the material from the cover got caught in his wheel, causing him to go down. He fractured his skull and broke his collar bone from the impact. Imagine if he was not wearing a helmet. Somehow, nobody else was hurt in the crash. All I was thinking was 'that poor kid, I hope he has health insurance'. Someone mentioned to me 'surely his team will have him covered'. From my experience in two different sports, this is never the case, and the responsibility of health insurance is always the burden of the athlete.

Later in the same ride, another crash, another broken collarbone. This time someone ran over a piece of metal on the road, flatting both tires and causing a crash behind. All I could think of was 'let this ride finish so I can be back at the hotel, safe and in one piece!' Earlier in that same ride, when the shootout was in full swing with us all racing along, a pack of wild dogs (yes, wild dogs in the desert!) ran into the peloton. Riders swerved and braked, one guy making an exit stage-left into the gravel lining the roadside, hopping rocks and somehow not crashing.

People often ask me the difference between skating and cycling. They are both incredibly difficult pursuits, both take a lot of focus and dedication. There is no arguing being on a bike is far more dangerous than skating in circles on the ice in the controlled environment of long track speed skating. Sport is dangerous. I know the reality and so does each and every athlete. Do we take care of ourselves and make sure to have insurance to cover the many potential dangers of the work we do? I can't say I always have. Sometimes, trips come at a short notice, or go longer than I thought, and then it's a matter of crossing my fingers and hoping for the best. As I've gotten older and matured, yes, I have been better with making sure I have the necessary coverage when traveling. This was easy as a speed skater because I was doing something that was not deemed 'high risk' and thus the normal travel insurance would suffice. As a racing cyclist, this is a whole different matter. I found it impossible to find the proper insurance to cover my racing needs.

I think often of that young Garmin rider with the fractured skull and broken collarbone in Tucson, and hope he is okay. I also think about my own close call last summer when I crashed at about 60km/h just before the National Championships in Ontario, smacking my head, luckily not getting concussed, and limping away with road rash and severe whiplash. I've been hit three times by cars in my life as an athlete while out training on my bike in pursuit of my athletic dreams. I've crashed so many times I lost count years ago. It's all part of the game but I'd be lying if I didn't say this all makes me very nervous.

I think about my young teammate I lost back in 2000, Nicole Reinhart, when she died from head injuries crashing in what would have been her biggest victory of her young athletic life. I think about South African cyclist Carla Swart who was a member of the HTC Highroad Team last year who lives on in the hearts of so many of my teammates on the continuation of that same team, the Specialized-Lululemon Team, after her shocking death when she was struck by a truck while out training on her new time trial bike last year. I think of the #2 ranked female bike racer in the world, Swede Emma Johansson, who was almost hit head-on by a vehicle making a dangerous pass a few weeks ago on a mountain road. Emma came away lucky, only two broken collarbones.

The list goes on as it always does.

I think of all this and I think of the life I've had in sport. Yes, there are risks, and for me these risks are not worth it if I only think of rewards. They are worth it only because the outlet of sport has allowed me to live with passion. I can say I've had this incredible path in life because of the passion that continues to live inside for what I do. This passion I am not willing to let go of and not live to its fullest.

The memories of athletes lost doing what they love lives on not just in me but, I think, in most athletes. I know they live on inside of me.

○ ○ ○

Clara returned to competitive cycling in 2010, with a view to competing in the 2012 London Olympics where she finished fifth in the time trial. She rode the Giro Donne – the women's equivalent of the Giro d'Italia Grand Tour – as a warm-up event.

Tuesday, 3 July 2012, Italy

There is a heat wave in Italy. It was as if the first five days of the Giro d'Italia Donne were raced in a wood burning pizza oven. Each day it feels like the cook adds more logs to the fire. It's like racing in an inferno. On day 3 the team car dashboard read 49°C. No joke.

The first day of the stage race it was scorching but we had a sea breeze almost making it tolerable. Being inland makes for oppressive and inescapable burn. I don't know if I've ever taken in so much water and concoctions of electrolytes. Powders, tablets and liquid versions of what seems impossible levels to maintain. So far so good, though, for this red-head.

The plan of attack which seems to work so far has been to start with three bottles: one water, one electrolyte fuel system (EFS) mix not too concentrated and then 'The Evie Bottle Bomb' I came to like when racing back in May. It was in the Exergy Tour in Idaho when my back was in so much pain that I couldn't reach into my pockets after crashing that I gave The Bomb a try. Much to my surprise, it worked! 'The Bomb' is named after my teammate Evie Stevens because Beth, our genius Goddess soigneur, came up with this solution for Evie back in April after she raced Tour of Flanders not eating a thing. Why? Because the race was and is absolute chaos and Evie just couldn't get to her pockets for food. So Beth made her this monster drink that lets her fuel for the intense races.

It's basically a First Endurance liquid gel (vanilla) that has 400 calories mixed with water. Yes, that equals 4 gels in one bottle. Perfect for the first hour of racing. I go back and forth with The Bomb and the water bottle in the first hour and a half, then move on to EFS mix, gels and chews. And more water. Water on the head, on the back, in the mouth and down the hatch.

It works out like that most of the time. Only problem is when the bottle of water you get looks like water but is actually lemon-lime flavoured mix. And when you're in a world of hurt like I was after leading Evie up the climb on day three to set up a moment to attack, and that leading took 11 kilometres of hard tempo to set her up ... well in that situation I don't really have the wherewithal to check if it's actually water being handed up from the team car when it passes the implosion formerly known as me up the climb and offers me a drink.

This happened and our sweet mechanic Sebastien said 'yes' when I grunted 'water' as they passed me. The beautiful cold water (or so I thought) felt so good in my hand and even better on my head and neck. How refreshing! It even dripped onto my face into my Oakley sunglasses, but I did not care. Until I took a swig of the fluid and realised it was not water but lemon-lime mix. Oh well. The cold did feel good.

And then there was yesterday when, again, we drilled it into the climb. The girls led Ina into the climb and it's not too fun to be on Ina's wheel when she is going until she blows and then you have to take your turn doing the same. Ina is too strong at the worst of times and I could only whisper, 'A little slower?' when on her wheel. I was hurting so much. I was the last to lead our Evie in pink up the 10km ascent called I-don't-know-what because all of these towns and cols are melding into one at this point.

Yes, that 'lead out' left me gasping for air and moaning in agony. How embarrassing is it when you are in such a state of hurt – like in a time trial or sometimes on the trainer in the basement – that you just scream out the pain because no one is around to hear. Well this time I had the world's best climbers all behind me when I was grunting and groaning up that climb in the heat of the scorcher of a day. And there was Evie behind me, whispering 'just a little longer Clara … just a little further … you can do it … just a little more …', and I am screaming in front like I am about to keel over.

My prayers to the cycling gods were answered when Emma Pooley of AA Drink attacked and I went ka-boom. Emma was my goddess that day because finally I could stop the torture. I could stop the pain of producing the power and gasp for some air for myself.

The funny thing was, today, in the flat-as-a-pancake race that saw us creeping through the countryside behind Tiffany Cromwell of Greenedge Orica, who must have been in a world of hurt herself some 12 minutes in front of us, Emma came to say hello.

'Clara, how was the climb for you yesterday, were you okay? There were some awful sounds coming from you … I felt bad to attack but to be honest I wanted to put you out of that misery… it sounded like you were giving birth!!'

Emma is from England so it was even more funny hearing this with an English accent. She also weighs about the same as one of my legs. Not one of my speed skating legs, but one of my cycling legs, which is a lot less baggage. Oh, if these little climber girls could only feel the weight of 67 kilos going up those climbs instead of the barely 50kg they don't even know they enjoy.

And that's the Giro in a nutshell. This is a race that has some beautiful courses, some epic days with climbs and heat and chaos, and we as cyclists come in all shapes and sizes. What is so unique about this sport is that one can feel like a winner in contributing to the success of other's abilities. We all punch above or below our weight at times when we help our climbers soar and our sprinters fly.

Thursday, 3 January 2013, Canada

Patterns long embedded follow wherever I go. Whatever I do. Somehow I thought after quitting sport life would be a little easier. At least in ways. But no, it seems, these patterns simply repeat. Patterns of punishment that go on inside my head. Thoughts of unrepeatable negativity scream out loud when I sit with myself too long. And now, these shouts of abuse are beginning to follow me into time spent with others.

For some reason I thought these verbal cues were a result of trying to be better at something. That something was sport. Sport that consumed me for over two decades and is now gone. Now it's just me. No pressure, no expectations, no need to be fast, good, strong or to even improve. Yet I can't let go of this idea that I always need to be more than I am. And it is eating me alive.

It's like what my neighbour said the other day (she being a former athlete as well), 'It's the permanent off-season'. Yes, that's exactly what it is. The time of the year where three or four weeks allowed freedom and recovery from months of physical and emotional output. I'd be easy on myself for about a week, maybe 10 days. Ultimately the guilt would creep in. Words inside my head asking why I was tired and why not out on the bike, trail or ice. Completely irrational words that prevented any kind of fun, let alone recovery.

And now life after sport is like a permanent off-season. There is no training plan to begin from scratch on and allow me to focus on. No daily goals that mean anything other than some personal satisfaction if I allow. Getting outside to be active means an experience that remains just that. Try as I might to enjoy these days and outings, I can no longer ignore these words in my head that beat like a tribal drum. These words that are at war with the seed of peace and satisfaction that is trying to grow inside of me, trying to sprout so that I can feel at ease in life.

There is no racing to work towards and as difficult as this is, I don't want it ever again. That part of me is utterly exhausted and there's no turning back. Knowing I can't go back to that part of me does not make it any easier. All I want is to settle down and enjoy life as it comes to me. The one constant is me and the person I cannot avoid is myself.

I suppose the only way to deal with the voices screaming inside is to do it like I did everything else. To face it head on and work to make it better, however long it takes. To work to improve myself in every way and then present these improvements to others. As an athlete I rarely gave myself a break. Perhaps this is why I was so good. Rarely a moment of sitting back and enjoying the ride. As much as I liked what I did, I don't want to live my life this way.

It's with these thoughts that I step not only into this new year, I step into each and every day of my life that is left. Each day, wake up; there is a decision to be made as to how it's lived.

In some ways life as a former athlete is like that of an addict. The comparison is quite normal to make of life as it was before with big goals, big dreams and big focus. In retrospect it seems easier but in reality it was torture. Just like the thought of a drink, a hit or a bet must seem like it would sooth the void. This comparison leads to melancholy because life will never be the same.

The goals I have now are small and most likely invisible to others. Goals of changing the words inside my head to nicer sentiments. Goals of simply enjoying what I do, no matter how small the deed. Even more than enjoyment, letting myself feel some sort of satisfaction and accomplishment with these small things. Not simply moving forward like a freight train though all the beautiful moments, forgetting to stop and feel the wonder of it all.

That's all I hope for and all I can think of doing to improve. That's life in the off-season. I'm going to learn to enjoy it for the first time in my life.

CHAPTER 26
CHRIS GARRISON
Seven Words

Chris Garrison moved from the roundabout capital of the US, New Jersey, to the roundabout capital of the UK, Milton Keynes, to take up a post as 'Trek Media Maven' (or Media Relations to you and me). She was industry legend Keith Bontrager's 24-hour race mechanic before, through a series of interesting and life-altering events, winding up in the UK after quitting her job on Wall Street. Chris hosts 'Ladies Night' events designed to help women get more out of cycling, and is a contributor to TotalWomensCycling.com and columnist for *Singletrack*.

🐦 @PunkassCG
🏠 www.trekbikes.com

Chris Garrison is one of the most forthright, intelligent and laugh-out-loud funny people you could ever hope to follow on Twitter and then meet IRL (in real life). She has a laser-like bullshit detector and cuts to the heart of any issue – particularly when it involves women and cycling, for which she is a passionate advocate. Chris was top of my hit list for women I knew I had to invite to contribute to Ride the Revolution *and finally – after much cajoling and flattery – I persuaded her to contribute the following piece, which is unashamedly Chris and absolutely fascinating. Much like the woman herself.*

I was wrist deep in grease while in the middle of a hub rebuild for a customer. By some small miracle, I'd managed to capture all of the loose bearings in my magnetic bowl, and they were in a state of containment that made Chernobyl look like a sieve.

I'd crafted a beautiful layer of grease inside the hub shell, and had already placed two bearings into their cloud of lubricant. I always thought it looked like the most comfortable place in the world, and if I was a bearing, that's the sort of bed I'd want to roll around in.

Bearing number three was just about to arrive in its happy place, when a customer came through the door. Our store had a hard and fast policy of customer greeting, and the rule was simple: no matter what you are doing, drop everything and acknowledge the customer, and see how you could provide assistance. This one rule became the keystone of customer service efforts that I not only practise to this day, but now teach bike retailers.

The store I worked in was called Wheel Life Cycles. It was near the Ivy League town of Princeton, New Jersey, and had a diverse customer base. The store had a massive basement in which we stored boxed and built bikes, and any other stock we needed. The workshop was on the main floor and was a feature of the store. Not buried behind any walls, it served as the go-to location for payment, and any questions. The store owner had strong feelings about the workshop being prominent. He wanted to demonstrate the investment in the tools required to do any bike work. His aim was to showcase the expertise and equipment required to build and service bikes properly. His secret objective was to discourage would-be home mechanics from deciding that they could do their own bike maintenance. The hacksaw wasn't quite so obvious. We didn't want to scare people, after all.

There was a red line at either entrance to the workshop area. This delineation created a virtual barrier that customers were not allowed to cross without express permission. This added to the notion that the shop was an area for experts only, and not for those who had purchased the *Idiot's Guide to Bike Maintenance*. Oh no.

That's where I was when I heard the seven words. In the workshop, at a bench, and surrounded by thousands and thousands of dollars' worth of specialist tools and Allen wrenches, while the scent of degreaser and lube diffused around me.

On this particular day, all of the other shop employees were downstairs organising a delivery that we'd just received when a customer walked in. I was the only one on the shop floor, and hence, it was up to me to live by the 'drop it and say hello' rule. Bearing number three went back into captivity in the magnetic bowl, and I picked up a rag to begin the somewhat futile attempt to remove the grease from my hands.

In a choreographed move that I'd done many times before, I stood up from my perch, turned around with rag in hand, and asked the customer how I could help him. It's important to note at this point that I was wearing a shop apron, and the distance from the workbench to where the customer was standing spanned about nine feet. My work was clearly visible.

His reply to my offer of assistance was that sentence of seven words. It led to one of those rare times when I was at a loss for an instant comeback of any description. I had to process what he said, and it sent my mind into a whirling dervish of thoughts, mostly in an attempt to make sure I understood what I'd just heard, in the face of all of the evidence in view of the customer.

'I need to speak to a mechanic.'

At this point in my life, I was in my mid-twenties. I had a degree in biology from university to my name, but a tumultuous end to a long-term relationship eventually had me working in a bike store, rather than the path to medical school that I'd been on since I was eight years old.

I can honestly say that until that very moment, in that bike store in central New Jersey, I never realised that the combination of my gender and the industry in which I worked could ever be perceived as an unusual one. Why should it be? I was a rider, after all.

Seven words delivered by one customer made me understand that it was possible for others to see me as somehow different to my male peers. It was like a veil had been lifted, and the obvious nature of the bike industry as being a 'male-dominated' one was evident to me.

Defining moments don't have to be the sort that are monumental life changers. Sometimes, they can just be little things that stick with you, and teach you some lesson from which you draw as you progress in life. Those seven words were one such moment for me.

When I recall the interaction with that one customer, I'm unable to determine why I didn't just chalk up his question to something simple, like some sort of super-human inability to grasp the obvious, or even a basic capacity to assess the situation taking place at the time. Instead, it seems to have triggered a feminist reflex that had been dormant until that very moment.

I moved on from the store to a stint on Wall Street, before eventually working my way back to the bike industry. My best friend and I have a theory that once you are in the bike biz, you may leave, but you never really get out entirely. It's like a gang. I was no exception to this. I flew the colours of a member of the trade, and even while suited and booted in New York, still had them stashed in a pocket of my attaché case. My co-workers learned that during three weeks in July, there was really no point in talking to me for the first hours of the day, as I clung to the early 2000's equivalent of a live race feed to watch the Tour de France.

Living in Manhattan meant that cycling was usually restricted to hot laps around Central Park with hundreds of runners, in-line skaters, horse drawn carriages, people crossing in front of you, errant soccer and footballs rolling into your path followed closely by children, and Type-A, testosterone-fuelled men on bikes. If someone was on a bike in front of them, it was like an enormous carrot being dangled in front of the hungriest Lycra-clad donkey you can imagine. Riding there made me imagine what it would be like to live in a world completely devoid of any sort of chivalry.

I left the money-driven world of high finance and went back into the bike business in 2005. I started my first role at Trek in a new program that was designed to get more women riding bikes and involved me driving all over North America in a Volkswagen Touareg towing a trailer full of bikes. My partner in crime the first year was Chrissy Redden, a Canadian Olympian who had just retired from an illustrious career as a professional mountain biker. It was a huge learning experience for so many reasons, which may or may not include figuring out how to drive the 100 miles between Salt Lake City and the Nevada State line with just my knees.

My programme was an experiment. Trek already had a bike demo programme that had been running for a number of years, but it didn't have any specific objectives to get women on bikes. Creating a demo team that was just about women was a risk, and not something that any of the big brands had done. So, I was sent out on the road as human litmus paper to see if women were into the idea of test riding bikes, and learning things from experts that would improve their cycling experience.

The next year, we added another demo driver. The year after that, a third rig. Then, a fourth. In year four, we teamed up with a woman running the Dirt Series, a successful string of women-only skills clinics operating between Whistler, BC and Utah. Women loved riding bikes, and they were hungry for other women to ride with, talk to, and learn from. We were providing a different type of support than what they got from even the most well-intentioned men. They weren't afraid to ask questions. They didn't feel marginalised if they were new and not very skilled. They weren't pressured to ride faster, unless they wanted to ride faster.

Every woman I talked to was like a plant that had been sitting in the sun just a bit too long, and there I was quenching their thirst for knowledge like a refreshing pitcher of water. There was palpable excitement everywhere I went. I told people basic pieces of cycling information that I had long since assumed was common knowledge, but for women had remained a mystery. I was actually helping people enjoy cycling and finding comfort on bikes. It was the most rewarding and gratifying occupation I've ever had.

Most of the resources available to women are men. Many women started cycling because of a man. The vast majority of store employees are men. And the bike industry itself is composed of far more men than women. My time on the road taught me that women everywhere had their own version of my seven words.

I'm now working as the media contact in the UK for Trek. Most of the people that do my job are men, and I'm fully aware that most of my peers are not of my gender. What I see now is that, while the amount of information available to women has improved, that same thirst for knowledge that I saw 10 years in the past is still very much part of the present.

Personnel in this trade isn't really the most glaring disparity any longer. Sure, it's still obvious what the gender breakdown is, but there are larger issues that extend far beyond the honorific people use when being addressed in emails. It's not just about the simple fact that girls can be bike mechanics. It's that people in positions of leadership have, for the most part, a lack of empathy. This spans the entire industry, from governing bodies and federations, to people in marketing who decide what images we show the world of cyclists in the pages of magazines and on websites.

The problem is that industry leaders still think that cycling is an activity dominated by men. And while it's true that, statistically speaking, there are more Lycra-clad men who ride than women, this assertion ignores the massive population of people who ride bikes that aren't made of the latest wunder material. Their numbers far outweigh the fraction of us who know the value of a good chamois and a wicking base layer.

Worse than percentages is the unrealised potential of having more women involved in the sport. It's like a volcano that's been tripping Richter scales for a while, and there's a few people trying to get others to understand just how powerful this eruption could be. Inevitably, there are the holdouts and disbelievers. Often, people come to their senses at the last minute and have to be reactive, rather than proactive.

Spending that four years on the road traveling around North America and speaking to women about bikes clearly demonstrated that there is a huge swell of people out there being largely ignored by the trade. There are bright spots and many positive changes, but overcoming old-school psychology isn't just a problem at retail, it goes all the way up to the highest levels of professional cycling.

That's what I think is the current state of women in cycling right now. Women have huge influence within households and communities. If we as an industry portray ourselves to be welcome to women, then the industry and the sport would both thrive. We'd see more advocates. More kids riding to school. More people working for better infrastructure. More of the things that those of us on the inside wish for with each passing Parliamentary debate or appearance before Congress. As women in the industry, it's no secret to us how all of these things can be achieved. We just aren't the ones calling most of the shots.

We have a saying in Trek that we believe the bicycle is a simple solution to many of the world's complex problems. I'm hopeful that, as an industry, we are becoming more and more aware that one of the best methods of delivery of that solution is through women.

I'm working off a different set of seven words now. One that I think applies to situations that extend far beyond the bike biz: I'm a woman, and I belong here.

CHAPTER 27

JESS DUFFY
What Cycling Means To Me

Jess Duffy rides bikes for fun, races bikes for Feather Cycles Racing team, and writes about cycling and the outdoors for several publications – then spends all her lunch break reading them. She has also captained the women's Bike Polo team to win the World Championships. A digital content and marketing guru, and National Standard Cycling Instructor, Jess likes fresh air, exploring Dartmoor, the sea and veggie food, which is why she escaped London for Devon.

🐦 @lapsandlanes

It was a tweet that led me to Jess Duffy. Something about promoting women's cycling that piqued my interest and prompted me to get in touch with her and ask her if she'd be interested in contributing to a book that aimed to promote women's cycling. It seemed like synchronicity and, when Jess agreed, my instincts proved to be decent ones. What follows is an intriguing, thought-provoking piece about what cycling means in one woman's life and what it might mean to all of us.

I didn't spend my formative years riding a bike, in fact, I learned to ride in a local park with my dad pushing me along as a young child, but as soon as I had mastered the actions required the bike was relegated to the garden shed and left to rust as 'cycling was too dangerous' in inner-city Birmingham where we lived. I never really got on a bike 'properly' until my late teens. I recall my first bicycle adventure when I was living in Australia with my then musician boyfriend. We went to visit his family in Mudjimba on the Sunshine Coast and were given a 'borrowed' beach cruiser that had a previous life as a hotel hire bike. We rode dirt tracks, beach paths and heat-soaked tarmac that day; I fell off numerous times and returned to our temporary home with legs covered in bloody memories. I was head over heels in love. But not with the boy.

I then went straight from Sydney to study at university in London in 2008 where I decided to chase an academic dream that wasn't destined to be mine. Things didn't work out with the boy and I couldn't hack the commitment my course required when I was so unsure of myself. But while living in Bow, I dabbled with my housemate's fancy custom fixed gear and found a burgeoning interest within myself. Not having the money or the know-how at the time, I decided to purchase a shiny blue 24" Raleigh Chopper from an online auction site. The bike was an instrumental learning tool in why people who know nothing about bikes should not buy them from the internet. I wobbled around the back streets of our neighbourhood with my housemate trying to do silly tricks on my silly little bicycle and decided promptly to sell it. The next bike I happened upon was a badly maintained Sturmey Archer 3-speed step-through named Ludo with a battered basket, peeling red paint and splitting sidewalls – but it was bigger and more comfortable to ride. By this time, I had quit uni, moved into a tiny first-floor flat with four maddening (but loveable) boys and was working in an achingly hip fashion store, where of course all of my colleagues rode to work on their tatty chic bicycles in a city where cycling was just enjoying a resurgence. I was still naively under the impression that London was this vast place that was impossible to get from A to B by bicycle and I only pootled from my house to local friends' rather than commute to work. Plus the stress of getting it in and out of the flat's claustrophobic elevator everyday was enough to put anyone off. However, I was intrigued by the city's hidden corners and kept making longer and longer journeys by myself to explore its gems.

A few months later, little Ludo was packed off to my home town of Birmingham as I decided to embark on an American adventure. I flew to New York in the early summer of 2009 and one of my first ports of call on the steaming sidewalks of Brooklyn was the 1234 Bicycle Co-operative, where for $80 I picked up a ratty bicycle and a ridiculously heavy chain. I was still a casual cyclist and not very confident on the road, but sometimes I like to do things on a whim and I foolishly decided to explore NYC by bike. Luckily, Manhattan's road network is based on a grid system and it was impossible to get lost on the avenues running north to south and the streets west to east. It was terrifying riding on the right hand side of busy NYC traffic and I had a pretty nasty altercation with a yellow cab but I came out of it laughing; full of exhilaration (as well as cuts and bruises) because nothing beats the freedom and sheer joy you feel when exploring a new place by bike! Sadly, I had to leave the bike with a friend while I headed to Philadelphia, the first stop on my 'Great American Road Trip' and didn't see it again for several months. By that time, I had decided I needed to go home and re-assess my life, and sold the bike to its adopted owner, a now famous musician and trend-setter.

I moved back home to my parents' place, in what I thought was a temporary solution until I could sort my head out and discover what direction I thought my life should be going in. Little Ludo languished in their conservatory, not keen on joining the heavy traffic in the poorly surfaced car-centric hellhole that Birmingham is to a bicycle. Then one night at a music show, I saw a young man who changed my life. He was tall, dark and handsome. He liked hardcore bands, he stood up for the radical and liberal politics that I believed in at the time, but most importantly, he rode a bike. A plain black, no-nonsense fixed gear bike that complemented his personality perfectly. Whenever I saw this bike locked up outside a music venue, my heart leapt a little and sure enough, it wasn't long before he had built me up a more practical bike to ride around on. It wasn't just a token of affection though, to me it became a symbol of much greater things and increased my own confidence and independence boundlessly.

The young man worked as a bike messenger and dreamed of opening up his own bicycle co-operative, and I worked in an arts centre and dreamt of discovering my life talent while making idle screen prints and meaningless photography projects. One day, while he was away on a mechanic's course, I decided that I wanted to turn my single-speed step-through into a 'real' bike. I converted it to fixed gear and swapped out some of the components with very little technical know-how but a lot of creativity. It was liberating to be able to do this myself and, soon enough, I joined the bicycle co-operative as a founding member and began dabbling in the workshop, trying to be helpful but mainly getting in the way! During this time, I was commuting to work on a daily basis, in love with the steady flow of riding fixed, feeling myself getting faster and preaching the benefits of cycling to all and sundry. I was then given the opportunity to train as a cycling instructor so that I could help our co-op reach out to the local community. It was a steep learning curve but one that benefited me intrinsically as a cyclist and which I am so thankful for – I've been able to pass on the basic skills that it taught me to hundreds of cyclists.

We decided to go away for my 21st birthday; to where else but the cycling mecca of Amsterdam?! We spent a glorious time cyclist-watching, visiting bike shops, riding to nearby towns and adventuring to lakes and parks off the beaten tourist trail. They are still some of my happiest memories; taking in the beautiful scenery with a basket full of fresh food, no pressure from other road users and nowhere to go but wherever our wheels wanted to take us. Soon after, though, I developed an illness which caused me great pain, lack of energy and terrible anxiety. I was constantly tired, couldn't eat and struggled to cope with my underlying worries about my life and what I was doing. I took them out on my partner and bit by bit our relationship fell apart. I was broken-hearted and felt like I had no-one to turn to. I left the co-op and I barely ever cycled due to my lack of energy or lustre for life. Then suddenly, I can't remember what changed, maybe I was fed up of moping in the house by myself all the time, but I started to go on little bike rides around the local area and re-discovered my love for taking pictures of old buildings and nature's little quirks. Then a cycling contact got in touch to ask why I hadn't done cycle training for the local council's project and I decided that I would give teaching a go by myself! I often had to cycle miles and miles across Birmingham to reach schools, but it gave me time to think and clear my head of negative thoughts. Working with young people never failed to put a smile on my face and it was (and still is) a positive rush when I managed to get someone cycling competently for the first time. Some people would laugh, some would whoop with joy, and others would cry. It was incredible to see. I decided to build a new bike from scratch, one that represented a new chapter in my life, and I found the whole process very therapeutic. My 'Steamroller' was born, through visits to cycle jumbles and forages in internet forums. A dark grey track frame with all black components, it looked dark and mysterious and it could not have made me happier.

Eventually, I had the confidence to start organising local cycling events such as 'At The Ride In' – an outdoor cinema for cyclists and also alleycat races, bike jumbles, themed rides, etc. I got involved with the monthly cycling event Critical Mass and helped to grow it through social media and of course, I became an avid blogger on all things bike. I started playing bike polo in Birmingham and I met two young guys who both rode fixed gear and liked to go on silly rides through the night just like me. One of them had recently lost his step-father and had this crazy notion of riding across Europe to raise money for Cancer Research in his name. I had never ridden further than our outer suburbs and back but I admired his tenacity and wanted to support him, so 'Birmingham to Berlin' was born. It was a zig-zagging bicycle adventure only passing through places beginning with B. We trained all summer and then managed to ride 988 miles unsupported in 11 days and raise over £8000 for Cancer Research supported by local company Brooks. Up until this point in my life, I had never felt like I had achieved anything, a constant disappointment to my family, always chasing that special something. This little ride, this was something.

When we returned from our trip, I started work at a local independent bike shop and realised my bike knowledge thus far was minuscule. I learned very quickly the makings of a good bicycle, the different kinds of frames, wheels and groupsets out there. I learned about the ideal kit to have and how to advise people on it. I don't claim to know everything about bikes; every day there is a new discovery, a new brand, a new development in technology and I'm happy that I'm always learning and then sharing this knowledge. I had still never owned a new bicycle at this point and I decided I would build myself a 'proper' polo bike as my badly converted track frame with a terrible habit of jack-knifing itself had outstayed its welcome. I bought a new single-speed frame, sturdy mountain bike forks, track wheels, a good-quality crankset and a whole host of other matching black parts, which with the patience of my mechanic at work I put together myself. I also decided to buy clipless pedals and shoes (despite never riding clipless before) because that's what all the good polo players were riding and, hell, I wanted to be good! Cue hilarious clipping-out fail in the middle of a busy dual carriageway with Time ATACs and so I reverted to SPDs to make my introduction to riding clipless a little easier. Amazingly, I didn't have too many terrible polo fails and I loved the new connection with my bike; I felt more in control, could accelerate faster and started to learn fancy tricks. Soon, all my bikes would have clipless pedals and I was never seen without my shiny Italian cycling shoes that I was ridiculously proud of.

I love that cycling brings together people from different backgrounds through the simple adoration of bikes; websites such as London Fixed Gear Single Speed (or LFGSS for short) helped me meet like-minded individuals and I would travel down to London to race, play bike polo and go on rides to seaside towns with complete strangers. I could not have achieved many of the things I have done today without the help of some of these lovely people. When I found the insularity of Birmingham too suffocating, I upped and packed my bags on a spur of the moment decision and moved back to London. Luckily, I found a job teaching cycle training in Hackney schools and I also worked weekends in a large independent bike shop. I barely had any friends despite knowing many London cyclists so I threw myself into playing bike polo instead. Bike polo is a welcoming sport; players come from all walks of life, and the mix of characters and the continuous improvement of my bike-handling skills kept me coming back for more. I became involved in the organisational side of things and after already helping to put on the UK Championships in Birmingham that year, I was voted in as co-chair of the London Hardcourt Bike Polo Association. I didn't put myself up for the position and was surprised and scared to find myself suddenly thrust to the forefront of an exciting sport. I loved working on new out-reach projects and developments in the sport but I also found it difficult to please all of the players all of the time. I increasingly found myself putting in more hours on LHBPA work than my own work and the lack of volunteers meant I put too much pressure on myself and I stopped enjoying the role.

Eventually, I also walked out of my bike shop job because of the low pay and poor treatment of staff, which is all too common in the lower echelons of the cycling industry. I was lucky to be able to work freelance for the London Cycling Campaign, Brooks, Le Coq Sportif and the Bicycle Film Festival during this time to help make ends meet. I managed to scrimp and save because I desperately wanted a new polo bike, now that more affordable polo-specific frames were being made and trends were changing. I ordered a forest green 26˝ Hija de la Coneja frame and collected some fancy parts to adorn it. It arrived two days before a major all-female tournament in Berlin and without a set of wheels or the conviction that I could play on a brand new bike, I rashly built it up anyway using a £20 set of Raleigh wheels my housemate had lying around. Luckily, the bike and I just clicked and I had never felt more at home on the polo court. Despite a frustrating start to the tournament, mainly due to the format, my team ended up finishing in second place, more as a result of sheer luck and a desperation to prove ourseves I think.

I have to pay homage to a little Gazelle Champion Mondial A road bike that came and went from my stable that year too. I bought her for cycle training as it was useful to demonstrate to children working gears while riding, but sadly she was cut through to steal another bike which was locked to her. Ironically, this happened outside of a well known cycling cafe while I was listening to a truly inspiring woman (and later friend of mine) who was cycling around the world. Donating the de-constructed skeleton of my little Gazelle to a local frame builder and friend seemed like a good use.

Not long after this incident, I was employed by Tokyo Fixed Gear, soon to be Kinoko Cycles, part-time. I knew that I was asked to interview for this job mainly because I was one of a few women in the cycling industry that had a good working knowledge of fixed gear bikes and had a CV chock-full of retail experiences. During my interview, I plainly stated that I refused to work for minimum wage (the poor standard for cycling retailers), pointing out that if you wanted good employees you had to pay for them! I was lucky that the owner and the then manager believed in me because I was paid a higher wage than some of my male counterparts due to my experience – and although it was still not good enough for this day and age, it was more than the industry standard. The shop was moving premises to a bigger location and wanted to create a women's range and to expand its road bike collection. I was excited to be a part of this and also to learn more about bike fitting, custom builds and developing brands in detail. Over the next few months, I filled in the gaps in my cycling knowledge with the help of my new colleagues and I became more and more fascinated with the technical developments and historical achievements that have moulded our sport and hobby for the better.

I also became more passionate about road cycling and bought my first carbon racing bike so that I could keep up on the fast-paced rides my male counterparts entertained most evenings after work during the summer. My first ride on that bike was a 140-mile overnight rollercoaster journey to the Durdle Door in Dorset. As our arrival on the beach coincided with the rising sun, I promptly passed out on the sand with only one shoe removed. I had never felt such a rush of delirious, delicious satisfaction as I dozed off. Surprised to see that I could keep up with the rapid pace set by the men (circa 20mph) with little to no training, I began to realise that if I cycled more I had the potential to do well in road competition. This realisation also came at a time where I had been competing internationally in Bike Polo (which is co-ed) for over a year, travelling all over Europe and the States for tournaments with no sponsorship or support compared to some of my male competitors. During 2013, I became the highest placed female player in the UK Championships, one of the few females to qualify and play in the European Championships in Krakow and one of less than 10 players worldwide to play in the World Championships in Florida. At Worlds, my mixed team was knocked out after the second of three days competing but I captained my women's team to the final, battled to a draw and then finally won it in extra time in the most exhausting mental and physical struggle of my life. Kneeling on the floor in 40 degree heat, salt encrusted and delirious with tiredness, I couldn't process the fact we had just won. I just felt empty.

When I got home with the World Champs trophy in hand, I still felt empty. I didn't take place in that winter's polo league and my custom-built bike languished on the balcony, slowly rusting away as I was voted out of the LHBPA and became increasingly sad about the sport. I found it frustrating and confusing that it was inherently co-ed yet women weren't picked for teams or sponsored by companies and that it constantly felt like a battle to improve the situation. When you did look for sponsors or help, you were branded as a sell-out despite giving up all your free time to develop the sport at grass roots level. In my head, the game was over.

A good experience for me in 2013 was picking up work as a bike messenger as the school holidays meant teaching work dried up. Bike messengers have always been regarded with equal parts wariness and admiration, but many of my friends were messengers and I respected the fact they rode their bikes all day for a living. It was the kind of riding I really loved; getting from A to B as fast as I could, up against the traffic, just pedalling my thoughts away come rain or shine. One day, with the wind on my face, it might hit me what I was supposed to be doing with my life, but right then I was just happy to be cycling. It was a male-dominated 'profession' and some messengers were downright terrifying, and I found many to be exorcising their own demons or riding away from other responsibilities just like myself. The few women I did know and see out on their road were truly inspirational people; two of whom I have the utmost respect and love for and feel like they are the unsung heroines of the cycling world. Steph, a smart French rider with a big heart runs the London Courier Emergency Fund, raising money for messengers who as self-employed individuals couldn't work when injured or involved in an accident. Emily, a gifted writer and blogger who I had followed for years, was mid-way through cycling round the world when a bereavement brought her back to the UK and working the roads of London. Emily's short snippets of her cycling adventures inspired me to put down in writing my own thoughts and feelings about cycling, and thus began a habit of voicing my opinions (sometimes a little too loudly) on blogs and in magazines.

Meanwhile, my fitness improved from riding all day and my confidence in joining the 'fast boys' on rides got stronger. I became good friends with one of them on a photo shoot for Vulpine and soon we were inseparable. As the seasons changed my enthusiasm for getting out on the bike started to die as I struggled with the winter blues, but a great group of friends and colleagues kept me riding early mornings before work and at weekends so that I didn't lose everything. We travelled to Devon in the New Year and spent a great week or so riding in the countryside, up and down the moors and along coastal roads. It was beautiful and therapeutic, setting me in good stead for the start of the cycling season.

Again, more opportunities came up to work on cycling projects and I travelled around Europe working on shoots, events and competitions. When I returned to the UK, many people were talking about racing and training camps but I didn't feel like I was good enough to take my cycling quite that seriously yet. It was only when a close friend and colleague at Kinoko suggested that we set up our own cycling team including women, I perked up. The traditional (and old fashioned) route into racing is to join a club as a young person and go to events with fellow club members, but for those of us who had gotten into cycling much later down the line and had our own way of doing things, clubs didn't always feel like the ideal environments to be in. Many clubs had very few female members due to their intimidating nature so I had never bothered to join one as I found other women through a variety of other local rides. Starting our own team from a solid foundation of strong riding friends and colleagues seemed like the ideal solution to our lack of club. None of us women had raced before and we were helped along with lots of support and advice from our male teammates on training rides, as well as reading and doing our own research into racing. We shouldn't have worried as racing bikes turned out to be far less scary than we had imagined.

Our base fitness was good from all the riding we had done that winter and so our major learning curve was based on tactics – something I still struggle with now after completing my first season of racing! Mid summer, I moved permanently to Devon on the simple basis that I wanted to 'work less and ride more', the spiralling cost of living combined with the poor wages bestowed by the cycling industry meant London was not a viable option to us anymore. We could be on the moors riding within 15 minutes rather than an hour's busy trawl through the suburbs to find a quiet Kentish lane.

The past summer has seen many positive changes for cycling and I have noticed more women out on the roads participating in rides and racing bikes than ever before. Well-publicised events such as the inaugural Women's Tour have, I'm sure, inspired another wave of riders and racers post London 2012. Cycling in the southwest of England is huge, no doubt because of the beautiful and wonderful countryside available to ride in. There are many races, rides, sportives and events to participate in for all levels of cyclist and I have really enjoyed organising women-only days out for local riders. Do I think segregation in cycling is necessary? No, not at all (apart from competition), but I do believe that the traditional male-dominated environment puts many less confident women off participating and that women-only events help to get them associated with the benefits and joys of cycling before getting more involved. It's still a bizarre past-time to many and I'm sure I'm regarded as somewhat of a cycling freak to my older friends but I cannot emphasise enough the great impact cycling has had on my life.

Anyone can ride a bike. Anyone can experience the freedom and fun that it brings with it. Anyone with passion and a desire to learn can start in the cycling industry, and it's usually from more experienced and passionate colleagues that you learn your trade, whether that be teaching cycle skills or fixing bikes. Many of us study and gain practical qualifications along the way but I genuinely believe it is only with experience ourselves that we become better cyclists and industry workers. If you don't know where to start, approach your local independent bike shop or community cycling project; put in the time and effort there and you will gain the experience and skills you desire to progress in the industry. Don't get me wrong, I'm no expert, and I'm still floating in the middle of this strange industry myself, earning greatly differing wages depending on who or what company I'm working for that day as a freelancer. I wish that skilled workers were valued more and I'm surprised to learn that the UK has some of the poorest wage levels for people in the cycling industry, but no-one (that I know of) works in this industry for the money. We work in it because of our passion for cycling. One day that may change, but right now we keep pedalling on ...

CHAPTER 28

KIMBERLEY RAMPLIN
The Tipping Point

Kimberley Ramplin is a cycling fan – a loud one. In her day job she's allowed to shout about sport in outlets as diverse as BBC World, The Age and ABC Lateline – and, yes, she can spot an offside trap – but from February to October, Ramplin can be found shouting at cyclists on a TV or laptop and live-tweeting the action with her Twitter 'family'.

🐦 @kimbo_ramplin
 http://thereferral.wordpress.com/

Kimbo is one of my 'go-to gals' on Twitter so she was an obvious choice to invite to contribute a piece to Ride the Revolution. *I told her she had carte blanche, and she contributed this thoughtful piece on doping in the men's and women's sports, and why women's cycling represents a golden opportunity for sponsors and marketers looking to promote a clean sport.*

People have a deep emotional connection to sport – as opposed to health or fitness. A successful narrative, one that appeals to sponsors, focuses on how sport makes you feel – and men's cycling has jerked around with how people feel about the sport for too long. When many of us think about women's cycling, what springs to mind is not the opportunities it provides elite athletes, but the problems that beset them. The gross pay disparity between women and men.

A lack of media attention. Less race coverage. Race organisation that can border on the farcical. Given these factors, it's easy to slip into a sort of institutionalised paranoia, a pervasive mindset that regardless of merit or achievement, the sport's foundations will continue to let women down.

It's time to switch things up. That is not to ignore these very real issues. Women should be paid the same as men. The women's competition needs the UCI to look at its racing calendar and relationships with race organisers. These are achievable (if long-term) goals, and they can be brought about if women's cycling exploits the clear advantages it enjoys compared with men's cycling. At all levels, women are arguably modern cycling's most valuable players. According to Bloomberg news agency, women make up approximately 40 per cent of the American television audience for the Tour de France, and one-third of its 12 million spectators. Women make crucial discretionary spending decisions, not only for themselves, but also for families. As one of three vice-presidents of the UCI, Tracey Gaudry is one of the world's top female sports administrators. Has there been a more celebrated rivalry in the velodrome in recent times than that between Britain's Victoria Pendleton and Australia's Anna Meares? Is there a contemporary male cyclist whose palmarès rival that of Marianne Vos? Most critically, women's cycling offers what the men cannot: the perception that it is clean.

Of course female cyclists have been hit with doping infractions, even lifetime bans. US star Rebecca Twigg admitted to participating in a systematic blood doping regime in the lead-up to the 1984 Olympics. Retired greats Nicole Cooke and Inga Thompson have both stated the culture of doping existed in the women's sport just as it had in the men's and that their careers were negatively impacted by their refusal to dope. That said, women's cycling has not been hit with a doping case so notorious that it became an 'affair' – as with Festina, Telekom, 'Oil for Drugs' – nor has a professional team been revealed years later to have been rotten to the core (such as US Postal). Despite anecdotal reports from the likes of Cooke and Thompson, there is little evidence in terms of positive tests or confessions that women cyclists are doping on the scale men were, and continue to. Ironically, the greatest scourge on the sport is the unique value proposition women's cycling can put to sponsors, race organisers and fans alike.

If the only benefits in life that really matter are emotional, the dopers and the culture that enables them to thrive in men's cycling – the awful omertà – can make the relationship between commercial sponsors and the sport toxic. In 2012, Dutch financial institution Rabobank made it clear it wanted out of the Dodge City of professional road cycling because the sport was rife with doping. It announced it would withdraw sponsorship from both men's and women's professional squads after the release of the US Anti-Doping Authority's reasoned decision against Lance Armstrong, earning the scorn of the rehabilitated former doper, David Millar, and the disappointment of the riders who no longer knew where their paycheck would come from. As well as being the biggest sponsor of Dutch cycling in monetary terms, its 17-year sponsorship association meant Rabobank and cycling went together like a horse and carriage.

At the time of Rabobank's announcement, the media concentrated on the fallout for the men's road squad. While the loss of Rabobank's sponsorship cannot be underestimated, the warning signs were there as far back as 2007, when, with the Tour de France victory seemingly in the bag, Rabobank withdrew, fined and sacked race leader Michael Rasmussen for lying to them about his whereabouts in out-of-competition drug testing. The team's zero-tolerance approach was in stark contrast to others whose sponsors were sullied by endemic and systemic doping. While there is a sound case for teams to protect and protest the innocence of riders accused of doping, and to rehabilitate them once bans are served, Rabobank's decision to axe Rasmussen was on point with the feelings of many frustrated cycling fans. USADA's report was the final straw for Rabobank.

It was no longer about the doping. It was the lies.

Throughout the shockwaves and recriminations of 2012, something strange happened. Rabobank didn't carry through with one part of its announcement. Instead, the company stuck it out as a major sponsor of professional road racing through the UCI Women's Team that started life as DSB Bank in 2005. The sky may have fallen on the men's team, but the bank flipped on its decision about the women's team. Today's iteration, Rabobank-Liv, is an excellent example of women's cycling as a more sound sponsorship option for companies and brands whose marketers are frightened or tired of seeing the sport associated with cheating. *The Cycling Sponsorship Report 2013* found cycling fans are among the most engaged with sponsor's brands and most likely to adopt new technologies in the world. Because women's cycling is brimming with stars who race across disciplines, they provide better value for money in terms of promoting bikes and kit, which suits bike makers. Giant's separate marque for women, Liv, also sponsors the Liv Pro XC Women's Team and Team Liv-Shimano. Its 'brand traits' – 'genuine, outgoing, confident, and optimistic' – are personified by the professional riders it supports, and none more so than the greatest cyclist of our generation, Vos. I say greatest without hesitation, and believe it denigrates Vos's astonishing achievements to add, *sotto voce*, 'if only she was a man'. In one season (2012), Vos held the Olympic & UCI World Championships road race champion jerseys; won the overall and points classifications at the premier women's stage race, the Giro Donne (now Giro Rosa) and the yellow jersey in the Tour Féminin en Limousin; the UCI Cyclo-cross World Championship and day races including Ronde van Drenthe, GP de Plouay and the only race where men compete against women – the Amstel Curaçao Race (where she finished 12th overall, ahead of some pretty handy types including Chris Froome, Joaquim Rodríguez,

Dani Moreno and Lieuwe Westra). While many male riders excel in stage and one-day races, the idea that today's general classification contenders – Nibali, Contador or Quintana, for example – would dominate different road disciplines and cyclo-cross in the same year is laughable. Vos has done this at a time where she has been consistently challenged, often bested, in groups every bit as select as the omnipresent 'heads of state' in a men's elite road race, by the likes of Wiggle-Honda's Giorgia Bronzini and its new signings, Mara Abbot and ascending star Elisa Longo Borghini; Boels Dolman's Lizzie Armitstead, Ellen van Dijk and 2015 signing Evelyn Stevens; Orica-AIS's Judith Arndt and Emma Johansson; and the now-retired Emma Pooley and Nicole Cooke. Nor is Vos an outlier in terms of crossover appeal and accomplishments. Her successor as women's road race world champion, Rabobank-Liv teammate Pauline Ferrand-Prévot, excels at road, mountain biking and cyclo-cross racing, winning La Flèche Wallonne Féminine 2014 and the U23 European XC championship.

Liv is not the only major cycling manufacturer to see women's cycling for what it represents: the long game. Specialized has technical relationships with men's squads, but its only naming rights relationship is in women's cycling, through the Specialized-Lululemon squad. Even a switch of teams in 2015 looks like it may play out well for the UCI Women's Championships. Specialized-Lululemon's decision to pull out of its eponymous women's squad and back the Boels-Dolmans squad looks disastrous on the surface. Instead, women's cycling drew yet another bike manufacturer – Cérvelo – back to the title sponsor fold. The company dipped its toes into men's title sponsorship with the Cérvelo TestTeam in 2009. Despite a strong season built around one-day success, stage wins and the green jersey in the Tour de France, the team was disbanded after just one year. While Cérvelo sponsored a woman's team between 2008 and 2010, it left title sponsorship in 2011 to form an alliance with Garmin. The Garmin women's team then folded, and it appeared

Cérvelo may have been lost to the sport's highest levels. This new deal is a triumph for women's cycling – and for clean racing.

Similarly, the clean reputation of women's cycling makes it ideal for sports marketers who are looking for value based on geo-demographics. In September 2014, Shane Stokes detailed the decision of the DeLotto (the Dutch National Lottery) and The Netherlands-based loyalty marketing company BrandLoyalty to step into the breach left by Belkin as major sponsor of the men's procycling outfit once known as Rabobank. As Stokes observed, the deal is an innovative one, bringing together cycling and speed skating (two of Holland's most popular sports) for the first time. With some trade teams such as Lotto-Belisol Ladies and UnitedHealthcare Pro Cycling Women's Team resembling national squads (and competing at the UCI World Championships in team events), there are clear synergies for corporations to sponsor women's cycling in conjunction with a different sport that appeals to the domestic audience they wish to target. The model is already at work in different professional sports around the world. In Australia, for example a partnership between the Sydney Swans AFL club and the NSW Swifts netball team sees the teams sharing training and recovery facilities and the support of the same major sponsor, QBE Insurance. Could this be the framework for sustainable sponsorship of women's professional cycling teams in the future?

Again, the clean reputation of women's cycling and the return of bike manufacturers to title sponsorship will help women's cycling press its claims for better racing opportunities. Championing the cause of running parallel races for men and women has had some impact. While La Course by La Tour de France 2014 was not the resurrected woman's Tour de France many, including Vos, had lobbied for, it was an unmitigated success. One of the reasons frequently used by race organisers for not holding stage races for women is the broadcasting cost. Cycling, with its day-long nature and need for helicopters and moto-camera operators to capture images, is an expensive sport to produce for television – which is why it makes no sense to hold premier women's races in anything but tandem with men's events. Women's Grand Slam tennis provides the obvious comparison. While men and women rarely compete alongside each other outside the sport's marquee events, there is pay parity between men and women at the Grand Slam level. Playing the four most prestigious tournaments simultaneously delivers the TV exposure sponsors demand, and not only on an individual level. Organisationally, cycling and tennis are similar, and just as casual interest in professional cycling spikes during the Tour de France, casual interest in tennis peaks during Wimbledon. As the Tour is owned and operated by the Amaury Sport Organisation (ASO), Wimbledon is run by AELTC, a wholly owned subsidiary of the All England Lawn Tennis & Croquet Club Limited. This allows both events to run without giving up their naming rights. Alternatively, a whole-of-championship underwriting sponsorship deal may prove the difference between women's cycling existing as a low-level team having a dream run in a purist, romantic FA Cup-style competition or playing for keeps in the Premier League. A naming rights sponsor secured by the UCI for the entirety of the World Championship series could give elite athletes the financial security they deserve through a minimum wage and encourage individual and team and sponsors to stay on board for longer contractual terms.

Women's cycling is at a tipping point. The talent is there. The audience is engaged, knowledgeable and hungry for a positive emotional connection with the sport. Even the sport's deep-set structural issues, such as race scheduling, can be brought to heel by the faith of sponsors. Opportunities abound if women's cycling adopts a reverse, 'build it and they will come' mentality. Women's cycling must exploit the one tremendous advantage the men gave away. Clean cycling does not rely on the emergence of a new breed of male road racers who eschew needles and pain relief, but quite clearly not the dented silence of the peloton. Clean cycling is not an alternative universe. It's here. With very few proven exceptions, it always has been. It's time for women's cycling, from the UCI through to trade teams, national structures and individuals, to start talking about doping by reframing the nature of the conversation. Cycling can confidently put women at the core of a clean cycling sponsorship sales pitch, whether it's a whole season deal, drilling further into existing vertical relationships with kit and bike manufacturers or exploring horizontal opportunities with different sports within the same domestic market. Failing to press this message home is nothing short of stupid.

CHAPTER 29

ANNA DOORENBOS
'As Easy As Riding A Bike?'

Anna Doorenbos is a bike lover and recreational cyclist who tweets, blogs and podcasts about her journey of discovery as a newly minted fan of professional cycling. Anna lives in Washington DC. She was inspired to write about one of the biggest difficulties facing women who want to start cycling for fun and fitness – the 'one size fits all' approach to women's cycling clothing design and the barrier to participation it presents.

🐦 @bloomingcyclist
🅱️ http://masteringtheuphillshift.wordpress.com/
🎙️ pelotonitispodcast.wordpress.com

Everybody loves Anna. As Blooming Cyclist she has become a fixture on Twitter, and it's been fun to follow her journey from newbie fan to knowledgeable and enthusiastic commentator on the sport through her Pelotonitis podcast. Anna is a very modern cycling fan, having grown up being able to access the kind of information on bike racing that I could only dream of when I first started watching back in the 1980s. Apart from our shared love of cycling we also share a mutual despair over finding fitness clothing that works for you if you're not a standard size (My own bug bear is being 'big up top'). Her piece on her struggle to find cycling gear that works for the average woman who just wants to get out and ride her bike for fun and fitness struck a chord with many of us.

'It's as easy as riding a bike.'

Like the saying 'easy as pie', this phrase doesn't actually make a lot of sense, as neither riding a bike nor making a pie is very easy. While the act of riding a bike might *seem* easy, the path to getting on the bike is full of obstacles. Not even including actually learning how to ride a bike, as an adult there are lots of things to overcome before a bike ride can become enjoyable: the intimidation of shops, the terrifying thought of riding with traffic, the overwhelming number of choices, the fear of Spandex, and on and on!

While the other obstacles are not for the faint of heart, I found looking for cycling clothing to be the most traumatic. As a female on the larger side, who wanted the comfort of sweat wicking Spandex, I could not have predicted the amount of stress the search for cycling clothes would cause. I must preface all of this by saying that riding without Spandex is perfectly acceptable and I often do ride without them on. While I'm firmly part of the Spandex Club, I also firmly believe that you should wear what you want to while riding. But if you do want to wear spandex, and are a female on the larger side ... good luck.

Cycling clothing has always been a point of stress for me. I've always imagined I'm not alone, but I've always held back admitting this and explaining why because of the fear of feeling embarrassed. But after a discussion on Twitter about the lack of cycling clothes for women inspired a friend to finally write her own body image post where she confessed her body issues and how the search for cycling clothes reinforced her self-esteem issues, I decided to screw up my courage to write about my own experiences, if only to empower more women to not be afraid to speak up about things that are considered 'taboo'.

I'm a plus sized girl. Always have been, always will be. That's just the way I am. I wear a US size 18 (UK 20/Euro 48). I have big thighs (made bigger by cycling!), big hips, a large waist, big boobs. And I would say that generally I'm able to convince myself that I don't really care about my size. Except when I have to buy clothes. That's when I feel fat. That's when I start wondering how people see me, if they judge me because of my body, if people are disgusted by me. And I shouldn't give a fuck! I'm a feminist, goddamn it. I know it's society that makes me feel ashamed! But I can't help it. When I think about clothes, and how I look in them, I always wonder how well I've hidden my stomach and if those who do see are disgusted by it. I know clothes that fit well and are flattering make a huge difference in how I look and my confidence. But damn, it is hard to find well-fitted clothes when you're a size 18 and have a large chest. And I care *a lot* about finding clothes that fit well, mainly because I'm concerned about how people see me. I'll admit – I've been brainwashed by society.

As the discussion continued on about cycling clothes for women on Twitter, I could feel myself starting to get emotional and stressed out. Buying regular clothes isn't a picnic, but at least I know there are a couple of places I can rely on to have my size. When it comes to cycling clothes, forget it. I've never been in a cycling shop that has women's sizes that will fit me. XL? Don't make me laugh! I'm lucky if I can get my arms inside an XL, let alone zip it up. The male cut might be roomier in the chest, but there is no way it's going to fit over my hips (trust me, I've tried). I don't even bother looking at cycling clothes in the store, because I know they won't fit.

This means I have to look online for my cycling clothes. And even online there are precious few options when it comes to extended sizes in cycling clothes. I hate buying clothes online – even everyday clothes. Even when they have good measurements, I still can't tell how the fabric lays and stretches, or if the cut will be flattering to my waist and chest. Plus, if it doesn't fit, I have to go to the trouble of sending it back. Buying cycling clothing online is even worse, because the sizing is awful. A nightmare. I spend *days* combing through sites, comparing sizing charts. I've even made a freaking spreadsheet. I need *at least* a 46-inch chest. Louis Garneau goes up to 3X. Sounds promising, right? Except their 3X is only 42 inches.

Castelli? Their XXL is only 45. And let's not ever talk about the high-end brands. Rapha? 40-inch chest max. Even discounting the fact that there is zero standardisation in sizing, how is sizing like that going to encourage more women to feel good about themselves on the bike?

I know I'm never going to look skinny on the bike, but is it too much to ask to have flattering cuts, non-elasticised hems, and jerseys that don't ride up? And this is just the technical gear. What about all the new 'stylish' every day biking gear? Rapha doesn't even have a women's casual line. And besides Vulpine (which doesn't have extended sizes), I'm hard pressed to even name another company that does casual riding clothes for women. And honestly, even if there were companies that did casual biking clothes for women, I wouldn't even bother to look to see if they had something to fit me, because I know they won't and it will just make me feel fat and ashamed when I see the sizing.

There are two issues at play here: body confidence and lack of options when it comes to cycling clothes. And I think the latter is affecting the former. When, time after time, I'm confronted with sizes that don't even come close to my measurements, the message seems to be 'We don't want you size here. Your size isn't normal and we can't accommodate for it.' How is one supposed to remain body confident in the face of that? Whether it's technical or casual riding gear, time and again, I'm reading the message that my size isn't 'normal'. Even if I didn't think of myself as fat, it would be hard to keep convincing myself of that when the only size that *might* fit me is an XXL – if I'm lucky. And even though I *know* they're just arbitrary letters and numbers that don't really mean anything, I can't quite stop myself from feeling ashamed of my size.

Could I be thinner? Yes. I could do things to help me lose weight. I've started Weight Watchers and have become addicted to spin class. But no matter how much weight I lose, I am always going to be plus sized. I'm always going to be 'big-boned' because that's the way

I was made. When will the cycling industry start recognising that most women who ride bikes aren't built like guys? We have curves, we have bellies, we have roundness. Women want flattering cuts to maybe help disguise some of the bits they don't like. And perhaps we want flattering cuts because we just want to look like a woman when we bike! Is it too much to ask that manufacturers create a cut that at least acknowledges we have HIPS and a WAIST? I've worn enough plus-sized, box shaped shirts to recognise the importance of defining a waist. I know I need to keep working on accepting myself, but it is hard to accept myself when it seems no one in the fashion or cycling clothing industry at the moment does.

I can understand how it's hard for clothing companies that make clothes for women – our body types vary *so* much. The combinations are endless: There are women with large breasts and small waists; or small breasts and small waists; or large waists and small breasts! And that's not even considering all the other body parts that can vary so much from woman to woman. Which means it's probably impossible for one company to cater to all female body types. But it's frustrating when it seems like no company is willing to make an effort to try and include even a portion of all the diversely shaped women. While there is no wrong way to ride a bike, it will be much easier to convince more women to ride if they feel they have choices when it comes to finding cycling clothing that fits them – whether that cycling clothing be Lycra or jeans or casual jackets or rain jackets.

But, in an ironic twist, I don't really care when what I look like when I'm on the bike. There is nowhere to hide when you're wearing technical gear. All of the lumpy bits are out there. But for some reason, I don't care. Even if shopping for cycling gear stresses me out to the max, once I've got it on and I'm on the bike, I feel comfortable. I feel *strong*. And I think, in the end, that's what makes it all okay. I know many women aren't like me, so I'm grateful I stop caring about how I look once I'm on the bike. And as long as I feel strong on the bike, I guess that is what is most important.

CHAPTER 30

KELTON WRIGHT

10 Reasons Why Being a Girl On a Bike Rocks!

Kelton Wright is a writer, a cyclist and a cat enthusiast. Kelton is also a Women's Ambassador for Rapha. Her writing on all things bike-related can be seen on Rapha, Machines for Freedom, and Bikes&Cat.

🐦 @KeltonWrites

🏠 http://www.keltonwright.com/ http://machinesforfreedom. com/

I first saw this pieces on the Machines for Freedom website and, when I'd finished laughing the deeply enjoyable laughter of recognition, I begged Kelton to let me use it for Ride the Revolution. *She agreed and here it is. The emphasis might be American but the benefits of being a girl on a bike are universal – and she's right, it rocks!*

Everybody knows that getting on a bike gets you svelte, but the perks to cycling don't stop there. From insta-friends to instant street cred, there's more to cycling than just feeling fit. Here are the top 10 reasons being a babe on a bike is rad.

1. Everyone loves an underdog.

Look, I'm not a fan of people having low expectations for me, but I am an enormous fan of proving people wrong. In high school, I used to roll up to stoplights in my Mustang and smile at the car in the next lane, ready to race as soon as the light turned green. The car is gone but the muscle is still there and I'm still revving at stoplights to prove that matching my lipstick to my kit has nothing to do with who's going to take the bike lane first.

2. Single scene.

Do you like to date athletic people with penchants for coffee and beer drinking, who also happen to share your favorite hobby? Well, welcome to cycling! Go to a crit or a gran fondo and enjoy the show because you're about to see the full package in Spandex, literally. Not only does getting on a bike give a girl insta-hotness among a sea of men, but there's no getting stuck at a table having awkward dinner conversation. The longest awkward conversation in cycling is only the length of a stoplight. Plus, no better way to judge a mate than seeing how they handle you bonking, or better yet, how they handle watching you drop them.

3. You can QOM all over this city.

On a sheer numbers scale, there are not as many women riding. You can QOM all over your hood because it's unlikely Marianne Vos or Mara Abbott are riding around Louisville, Kentucky. So while the guys have 700 other dudes who've ridden that segment, it's a little easier to crack top 10 when there's only 40 women who have.

4. People want to fix everything for you.

I know how to fix a flat. But I've also very recently learned how to give myself a cool manicure, so when my tube punctures and a guy offers to fix it, who am I to say no? Look, I get it, it's rad to do it yourself, but it's a little ridiculous to not be appreciative of the fact that if you're bonking and mad at the road and your tyre pops, it's likely that one of the guys on the ride with you will offer to fix it. I'm not much of a damsel in distress, but I'm happy to be a damsel in appreciation.

5. Insta-friends when there are other girls.

There's nothing like going for a group ride with all guys to have another woman roll up. It's like hearing someone drop a 'y'all' on a train in Brussels – good God, are you from North Carolina, too? Sweet tea'n' biscuits, give me a hug!

6. Six hour slumber party.

It's great to get drinks with friends or grab a nice meal, but two hours in a public setting can only get so intimate. Six hours on a bike in the heat of the day in the middle of nowhere gives you time to get slumber party weird with people. By mile 30, I know how you feel about your boss, but by mile 70, I know how your boss feels about your new co-worker in the bathroom at the Christmas party.

7. I can eat EVERYTHING.

The major bonus to burning 2,000 calories on a ride is that you get to eat those calories. From waffles and rice cakes to Coca-Cola and Paydays while you're on the bike, to hamburgers slathered in sauce, dripping with cheese, and wrapped in bacon as soon as you're done, you get to eat everything and still have *Fitness* cover arms.

8. You're allowed to be aggro.

The struggle to be all things all the time is a real issue for women, but on the bike, you don't need to be sweet and polite while simultaneously being strong – you just get to be aggro-as-hell. And it's encouraged. Make that bike face, drop people, climb harder, and when you pass the bro who thought you couldn't keep up, flick your braid and smile.

9. The cattiness is gone.

Whatever reputation women might have for being catty in the workplace is evaporated on the bike. This is a sister-help-sister environment. We'll get through this. We'll get over this hill. We will get to the finish. There are few things more satisfying in this world than chasing a line of ponytails down a mountain.

10. You look rad.

Let's face it – seeing a chick bombing down a mountain in her favourite kit on her dream bike is about the coolest thing ever. Having someone ask how far you biked and seeing their face when you say '65 miles' is a better confidence booster than three margaritas.

BIBLIOGRAPHY

Want to know more about women's cycling, or read more women's cycling writing? Then start here:

Bella Bathurst *The Bicycle Book* (Harper Press)

Gale Bernhardt *Bicycling for Women* (Velopress)

Kathryn Bertine *The Road Less Taken* (Triumph Books)

Beryl Burton and Colin Kirby *Personal Best* (Mercian Manuals)

Cathy Bussey *The Girl's Guide to Life on Two Wheels*
    (Ryland Peters & Small)

Nicole Cooke *The Breakaway* (Simon & Schuster)

Bálint Hamvas *Cyclocross 2013/14* (Cyclephotos)

Juliet Macur *Cycle of Lies* (William Collins)

Sue Macy *Wheels of Change* (Random House)

Kimberly Menozzi *27 Stages* (Good to Go Press)

Freya North *Cat* (Random House)

Emma O'Reilly *The Race to the Truth* (Transworld)

Victoria Pendleton and Donald McRae *Between the Lines*
    (HarperCollins)

Marijn de Vries and Nynke de Jong *Vrouw & Fiets*
    (Atlas Contact, Uitgeverij)

Frances Willard *A Wheel Within A Wheel* (Applewood Books)

Selene Yeager *Everywoman's Guide to Cycling* (New American Library)

ACKNOWLEDGEMENTS

To all the inspirational, extraordinary women who gave up their time to speak to me and to contribute to this book, huge thanks and admiration for the ways you have each helped to shape the sport of women's cycling.

To all the inspirational and extraordinary women over the years whose stories may not figure in these pages but who, in their many and varied ways, have fought for their sport and made it what it is today – huge thanks and admiration for everything you've accomplished.

Charlotte, Sarah (and mini me) and all the team at Bloomsbury who held my hand through everything and taught me how to do this – the learning curve has been steep and endlessly enjoyable and I quite literally could not have put this book together without you.

To my family, close and extended, who listened politely as I babbled excitedly about the stories I was telling – as ever, my love and gratitude and all that good stuff – and thanks for being genuinely interested in my work.

To my cycling and non-cycling buddies who gave me advice, ideas and support and have been as excited as I am as this book has taken shape.

Rory and Don, Scott and John – for mentoring and support services rendered – always appreciated and duly acknowledged.

To Paul Campbell – thanks for giving me a break and encouraging me to write from the heart.

INDEX